The SAFFRON PEAR TREE

· AND OTHER KITCHEN MEMORIES ·

*These memoirs are dedicated to my husband,
who has walked such a long part of
life's road with me.*

Oshun

Published by Oshun Books
an imprint of Struik Publishers
(a division of New Holland Publishing (South Africa) (Pty) Ltd)
PO Box 1144, Cape Town, 8000
New Holland Publishing is a member of
Johnnic Communications Ltd

FIRST PUBLISHED 2005

1 3 5 7 9 10 8 6 4 2

www.oshunbooks.co.za

Publication © Oshun Books 2005
Text © Zuretha Roos 2005
Illustrations © John Hall/Oshun Books 2005
Front cover image of pears © Alamy

Publishing manager: Michelle Matthews
Editor: Ceridwen Morris
Designer: Sean Robertson
Illustrator: John Hall
Proofreader: Joy Clack
Production controller: Valerie Kömmer

Set in 10.75 pt on 14.75 pt Adobe Caslon Pro
Reproduction by Hirt & Carter (Cape) (Pty) Ltd
Printed and bound by Paarl Print,
Oosterland Street, Paarl, South Africa

ISBN 1 77007 038 9

~ CONTENTS ~

CHAPTER 1

~ A WOMAN'S KITCHEN ~

... OH, GREEN AND GLORIOUS! O HERBACEOUS TREAT!
'T WOULD TEMPT THE DYING ANCHORITE TO EAT:
BACK TO THE WORLD HE'D TURN HIS FLEETING SOUL,
AND PLUNGE HIS FINGERS IN THE SALAD BOWL!
SERENELY FULL, THE EPICURE WOULD SAY,
"FATE CANNOT HARM ME, I HAVE DINED TODAY".

Sydney Smith

On a large wooden board lies a young *kabeljou*, a kob, of about 40 centimetres. It is sea-fresh: it was caught off a boat today. I am going to fillet it, and prepare a beer batter. I shall cut each fillet in two, dip it in batter and lower it into boiling hot oil. In seconds the fish will emerge encased in a crisp golden crust. It will be delicious. There will be new potatoes and peas, and chilled wine. Perhaps I'll make a pudding; it is cold and the day draws in.

From where I stand in the small kitchen of our beach house, I have an unbroken view over ocean and rocks and crashing waves. It is a great blessing to live within all this pure space: if the earth was flat, I would be able to see all the way to Antarctica.

The dusk deepens suddenly: a wall of cloud moves in rapidly from the west. The windsock stretches out and flaps its gaily coloured tails in the wind. Tonight it will rain. I start to fillet the fish, carefully.

A large old-fashioned kitchen is what I would love to have most. I'd choose an old-time kitchen like my grannies' over the beautiful modern ones. There should be lots of cupboards and a cosy table. I would like to smell again the woodscent from an old stove, and there should be a comfortable woman with a white apron bustling around to keep me company and to help me with chores.

Food and kitchens and the cycle of life: in the lives of most ordinary women these three concepts are almost inseparable. Invisible threads connect womankind to kitchens: their mother's, their own, those of their friends. It is in those first kitchens, our mother's, our grannies', where we first measured the slow passing of our babyhood against the height of the kitchen table until, one triumphant day, we can peek over the tabletop and, at last, see what is up there!

Then time starts speeding up, and the day comes when we find ourselves in a kitchen of our own, perhaps small and cramped. Later there might be a baby in a high chair, or a toddler on the floor.

And how fortunate is the woman who grows old in her own kitchen, among her familiar possessions. She will have dented pots and bent forks and wooden spoons worn down with stirring. Her once gleaming cutting knives will have worn thin with sharpening. Her plates might have cracks and her table will be grooved and marked. Her cat might be as stiff and old as she is. But she will be happy as she sits near the stove with her mug of coffee and her memories.

CHAPTER 2

~ OUMA SANNIE ~

... SAY, IS THERE BEAUTY YET TO FIND?

AND CERTAINTY? AND QUIET KIND?

DEEP MEADOWS YET, FOR TO FORGET

THE LIES, AND TRUTHS, AND PAIN? ... OH! YET

STANDS THE CHURCH CLOCK AT TEN TO THREE?

AND IS THERE HONEY STILL FOR TEA?

Rupert Brooke

How sad, when a child has to grow up without grandparents. Maybe there are indifferent or sick or faraway grandparents; perhaps even horrible grandparents: that cannot be changed. But for a child to have a dear granny or a granddad close by is one of life's great privileges.

Grandparents are very much like a second pair of kindly, older parents, who do not have to discipline you unless you are being very naughty. They always seem to have time for you.

Oupa John, my paternal grandfather, died when I was just seven-years-old. He was short and stout and he worked very hard in his vineyards. When he was not working, he wore formal suits with waistcoats. He was, it was later said when I was older and he was dead, that he had been a "difficult man". When I see those old sepia photographs of collections of Edwardian men in striped suits, with moustaches and stern expressions, I see my granddad among them.

After his death Ouma Sannie stayed on in the old Victorian homestead on the family farm, just across the road from where we lived, in our post-war house with the red-brick flowerboxes.

Ouma's huge, two-gabled farmhouse had been built by Oupa John at the turn of the previous century. Uncle Uli, my father's brother, inherited the family farm, and he and his wife Aunt Moya lived in their own, modern home. Ouma's homestead was, however, far too large for her alone: the farm manager and his wife stayed in the other wing.

In the mornings my Ouma sat at the table in her pantry where the sun streamed in through the sash window, and ate her *mieliepap* with sugar and warm milk. I often curled up on the deep wooden windowsill, my arms around my knees. Ouma would have the morning paper folded next to her plate, and she would lift up her lovely old patrician face to peer at news items through the bottom of the glasses on her delicate nose. I would quietly amuse myself by peeking this way and that through the pebbly, pale green glass panes, which pulled and stretched the rose garden and the vineyards beyond it out of perspective.

In the kitchen next door women's voices murmured like tranquil water slipping over smooth river stones. Vegetable peels and scrapings plip-plopped into a pail.

Ouma ate slowly, as if she didn't really want to, like an obdurate child. She suffered from unspecified "problems of the digestive system". These problems sometimes provided an excuse to spend a day in bed, to complain of her pains, to get solicitous attention from her daughters-in-law.

Ouma was fashionably thin and well-groomed. She was not an embracing and kissing grandma – you did not clamber on to her knees. Yet her affection for us all was unmistakeable; we did not need kisses to know that. Children can sense love – they have the delicate feelers of butterflies.

Ouma bought beautiful clothes. Her favourite colour was red, red into old age. She wore printed cotton shirtwaists at home – her house dresses. But she never ventured, even into our humble and ugly little town, in those dresses – she "got dressed". On Sundays she walked into church in one of her well-cut suits, always straight-backed, clutching her psalm book with its ivory covers and leatherbound spine. There would be red somewhere in the pattern of the suit, and a red hat on her head.

She was well off. She had a cook and a succession of young maids-of-all-light-jobs. A "day girl" also came in, to vacuum and dust and sweep industriously, to polish her silver and furniture.

Later, much later, I realised that Ouma had led a life of serene schizophrenia – not the psychological condition, but regarding her personal perception of South African life …

Sometimes she would call suddenly towards the kitchen: "Emma! Eena!" Thin Emma and fat Eena would appear, drying their hands on their aprons.

"Listen," Ouma would say and lift up her paper, opening it up and shaking it, peering down her nose through her glasses. "Listen to what Dr Verwoerd said yesterday …"

What would she have made of South Africa now?

"Mother," my father pleaded with her more than once, "leave the servants out of politics! It's *white* politics, Ma!"

"They must know what is going on in the land," she replied stubbornly. And she carried on calling them, to come and listen to some snippet from the newspaper. There was no ambiguity or malice in this habit. She shared the newspaper's political reports and ordinary gossip items with them equally. She believed she was expanding their horizons; she believed, I think, that they saw things through her eyes.

She admired all people in power – she saw them as larger than life, and party politics played no real role in her life. When Mr Leabua Jonathan was Prime Minister of Lesotho, Ouma would smile whenever she saw his picture – his large, smiling black face – her head tilted as if to see him more clearly. She always exclaimed something like, "Dear old Jonathan!" as if she knew and loved him well. So what Dr Verwoerd had to say was important to her only because he was the leader of the country. Equally important was what British royalty did or said: "The Queen opened Parliament today …" she would announce, and smiling, her head tilted, study the picture accompanying the item, as if she and Queen Elizabeth shared a secret between them.

She also doted on the Royal houses of Belgium and the Netherlands. Once Prince Bernhard came on a visit to South Africa. This excited her; she scoured the paper first thing to see what he had done or said the previous day. She spoke of the prince in familiar and affectionate tones, as if he were a neighborhood Afrikaans boy: sometimes she called him "Prince Barnard".

Although she clung to the more genteel times of the turn of the 19th century, she had an endearing common touch. I often found her at her kitchen table with her "staff", drinking her impossibly strong coffee and gossiping with them. She liked to know what was going on in the small, whitewashed houses among the vineyards; who was expecting a baby again; and was it true that Liesa had run away from her husband?

"Last Saturday night Uli had to go and break up a drunken fight again. You people drink too much."

"Madam! Not us! It was Jan again; he started it all …! I just shut my door. I want nothing to do with that scum, and do you know what …?"

And Emma's voice would drop; she would lean forwards towards Ouma, who also inclined her head to hear better, and Emma would impart a scandalous bit not meant for anyone else's ears. Ouma would shake her head and take another sip of coffee. "Ayy …" she would mutter.

Ouma made us laugh often, unaware that she had said anything funny. Her blood pressure was too low: her doctor had told her to take a tablespoon of whisky in the morning and in the late afternoon, and doctor's word was law. She would stand in her kitchen with her tiny liqueur glass of whisky, mumbling to herself before swallowing the potion. Once Dad, coming into the kitchen by way of the back door, caught her at this little ritual, and kidded her.

"Isn't it too early in the day to be hitting the bottle, Ma?"

Ouma gasped in indignation. "My child! It's doctor's orders! My son, every time I swallow this evil stuff, I first lift up mine eyes and I pray, 'Jesus, please forgive me, You know that I *must* drink this!'"

It was a time long before political correctness. So when her trusty cook, Eena, informed Ouma that she was expecting a seventh child and would shortly go off on maternity leave, Ouma was silently furious and frustrated. She doted on Eena, but a seventh baby?

"They have far too many babies!" she complained to my father. "If I were Verwoerd, I'd get up in Parliament and I'd proclaim a law for these men: chop it all off!"

The farm kitchens of my childhood were alive with day-long activities. They were *working* kitchens. Fresh Jersey milk was carried into Ouma's kitchen in the pale cold dawn in white enamel pails and handed to the maid responsible. Fresh vegetables – bunches of carrots, heads of cabbage, green beans, new onions – were brought to the kitchen door by gardeners in the strong cane baskets which were used for grape-picking in season.

At times this kitchen clattered with crockery, sizzled with the enticing smells of meats, chattered with the voices of women: white, brown and black. At other times perfumy vanilla swirled in the air. Utensils were close at hand, hanging from hooks or in cupboards; nothing was for prettiness or show.

Here three meals were still prepared daily. The Aga stove sang cosily in its hearth, while women moved in and out to attend to their chores, to talk, gossip or clean, or to rest briefly by the kitchen table with a mug of coffee.

The only time Ouma Sannie's kitchen was deserted and the Aga hummed to itself, was in the drowsy hour after midday dinner, when everything had been cleared away and scrubbed clean, and Ouma rested in her cool, high-ceilinged bedroom behind closed shutters. Outside, under the eucalyptus trees, the maids sat placidly chattering, legs outstretched, with plates of food piled high.

Cooked food, I am convinced, does not taste as good today as it tasted then. There was something about a solid fuel stove – an old black Welcome Dover, a cream-coloured Aga, an Esse or an Ellis de Luxe – which imparted a certain extra flavour to foods. Maybe it was the constantly varying degrees of heat or the fragrance of burning wood which lightly permeated the food; maybe the old pots had something to do with it.

These kitchens were places which nurtured and soothed. You could sit down in a chair at the kitchen table, put your elbows on the surface, rest you face in your hands, and watch and listen. You would hear a snatch of juicy local gossip, or be given a cup of sweet tea, a cookie, or a mug of coffee. You could watch a maid unhurriedly preparing vegetables, or, in November, watch Ouma rolling out cookie dough as she prepared for the December holidays by the sea. As long as you were not in her way: then she would tell you to be off; she had a lot to do.

Despite the cook she always had, Ouma was extremely capable in the kitchen. But she didn't have to cook and bake unless she felt like it. As she grew older, more inclined to digestive problems, her cook made all her simple meals.

But those generations could not cook green vegetables properly.

They made superb roast potatoes, sweet potatoes, carrots rich with sugar and butter and nutmeg. But they always overcooked their greens.

Dinner at Ouma's was at midday, but by ten in the morning vegetables were already simmering away on the stove. Cabbage was invariably a khaki-coloured, smelly mess, and my own mother's wasn't much better. I hated cabbage until long after I was married, when I found out how to cook it properly. Young green beans were always chopped up and cooked until olive-coloured. Not much was known about nutrition: meats were the most important foodstuff. It was a pity, considering everything came fresh from the farm gardens.

This is what my mother tells me: when Granddad was still alive, Ouma took pride in her "table": in the quantity and quality of the food which appeared on her dinner table. Unexpected guests were frequent and always welcome.

But although there would be two or three meat dishes at the main midday meal, Ouma frowned on hunger expressed with too much enthusiasm, and she found lusty appetites indecorous and coarse. Of plump women she said, with a feigned sigh at such robustness; "She looks so healthy …" But she fooled no one. She considered overweight as vulgar, as somehow "not refined" – unless we're talking Queen Victoria, one of her role models. Queens, nobility and reigning heads of state presumably were not judged on their figures.

Yet she indulged my Oupa's peculiar tastes, which might have caused his relatively early death.

Oupa rose at four, winter and summer, and this meant that, before the eight o' clock breakfast, he had already put in a few hours of hard work in the vineyards. His favourite breakfast was a piece of fatty pork roast ... And only Ouma's Malay cook of those times, Tima, could bake this to his satisfaction.

"I was stunned," Mom told me, "when I was visiting the family for the first time, and I saw Tima taking the sizzling pork from the Aga's oven ... at eight! And his other favourite for breakfast was old-fashioned bean soup with those dice of pork fat ..."

Oupa also indulged in a shot of his home-distilled witblits – "white lightning" – at eleven, and again at four. That was all he ever drank.

It's hard to reconcile the fastidious eating habits of my delicate granny with such a wanton appetite. And I always wondered if Tima, originally from Cape Town, was a Muslim ... she, who had to prepare pork so often. No one could tell me. But Tima, long gone, still lives on in family lore, remembered with great affection by my uncles and aunts for her exceptional skills in the kitchen. No one before or after her, according to Ouma Sannie's big family, ever cooked so well. But she probably also overcooked the cabbage. I think Ouma believed it was more digestible that way.

I left home, left the Hex Valley to go to university and the bright lights of Stellenbosch. One of the pleasures of returning home for holidays was to stroll across the road, through the farm gate, and up to Ouma's backyard. A huge mulberry tree overhung the outside cement sink where pots and pans and other really dirty things were scrubbed clean with fine sand. Her beloved chickens would cluck contentedly in their large coop in the shade of the rustling eucalyptus trees. Cement stairs led up to the screen door, which would squeal when I opened it. The back door led into the scullery; the old milkroom opened to the left. Then I was in the kitchen, with its unique scentprints of waxed linoleum, soap, smouldering coals and fresh firewood, overlain with the faint perfume of coffee. It was also, like returning to my parents' home, a homecoming for me.

Once, back for a holiday, I stopped in the kitchen, absorbing the achingly familiar atmosphere. Tears of self-pity welled up because a love affair had just ended. I could not talk to my mother about it; she considered university romances as fleeting incidents, ships passing in the night, not to be fussed about.

"And this, child?" Ouma asked when I curled up on the window-sill in the pantry. "Why are you so sad?"

I told her about the boy, how beautiful he was, with his blue eyes and golden hair, his broad shoulders. I told her how much I loved him, but that he'd spurned me for another girl …

"Child," said Ouma, "let's make some fresh coffee …" I followed her into the kitchen, where she busied herself with a bag of coffee and fresh water and her battered enamel coffee pot.

The kitchen was empty; the servants were off duty. We sat at the kitchen table while the coffee steeped for a while on the singing Aga. Ouma listened to my tale of love lost without once interrupting or belittling my heartache. Then she stood up, and took the coffee pot off the stove with a kitchen cloth. She poured the black, dangerously strong liquid into our waiting cups.

"Child," she sighed and sat down again, "you should understand … a woman's love is like her private parts, all neat and hidden away, deep and mysterious, able to bear new life and cherish it. A man's love, on the other hand, is like *his* privates. It all hangs out, weird-looking; it's all superficial, and it's there for anyone to use and he doesn't mind who. No depth to it. That's a man's love."

No gentle quoting of Victorian verse to me or too-careful pandering to my romantic mourning. I burst out laughing. The sorrow of lost love began to lift.

Pork Chop Marinade

Simply reading this recipe makes one realise it is ancient, because it's so different from modern recipes. This is one of the very few recipes we have from Ouma: her daughters-in-law copied it, and from them it came to us, the numerous female cousins. Pork loin chops tend to be dry. This marinade not only preserves the meat, but somehow makes it succulent. It is obvious that pork chops would have lain in this marinade in the days without refrigeration, and then pan-fried, perhaps, although they are far better grilled over wood coals. Please note: the marinade is not eaten … and exact quantities are not that important. It's a piece of Africana, this one, and you'll be pleasantly surprised at what it does to the chops!

½ cup soft, dried apricots, firmly pressed into the cup when measured OR 1 cup, loosely tossed in

3 very large onions, sliced into thin rings

2 cups grape vinegar OR 1 cup grape, 1 cup cider vinegar

6–12 well-bruised lemon leaves OR, if you don't have any, use strips of lemon peel

1 tablespoon curry powder

2 tablespoons sugar

½ teaspoon salt

1 teaspoon turmeric

1 tablespoon crushed breyani spices OR other crushed spices such as cardamom, cumin, anise and pepper-corns

Boil the apricots in water until soft. Enough water should be left in the pot to be able to liquidise the apricots (or mash it, like Ouma did). At the same time, boil the onion rings in the vinegar until tender. Then mash the apricots (or use a blender) and stir into the boiling onion-vinegar mixture. Remove the pot from the heat, and stir in the remaining ingredients. Let the mixture cool. (And don't worry about the tremendous sourness: you're not going to eat it).

This is enough to marinate 10–12 chops depending on size. If the marinade is too thick, thin with a little water. Use a glass or porcelain dish which will not react with the acid. Ladle some of the mixture on the bottom, spreading it. Pack a layer of chops tightly together. Layer over more marinade, then add more pork chops and the last of the marinade. How you do it, will depend on the size of your container. Make sure all the chops are in contact with the marinade. Cover with plastic film and keep in the fridge. It's a good idea to turn them once or twice, making sure they are marinating all over.

You can safely keep them in the fridge for 2–7 days before use.

To use: Scrape the marinade off the chops with a spatula, and discard. The chops don't have to be frantically scraped; just get rid of most of the marinade. By far the best is to grill the chops over open coals. Don't overcook them, and only salt them lightly after grilling.

CHAPTER 3

~ Beach Sand and Beskuit ~

THE SEA, THE SEA, THE OPEN SEA,

THE BLUE, THE FRESH, THE EVER FREE;

WITHOUT A MARK, WITHOUT A BOUND,

IT RUNNETH THE EARTH'S WIDE REGIONS ROUND;

IT PLAYS WITH CLOUDS, IT MOCKS THE SKIES,

OR LIKE A CRADLED CREATURE LIES.

I'M ON THE SEA, I'M ON THE SEA,

I AM WHERE I WOULD EVER BE,

WITH THE BLUE ABOVE AND THE BLUE BELOW,

AND SILENCE WHERESO'ER I GO.

IF A STORM SHOULD COME AND AWAKE THE DEEP,

WHAT MATTER? I SHALL RIDE AND SLEEP.

Barry Cornwall

My father is now ninety-three years old, the second-born of six children. Ever since he was a small child, he and his family used to go on a summer holiday to Kleinmond on the West Coast, in December and January. He tells me what he remembers.

In that time far beyond my memory Kleinmond was no more

than a tiny collection of simple dwellings hidden away in dense bush on the edge of a primeval coast.

If you ventured into that wild wilderness, you were on your own: if you forgot something vital at home, too bad. Like almost the entire coast then, it was pioneer country. Long ago small bands of *Strandlopers*, the early tribes, wandered there, living off shellfish and edible bulbs. As often happened in Africa, they have wholly disappeared, leaving behind faint traces of their fragile lives in the form of mounds of shells where they ate and slept. Even these have been shrouded in sand and sedge by the winds of time.

This was the place my Oupa chose for his annual seaside holiday. My father cannot remember many details from those early days, except for their joy and exultation at being in the wilds. They stayed in one of those primitive houses in the bush, augmented later by tents for the older children and the servants.

"It was a paradise," Dad recalls. "The entire coast was a tangle of shrubby coastal bush and *fynbos*, wildflowers, and those stunted trees you find near the sea. There was nothing of civilisation; every excursion we made was an adventure into unknown territory …" No big trees grew near the Kleinmond encampment except for some tall eucalyptus, no doubt planted by an ancient and far-seeing wayfarer.

"What about snakes, Dad? There were always snakes in the bushes, even when we were kids?"

Dad laughed, another amusing reminiscence for him: "Thank heavens we were never bitten!"

Naturally it fell to the womenfolk on the farm to prepare for those momentous weeks in the wilderness; to make sure all needs would be met. Ouma and her maids were busy for weeks. They saved up eggs, rubbing them with pork fat to seal the shells and so preserve them. Then the eggs were packed carefully in wooden boxes in wood shavings – the thin shredded "wood-wool" in which the export grapes were packed. Slaughtering took place, and slabs of pickled pork and beef went into brine in an oaken vat of about five feet high. Butter was wrapped in greaseproof paper, and added to the brine.

Every possible household necessity was taken along. Flour, salt, sugar, coffee beans, pails of snow white pork fat, pots and pans. Extra mattresses, bed linen, towels, soap, medicines.

And Oupa's family of six children had to have fresh milk.

A week before the departure date Oupa would load a Jersey cow in milk on the train, with a man still remembered as "old Hans" as her minder. This journey of Hans and the cow was amazing ... Feed had to be loaded for the cow and provisions for old Hans. Somewhere en route to Cape Town, probably at Eerste River, Hans and his cow had to change trains.

From Eerste River they travelled as far as Bot River, where the two finally disembarked. Bot River was still several miles from Kleinmond. So Hans and his charge would tackle the last leg of their journey on foot – slowly and gently, so that her milk would not dry up. Hans milked her when necessary, watered her, let her rest. So they ambled their way to the sea, which probably took another two days.

"Near the Kleinmond house was a nice protected clearing in the bushes," Dad tells me, "where the cow stayed. Father brought along bales of lucerne for her ..."

Oupa was a very hard-working farmer used to rising before dawn. The seaside holiday was his only break of the year, and the prospect made this taciturn man with his brooding eyes act like a child. He annoyed his entire family immensely by refusing to go to sleep the night before departure. He was too excited. He wound up his gramophone and listened to his scratchy records into the early hours. By 2 a.m. he would rouse the house and the farmyard: "Up, up! We have to be off!" The dogs started barking hysterically. Everyone crept blearily from bed, not having slept at all well.

Ouma was highly irritated at her husband, who had kept her from her sleep with his "childish nonsense". Outside the loaded truck was waiting. The portable little chicken coops had been hung beneath the lorry the previous night: Ouma never, in all the years I knew her, went on holiday to Kleinmond without her chickens. The children, servants and all the pets clambered aboard the truck. Ouma and Oupa themselves followed behind the lorry in Oupa's old gunmetal-blue Chevvie.

"My father had no head for mechanics," Dad chuckles. "He'd heard from someone that a car can "seize" if it did not have enough oil. So for this journey he always poured far too much oil in the sump. By the time we hit the first bad hill just after Villiersdorp the engine would be flooded with oil and the clutch would start to slip. Everything came to a dead stop. We jumped off the truck and ran to find stones to put behind the Chevvie's wheels so it would not run backwards."

Today, it's a trip of maybe an hour. Then, over untarred, dusty, winding roads, up and down hills, with a Twenties Chev and a creaking farm truck loaded to the gills, it was a journey of adventure. The car boiled often. The truck boiled. It seems boiling engines were a normal feature of any journey then.

When they arrived at last, Ouma and the servants would first have to clean the dusty, spiderwebbed house. The windows were washed, the rooms swept and swabbed, bedrooms cleaned out and beds made up with Ouma's fresh linen. The very basic kitchen with its little black coal stove was scrubbed clean. My father does not remember – and as a child he would not have cared less – whether there was running water. Probably not; the house probably had one or two rainwater tanks.

And every year Ouma was absolutely infuriated when Oupa waited only until the first bed had been made up in a cleaned room. He'd undress and get into bed with a satisfied sigh, and fall asleep.

But women have to carry on regardless … Ouma, like many thousands of women then and now, had to contend with far more primitive conditions on holiday than those in the comfort of her own home. And sea air made the many mouths ravenous. "What could not be cooked inside," Dad says, "was done outside on small cooking fires." Strange as it seems now, grilling meat outside as a social ritual – *vleisbraai* – apparently did not exist.

My father and his brothers became ardent anglers. Fish were plentiful. "You cast in, and you hauled out a fish. No exception," says Dad, perhaps exaggerating. At some stage during the holidays, however welcome fresh fish was, Ouma forbade them to come home with yet more fish. There was no way to preserve it. Electricity was a long way off in the future. The notion, then, that the seas could be fished out one day was, of course, unthinkable – as far-fetched as a strange nightmare.

Bait for angling was usually redbait and white sandmussel. White mussels, scarce now, could be found in colonies just below the sand on the low tide line. They were pried open, the meat taken out, and, if not used for bait immediately, they were salted and put on gunnysacks to dry in the sun.

Mum remembers: "When I was already married to your father and your Oupa rented a big house – Kleinmond was a tiny village by then – we would still travel on the truck itself. The two youngest boys went in the car with my in-laws.

"The truck was a travelling circus ... Children, servants with babies, the dogs, the cats ... Always mountains of household stuff, like extra mattresses, blankets, folded tents, suitcases, trunks, cardboard boxes full of food, piled high and secured with ropes ... the meats sloshing around in the brine in the capped wooden vat ... And every single year, as we travelled through Worcester long before dawn the damned rooster would start crowing. We were a sight worse than any troupe of medieval raggle-taggle gypsies. The rooster would crow and the dogs would yap and bark and people would open their windows to stare at this cavalcade ... I nearly died of embarrassment!"

After Oupa's death some years after World War II, Ouma carried on with the same holiday traditions. Later still my Uncle

Uli, by then farming the old family farm, sent a truck ahead with maids, the pets, and a few strong young men. The house, above the beach, would be cleaned and the yard cleared of weeds and devil's thorn – the latter could be hell on grandchildren's feet. By evening the lorry would return home, but Ouma's cook and a second maid would stay behind to keep house and wait for her to arrive in comfort in someone's car.

Not far from Kleinmond there used to be a picturesque little harbour, reached, in olden days, by nothing more than a few footpaths through the *fynbos*. Later a gravel road turned off the main road and meandered down to the harbour. This was Visbaai, a small community of Coloured fisherfolk who had lived there since time immemorial.

The little harbour was dangerous. The swell, as it rolled in, was huge, and those fishermen had to know the exact moment when they could shoot past the breakwater to come back in. In stormy weather there could be no fishing. They used small wooden boats called *bakkies*, which were no more than rowboats way back when. Later they were equipped with outboard engines and later still they became bigger and sturdier. Those early boats were mere acorn husks on the eternally heaving Atlantic.

It was a poor and very isolated community who lived from the sea and grew sweet potatoes and pumpkins in little plots scratched from the sandy earth. There was a fish-drying shed with a thatched roof. Here the bokkems – salted *masbanker*, mackerel and *hottentot* – hung in long rows like dark spiky necklaces. When the icy northwester howled in winter, and there was no fresh fish, these would be eaten and sold: dried fish to eat with home-made bread and sweet milky tea. To me, this is a treat to this day, a comfort food, although bokkems are now as scarce as truffles in Provence.

I recall so well, during all the years of our holidays with Ouma, standing high up on a rocky ledge with my cousins as we waited for the boats to come back. This was usually around eleven o'clock. "There they come!" the shouts would go up as the tiny black dots appeared far out on the green waves.

Those people had a hard life, a much harder life than I could appreciate then. I saw Visbaai as merely picturesque; a place where kindly old fishermen took us along to watch them take up their lobster traps, where weatherbeaten women in *kappies* leaned on their lower doors watching the sea through eyes narrowed against the sun. Sometimes they asked whether we'd like a few *bokkems* or a *vetkoek* – dough pinched off from bread dough and baked in a pan sizzling with fat. Even our hikes to Visbaai, through grasses and bushes higher than our heads as we jogged along the footpaths, were magical mystery excursions.

One should never go back to places where you were happy as a child. After an absence of more than two decades, I saw Kleinmond again. It would be unreasonable to expect any coastal village not to expand, but still I was shocked.

I saw a vast urban sprawl which had swallowed up the wild bushland, the fields of rushes, the *fynbos*. The small game have been chased away and the untamed natural beauty eradicated by money and greed. The town now stretches as far as the Palmiet River, once a black, lonely and mysterious Styx.

There might be beautiful houses and lovely gardens tucked away, and the inhabitants surely love their town, but for me all the old enchantment has been ruined. The only aspect that could not be entirely destroyed is the rocky coast, the endless beach and the sand dunes. And yet even this magnificent coast now seems diminished, hidden from view, incidental to the grid pattern of nondescript houses. The beach opposite the hotel looks trampled and tired; the sand has lost its clean golden hue of long ago, as if too many careless feet have trodden it over too many years.

When I saw the remnants of Visbaai, it broke my heart. The old slipway was deeply pitted, and the harbour was surrounded by the usual hideous late-twentieth century shoebox buildings. The harbour wall had cracked in two and was drunkenly listing into the endless breakers. Nothing, nothing was left of the original white-washed houses with their distinctive chimneys. As I stood there in the wind watching the swaying bamboo fronds beyond the broken breakwater, I sensed clearly that the spirits of the fisherfolk who had lived out their humble lives around Visbaai had fled long ago. Nothing was left of them; the very air around me had changed.

Our December holidays with Ouma in Kleinmond form one of the pillars of my happy childhood. Our Christmas was a simple affair, the dinner on Christmas Day being the high point. "Father Christmas" appeared magically during the night of Christmas Eve while we were all asleep, and we woke to see that the empty pillowslips we'd hung on the ends of our beds were now full!

One of Ouma's major culinary achievements, her wonderful boiled Christmas pudding, seemed to be all in her head. No one ever saw the recipe; she certainly never used one when she made it.

It was a rotund queen of desserts.

Two days before Christmas she sat down at the kitchen table of the Kleinmond house with a young maid at her elbow. The mixing of the pudding was something of a magic ritual. Little piles of ingredients had been put on the tabletop within arms' reach – brown sugar, spices, raisins, dried fruits, salt. Dates and glistening glacé cherries. Nuts. A tin container of flour. If she'd forgotten something, she would send young Emma to fetch it.

I see her: tranquil, pale features, mouth slightly pinched with concentration, as she measures off flour roughly and puts it in a huge ceramic mixing bowl. The bowl has a creamy yellow glaze on the outside. She adds ingredients to this bowl by pinching her five slender fingers together and picking up the amount she wants from the piles: her fingers are her measuring spoons. Sometimes, thoughtfully, she adds a tiny bit more of the same ingredient. She is quiet. But there is never a recipe she reads from. She knows it by feel, by heart.

The pudding has its own special cheesecloths, which will be well-floured before the batter is encased in them and tied with string. The pudding will be boiled on the Ellis de Luxe, and then cooled. On Christmas Day it is heated again, and Ouma prepares two sauces for the pudding: a cinnamony, milky sauce for herself and the children, and a heady brandy sauce for the rest. Sometimes Dad sneaks in and adds more brandy to the "adult sauce".

Mom reminisces: "Moya and I sat down with Ma and copied what she did as best we could. Then we tried making that pudding exactly the same way. It didn't work. It simply wasn't the same at all."

After the Christmas dinner around the table in the beach house – a rowdy affair with aunts and uncles and cousins – a maid would carry in the round, fat Christmas pudding on a platter: the little scene came straight out of a fresco showing Romans at feast. The only difference was that we were not reclining on benches. The remnants of the vast dinner would still be on the table; an uncle might be stretching a last fork towards a piece of chicken skin or pork crackling. The maid would put the platter down in front of Ouma, naturally at the head of the table. Ouma carved her pudding: large round gleaming slices that turned over gracefully in the platter. The pudding had none of the overly rich stodginess of fruitcakes or plum puddings, which plop heavily into the stomach. There was something different about it, a lightness which belied its solid texture. It was deeply seductive. Even after the superabundance of the Christmas dinner we all still had room for that pudding.

But only Ouma knew its secrets. When she died her Christmas pudding died as well and is interred with her bones.

I do not know whether Ouma ever had a scrapbook of recipes, but surely she did not make all her cakes and cookies from memory. But I cannot recall such a book, except for an old printed hardcover book which I was allowed to have after her death.

This piece of Africana is called *Die Suid Afrikaanse Kook-, Koek- en Resepte Boek* and was written by the well-known Mrs E. Dykman of Paarl. Inside, Ouma had written her name: Sannie Coetzer. It had been given to her by a Mrs Roper. It is the eighth edition, and does not have a publication date, but it can be deduced from the advertisements inside that this edition could have been printed no later than 1912, before the days of formal Afrikaans language rules and hence the proliferation of what would now be considered spelling mistakes. The pages have yellowed, but the book is in fairly good condition. It is clear from the lack of pencilled notes, food splotches and other signs of use that Ouma did not cook from it.

As for Tima's legendary cooking, only a few scraps of information are left.

Soetkoekies (Sweet cookies)

This is a very old traditional South African recipe. As with all traditional recipes, many variations exist. It's worthwhile trying, as it keeps, airtight, for ages, and it's delicious. I have only metricated where metric weights are easier to use. A cup is always 250 ml.

5 cups cake flour

2 cups yellow sugar

1 teaspoon bicarbonate of soda

1 teaspoon ground cloves

1 teaspoon allspice

2 teaspoons ground ginger

3 teaspoons ground cinnamon

Optional: 1 teaspoon grated nutmeg

2½ teaspoons salt

125 g soft butter

125 g rendered soft pork or mutton fat*

125–200 ml sweet wine like muscatel or sweet sherry

2 jumbo eggs, whisked well

Preheat oven to 190 °C. In a large container, mix the flour, yellow sugar, all the spices and the salt. Rub in the butter and fat with your fingers and palms, until the mixture resembles bread-crumbs. Add just a little sweet wine to the whisked eggs, then stir into the dry mixture. Now add just enough of the sweet wine to form a fairly stiff dough. Knead, then roll out thinly on a floured surface. Press out large round shapes, carefully place on greased cookie trays, and bake for about 12 minutes in the preheated oven. Check after 10 minutes. You will need to bake them in batches. Remove with an egg-lifter and let them cool and harden on racks. Store in airtight tins.

* To obtain the rendered fat, ask your butcher for clean pork or mutton fat. We prefer pork fat in this case. Cut it into small cubes, and render over low heat. The fat will slowly liquify and bits of crackling will form, which you don't want for the recipe, but which taste great with a bit of salt … Pour off the fat at frequent intervals into a suitable container to prevent it browning. It is worth your while to use rendered pork fat, as it makes a difference to the taste and texture of the cookies.

This recipe should yield about 50–60 cookies depending, naturally, on how thickly the dough is rolled out and the size of your cookie cutter.

Ginger Cookies

625 ml flour

200 ml sugar

3 ml salt

5 ml mixed spice

5 ml ground cinnamon

15 ml ground ginger

170 g butter

30 ml golden syrup

10 ml bicarbonate of soda

60 ml milk

Preheat oven to 180 °C. Sift the flour, sugar, salt, mixed spice, cinnamon and ground ginger together. Rub in the butter with your fingers until you have a crumbly mixture. Mix the syrup, bicarbonate of soda and milk. Add to the dry ingredients and mix to form a soft dough. Roll into golf-ball sized balls. No need to press down. Bake for 15–18 minutes. Makes 36 or more.

Basic Sweet Biscuits

250 g butter

300 g castor sugar

2 jumbo eggs

5 ml vanilla essence

500 g flour

15 ml baking powder

3 ml salt

Preheat oven to 180 °C. Cream the butter and sugar until light. Add the eggs one by one, beating well after each addition. Beat in the vanilla. Sift together the dry ingredients. Fold it into the butter mixture, to form a soft, rollable dough. Rest dough for at least 30 minutes. Roll out to 4 mm thickness. Cut into shapes. Bake for approximately 15 minutes. Dust with castor sugar while still warm. Makes about 50 cookies.

Bobotie

Countless variations exist, of course, for this traditional dish.

1 onion, chopped	1 apple, peeled and coarsely grated
oil for frying	2 thick slices of white bread, soaked in milk
20 ml good curry powder, or to taste	A handful of sultanas
5 ml turmeric	2 eggs
750 g–1 kg minced lamb or mutton (traditional)	Bay or lemon leaves
30 ml red grape vinegar	Almonds (optional)
30 ml smooth apricot jam	About 125 ml milk
About 7.5 ml salt (to taste)	

Preheat oven to 180 °C. Fry onion in oil, stirring, until soft. Add curry powder and turmeric, and fry for a minute or so. Add the meat, vinegar, apricot jam, salt and apple, and stir to break up any clumps. Take the bread from the milk, and squeeze very lightly; it should be wet. Break up and add to the pot. Add the sultanas.

Put the meat mixture in a greased oven dish. Beat 1 egg and stir in well. Smooth the top, and stick lemon or bay leaves and almonds into the bobotie in an upright position. Bake for about 45 minutes.

Beat the other egg with the 125 ml milk. You can stir in a little turmeric to add colour. Take the bobotie from the oven, pour over the custard, and bake further until the custard has set, for about 10 more minutes. Serves 4.

Ouma's Snoek Tart

125 ml grated Cheddar
300 ml soft breadcrumbs
10 ml soft butter
375 ml milk
20 ml cornflour
2 eggs
White pepper and a tiny bit of salt
250 g smoked snoek, boned and flaked

Preheat oven to 170 °C. Mix the cheese into the breadcrumbs and press into a small buttered pie dish to form a kind of crust. Whisk the butter, milk, cornflour and eggs together. Season with pepper and a little salt (remember that the snoek is salty). Stir the flaked snoek into the milk mixture, fill the pie crust, and bake until set (about an hour, but could be less).

Palates more partial to a bit of zing might like to add a few dashes of Tabasco, and an extra sprinkle of cheese over the top when nearly done and puffing up. Makes 4–6 servings.

Liver Patties

Some people detest liver. Ouma believed it to be, quite rightly, a most nutritious meat, rich in iron. I found this scribbled on a piece of paper in a drawer in her kitchen after she died.

1 sheep's liver, skin removed and soaked in milk*

1 large onion

2 tablespoons flour

2 eggs

1 cup milk

1 thick slice bread

Salt, pepper, grated nutmeg

1 tablespoon grape vinegar

1 teaspoon Worcestershire sauce

Butter

(*Presumably the liver had to soak for a few hours.)

Mince the liver and onion and stir in the flour. Whisk the eggs and milk, and soak the bread in it. Crumble the bread and add to the mince with the eggs and milk. Season well with salt, white pepper and nutmeg. Add vinegar and Worcestershire sauce. Mix well, form patties and fry in butter. Serve with mashed potatoes and chutney. Makes about 6 patties.

Ouma's "Mayonnaise" for Fish

This preposterous recipe lives on in one of my old recipe scrapbooks. Do not scan over it and dismiss it. It's cheap enough to try. It does go very well with all pan-fried fish, unlikely as that might seem! It can be made well ahead of time, put into clean bottles and refrigerated: it lasts forever. Change quantities given to suit your own tongue-taste test, but it should be on the sweet side. The slight condensed milk flavour which tends to come through goes away if the "mayonnaise" is allowed to stand in the fridge for a few hours. You're supposed to put a blob on the side of your plate … When we were kids we ate more "mayonnaise" than fish.

1 x 385 g tin sweetened condensed milk
½–¾ tin* white grape vinegar
20–25 ml hot English mustard
3 ml salt

(*Note that you use the milk tin to measure the vinegar. You can also replace some of the vinegar with lemon juice.)

Mix everything together, using a whisk. You might want to add more vinegar, but the mixture must be on the sweet side of sweet-sour! A pinch of cayenne pepper or dash of Tabasco can also be added. Makes about 350 ml.

CHAPTER 4

~ A MIDNIGHT PEACH ~

WHAT WONDROUS LIFE IS THIS I LEAD!

RIPE APPLES DROP ABOUT MY HEAD;

THE LUSCIOUS CLUSTERS OF THE VINE

UPON MY MOUTH DO CRUSH THEIR WINE;

THE NECTARINE, AND CURIOUS PEACH,

INTO MY HANDS THEMSELVES DO REACH;

STUMBLING ON MELONS, AS I PASS,

ENSNARED WITH FLOWERS, I FALL ON GRASS.

Andrew Marvell

They roll out of the thin plastic bag: three cling peaches, the size of my palm.

I wash one under the tap. I bite into it. It is faintly sweet, but with an overriding acerbity. I cannot chew it, much less swallow. I go to the window and throw it on the lawn. A hopeful seagull screeches overhead, then realises it is nothing that he will want to eat.

It is possible that I will never again find the perfect peach. We do not have a peach tree and I have to buy peaches. I would love to eat, just once, a Tuscan peach again.

A summer night, a long, long time ago ...

Although the windows were wide open to catch any night breeze, and the back door had been left open to let in a draught, the room was still too warm. I tossed restlessly while my younger sister slept curled up and motionless, like a little hedgehog, on top of her bedclothes.

Outside, a huge full moon was stuck in the fronds of Mom's flowering creeper. I rolled from the bed. My cat looked up quizzically from where she slept at the bottom of my bed, and fell asleep again.

A craving had taken hold of me as I tried to relax into sleep, tried to ignore the heat of the day which still hovered below the ceiling. This hunger and thirst had to be appeased before sleep would come.

I climbed through our bedroom window. A dark shadow snuffled joyfully into my patch of moonlight and rubbed against my thigh: our doberman, Sentry. He wagged his short tail and made whiny sounds: soft dog laughter of pleasure at such unexpected company from a member of his family while he's on his lonely nightwatch duty.

The night air was cool against my body in its thin nightdress, the soil pleasantly rough under my bare feet. Sentry and I walked along the gravelly garden path in the still moonlight. Across the road, on my uncle's farm, the frog chorus clacked happily in the earth dam, and a "whoosh!" alerted us to a barn owl, probably one of the family of owls who had lived in the attics of the farm outbuildings since time immemorial. Ouma's house slept solidly and smugly under its gables, in moon-dappled darkness under the eucalyptus trees.

In the oldest part of our large, rambling garden was a magnificent peach tree. Where it had come from, no one knew. Perhaps my grandfather had planted it a very long time ago.

In summer this tree bore enormous, fragrant cling peaches. It was a magic tree, for it seemed to be the only one of its kind in South Africa. I was never again to taste that particular peach after I left the Valley, but I did not know that then.

Dad called it a Tuscan: the Tuscan peach tree. Whether it really was of Italian descent, no one knew.

In late summer and autumn it drooped with orangey fruits more flavourful and juicy than anything Eve might have discovered in Paradise.

Sentry sat on his haunches now, tongue out, watching me as I stretched up to pluck a ripe peach close to the moon. I leaned forward to let the juice spill on the ground, and bit deeply into the sweet, perfumed flesh.

"Sentry, hmmm, it's just gorgeous! What a pity you don't eat fruit!" And I reached towards the moon again and plucked a second peach.

Only when my tummy was full with the ambrosial fruit, my fingers and my face and nightie sticky with its juices in spite of bending over, did I walk back towards the bedroom windows, Sentry at my heels.

The Tuscan peaches were solely for eating. For bottling, Mom bought big cane baskets full of other types of cling peaches. Most of the time she was simply *given* basketfuls for free. It was hard work, to bottle those golden fruits of summer. But they were beautiful when the shiny orbs in syrup had been arranged carefully in their bottles, and stood in sealed perfection on a cool, dark pantry shelf.

I take the two miserable shop-bought peaches which are left, and skin them partly. Then I go and put them near the birds' water bowls. Maybe the starlings or the mousebirds will peck at them: they do not know any better, and domestic fruits are scarce here on the sea. Somewhere in Europe, perhaps at this very moment, a child is biting into a fragrant, juicy, imported South African peach. And somewhere in South Africa beaming farmers still carry cane baskets of big, healthy cling peaches into the kitchens of industrious housewives.

I seldom bother any more with the half-ripe peaches offered in shops. Sometimes I buy a tray from one of the farm trucks selling them on the side of the road as I drive into Jeffreys Bay. That's the best bet, and I have been lucky this year to find really good, sweet clings. But these peaches which I now offer the birds have been a mistake: I bought them in a supermarket and I should know better by now.

Once you have known perfection in a product it is very difficult to settle for second best: all through my childhood and youth we had the Tuscan peach tree.

An old, gnarled loquat tree grew on the edge of our garden. It might have been a century old; it might have been planted by my great-grandfather: this soil had been in the same hands for four generations. Or a bird might have dropped its seed there thousands of seasons ago.

The loquat tree bore its small yellow fruits in bunches, and all the best ones were always highest up. But the loquat had decided early on in its long lifetime to be a tree for children; its branches were good for climbing: black and strong, and with many forks in which to sit.

So the loquat tree became a refuge for a sorrowful child. No matter what the passing sadness was about, the child would drag itself across the lawn, through the flower beds and the shrubs, to the loquat tree. The places on the lower branches where we had found the best handgrips had been rubbed smooth by the grip of many childish hands. A child could haul itself up, up, into a comfortable fork, and eat loquats, if there were any, or just sit there and pity itself and sob until it felt better. It was a good, sheltering tree.

I was shocked to find out recently that loquats are classed as "undesirable aliens". Our beloved loquat tree died of old age, long after I left home. I am glad no one can approach it with a hacksaw now, to kill it and call it an alien.

Somewhere women in aprons, with secret smiles, must still be baking seeded quinces filled with sugar and sultanas for dessert, and taking pleasure from their seductive fragrance. Or making clear honey-coloured quince jelly? Are there still pomegranates ripening in tangly trees, and do children still break them open for the sweet, shiny rubies inside? Do kids still seek out wild brambles, to pick blackberries, of which you could never get enough for your mother to do anything useful with, like making blackberry jam? They used to grow wild along the Hex River.

These are among the tastes I miss, for they have become scarce. Once, these fruits simply *were there*. You passed a pomegranate shrub – those I knew were more like snarled shrubs than trees – and plucked out a hard beige fruit. Once cracked open, it was a fruit you eat contemplatively somewhere under a shady tree, picking out the sweet, red seeds a few at a time, while your mind wandered elsewhere.

Quinces, as they ripen in storage, have a most alluring fragrance. But they are not often eaten raw. They can, however, be sliced, processed and bottled. They can be baked, with sugar and honey and cinnamon. I have a friend who does eat them raw, with salt.

Some three decades after the time I'm talking about, I had to discuss, as a lecturer in Johannesburg, a short story with a large class of college students. The fragrance of ripe, stored quinces played an important role in this tale, and I asked the class whether they could recall the particular fragrance of overripe quinces. They could not. They had no idea what quinces were.

Near the front door of my childhood home an apricot tree as ancient as the loquat crouched on a corner of the lawn. It delighted us with its blossoms in spring, and faithfully bore its fruits at summer's end. This tree also had a child-friendly gnarl of branches along which to crawl; the thinner ones, brittle with age, creaked under our weight, but did not break. Its fruits were perfumy, sweet, a pinky-orange. You squeezed the apricot along the shallow ridge which marked its downy roundness, and it would softly open up into two halves. We did this to inspect the area around the pip for the tiny, wriggly white worms which sometimes lived in ripe apricots. No doubt we ingested the worms now and then. But we came to no harm.

We would often keep the smooth brown pips. These we would sand down on a rough brick or a piece of cement until the kernel appeared, which we extracted with a bit of wire or splinter of wood. The kernels tasted like almonds. Of course, none of us had yet heard of laetrile, a doubtful cancer cure made years later from apricot kernels. We just liked that almondy "nut" inside the pip.

Our mothers and grandmothers all bottled fruits. Their pantries were their showpieces, small museums to their industriousness.

"I was lucky with my quince jelly this year," Mom might say to women visitors, and proudly take down a bottle to hold against the light, to be admired. If they considered their preserves good enough, they might exhibit it at the Women's Agricultural Association's annual show. Oh, to win a first prize for bottled apricots or whole-berry hanepoot *konfyt*!

As children we were blasé about grapes. The vineyards were all around us in serried trellised ranks; from December to April the different varieties swelled and expanded into green and purple berries which burst under our teeth, releasing their special scents and tastes. We were choosy. We pretended to like only this cultivar and not that one. We preferred to gorge on the *natrossies*, left on the vines because they were too small. These tiny spurned bunches became honeyed by the hot sun and yielded nectar until the weather grew cold and the seasons started changing.

The voluptuous colours of the autumn valley, that rich quilt of red and yellow, green and brown patches of vineyard, vanished with the first frosts. Icy northwesters blew in winter, and the vines turned into brown naked limbs which curled stiffly around their trellisses. As snow clouds covered the Hex River Mountains like grey shrouds, Mom would open a bottle of peaches for dessert, add a touch of vanilla, and warm it gently.

And we would eat the sweetness of preserved summer with hot custard while the winter winds blew outside.

But summer and autumn with their mellow fruitfulness would come around again, and the Tuscan would bear its fragrant fruits again and again, forever.

I did not know then that forever is but a short span of time. The past is a tender country, one to which we cannot return. We are exiled into the harsher present.

Apricots in Brandy Sauce

750 g firm fresh apricots (about 4 cups when halved and stoned)
250 g sugar
125 ml water
65 ml good brandy
30 ml fresh lemon juice
5 ml vanilla essence

Break or cut the apricots in half and remove the stones. Combine the sugar, water, brandy and lemon juice in a pot, and bring to boiling point, stirring frequently, until it thickens and changes colour (you want a caramelly sauce). Add the apricots and vanilla. Simmer about 5 minutes or until the apricots have softened – they should not be mushy.

If you prefer a stronger brandy taste (the alcohol boils away), add a little to the sauce after cooking the apricots. Serve warm or at room temperature with ice cream and slices of plain sponge cake, which you can buy in most shops. The cake slices should soak up some of the syrup. Enough for 6.

Peach Brûlée

This egg yolk sauce should not come near boiling, or it will curdle.
Use a thick-bottomed pot or a double boiler.

5 egg yolks
50 ml castor sugar
500 ml thick fresh cream
Pinch salt
10 ml vanilla essence
8 canned or bottled peach halves, drained
65 ml brown sugar

Beat the egg yolks and castor sugar until the mixture is thick and creamy yellow. Whip in the cream gradually, and add a pinch of salt as well as the vanilla. Heat the mixture, stirring with a whisk, until it thickens. Use a wooden spoon to test: when the spoon is lifted and the mixture coats the back of the spoon, the sauce is ready. Remove from the heat and whip for about 2 minutes longer.

Pour the custard into a heatproof serving dish, and cool. Arrange the peach halves, cut side down, on the custard. Sprinkle over the brown sugar and place the dish under a preheated grill until the sugar melts and starts to caramelize slightly. Can be served with vanilla ice cream. 4–8 portions, depending on appetites.

Sole with Grapes and Cream

This is delicious. It's easy; the only fiddly bit is that you have to peel and de-pip the grapes, but it's worth it. For 4 portions:

4 prepared soles

Seasoning salt of your choice

Ground black pepper

½ lemon

250 ml fresh cream

1 big bunch grapes, any cultivar, peeled and seeds removed

30 ml butter

Finely chopped parsley for garnish

Preheat oven to 160 °C. Butter an ovenproof dish. Put in the soles and season. Squeeze the ½ lemon over the sole fillets. Pour over the cream and add the grapes. Butter a large enough piece of foil, and cover the dish well. Bake in the oven for 15–20 minutes. Garnish with chopped parsley. Serve with unpeeled steamed baby potatoes, young peas, baby carrots and a green salad.

Preheat oven to 160 °C. Wash quinces well, and remove stem. They don't have to be peeled or cored. Pack them stem side upright in a deep oven dish, and fill up with about 2 cm of water which has been flavoured with 10 ml vanilla essence. Cover with foil or a lid and bake about 3 hours or until the fruit is tender. Add more water during the baking time if necessary. Serve as a dessert to be eaten out of the skins with fork and spoon. Serve with lots of runny honey, golden syrup or maple syrup, and cream whipped with sugar and vanilla. One quince per person is ample.

Because a quince is so tart, you can also core the fruit and fill the hollow with yellow sugar and sultanas before you bake it.

Brandied Peaches

For this you need perfect, just-ripe cling peaches, firm, with good colour and without blemish. Less than perfect peaches will not have a good flavour and aroma.

12 ripe, firm cling peaches
500 g golden brown sugar
1.5 litres water
1 litre brandy

Use large-size canning bottles with new or well-fitting lids. Wash them, rinse, and stand them in an oven dish. Put into a cold oven and heat oven to 160 °C. The bottles should be left at that temperature for at least 10 minutes or until you need them for the bottling.

Wash the peaches well, and cut them down to the stone, all around from the stem end. Use the thin "fold line" on one side of the peaches as a guide. Then take the peach firmly in both hands, and twist ... With a little practise, the two halves should come apart neatly. Remove the stone. Scald the peach halves in boiling water, then remove and plunge into very cold water. Remove skins. Add brown sugar to the water, and heat gently, to dissolve the sugar. Add the peaches. Simmer about 5–8 minutes, until tender – watch carefully, you don't want them to be mushy. Ladle the fruit into the sterilised bottles. Pour equal quantities of brandy into each bottle, then fill up with the simmering syrup. Screw on the lids, and wipe the bottles carefully. Keep in a cool place and allow to macerate for 1 month before use. The bottled peaches have an almost indefinite shelf life, but it's better not to keep them for years, as they will discolour and might lose flavour.

CHAPTER 5

～ A SHEEP AT LARGE ～

HAPPY THE MAN, WHOSE WISH AND CARE
A FEW PATERNAL ACRES BOUND,
CONTENT TO BREATHE HIS NATIVE AIR
IN HIS OWN GROUND.
Alexander Pope

In 1948, after the war, my father built us a house on the strip of land he had inherited – about six acres – which was part of the old family farm. His four brothers all received farms, but Dad had elected to go to university and become a teacher. Oupa did not believe in higher learning, only in farming. He did pay for Dad's studies and bought him a small car with a canvas roof, but Dad could not expect a farm if he was going to be a teacher and Oupa had already spent money on his education. So he was only given the small plot planted with vineyards and Elberta peaches.

This postwar house was the home in which I grew up. It was a very ordinary house, with a gable on one side. The ubiquitous red facebrick so popular after the war was used for the built-in flower beds which ran around the stoep. Three bedrooms, one bathroom. A sitting room, a dining room, a kitchen, a small study for Dad. From the bedroom allocated to me and my sister, Annie, we could see Ouma's house just across the road that bisected the farm. Later, our brother, George, would also be born.

We did not have much money, just lots of space. So we kept a Jersey cow which provided us with milk and rich golden butter, and Mom kept poultry and muscovy ducks in large coops under a grove of eucalyptus trees. She sold her glut of butter and eggs to the local co-operative store for pocket money. Sometimes a pig was fattened and once we kept a sheep.

Our kitchen was huge, because this was what my mother had desired most: a large kitchen where a table could stand comfortably in the centre. The walls and the cupboards were cream-coloured with pale green trim. Shiny cream was the colour of the Fifties: there wasn't much of a choice of paint colours then. Mom's kitchen had lots of counter space, glass-fronted cupboards, that essential table, and a scullery with a twin tub washing machine. The new electric stove was an extremely hardy and reliable Swedish model, a Husqvarna.

But it was not a cosy kitchen. It was too noisy; the acoustics could be unbearable and sounds reverberated. This was before Novilon and its family of soft floor coverings, and linoleum was not in fashion any more. So the floor was of some strange, hard tile. It amplified all sound. It had to be washed and polished laboriously. Mom would push the polisher up and down over the floor to wreak as much shine as possible from her cream-coloured floor, and the machine was as noisy as a steam train.

When that floor was polished and shiny, it was also slippery. More than once my dad, wearing his teacher's dark suit and smooth-soled shoes, slipped and fell, feet briefly higher than his head. We would go and snigger elsewhere, and Dad would pick up himself, his briefcase and his wounded ego, and stalk sulkily to his study with Mom's laughter following him. Dad hated that floor.

On drowsy summer afternoons, when the sun beat down like a hammer outside, Mom and Aunt Moya would sit at the kitchen table in a scent of coffee and gossip: the kitchen was always cool and shadowy in summer.

In that echoing kitchen the two women talked in low, intimate voices so a child could not overhear, and drank coffee.

"… You know, Elize came charging in on Tuesday morning, in a terrible mood as usual, because …" a voice would drop and the heads bow closer together, then the voice rose a little again. " … And apparently that spoilt brat of hers was in trouble at school again, but according to her it's all the school's fault, so …"

More whispering. An empty cup said "clunk!" irritably as it was put down firmly in its saucer. "No wonder poor Larry drinks … I said to Uli, no more going with Larry to rugby games at Newlands. In the end it's nothing more than a … whisper. You know."

Both Mom and Aunt Moya were radiantly healthy, but an observant, unseen child could deduce that other women's "women's troubles" also interested them greatly. "Yes … a full hysterectomy! Poor Miranda, and she wanted one more child at least … And I hear that Sarie …."

We did not know the terms they used, but children have an uncanny sensitivity to arcane subjects. So we eavesdropped about Aunt Poppy's uterus, Aunt Elna's caesarian and Aunt Molly's menstrual trials, none the wiser, but puzzled by the awful intricacies of the adult female world.

Sometimes Ouma would appear, her hands full of dirty papers or crumpled newspaper, complaining: "The people who walk down the road are forever littering! And I always have to pick up after them!"

Ouma would drop her pickings into the rubbish bin outside the back door; the mesh screen door would howl as it always did; was it ever oiled? Did we simply become used to creaking screen doors? And Ouma would wash her hands over the scullery basin, and then pull out a chair – the chair always screeched on the hard floor – and sit down with a sigh for all the troubles in the world. Mom would pour her a cup of coffee.

"Mother, we were just talking about …" and the voice dropped. "It's the talk of the town; only her husband doesn't know …"

Ouma would sip her coffee, always with a small, contented sigh. She loved coffee.

"The day Jan married that hussy we all said she would be the end of him yet. Even Emma tells me (even the servants know!) that Piet's red car is parked in a street somewhere near her home at least two, three times a week when Jan is at work."

"It's only a question of time before …"

I might be doing homework in Dad's study; it was easy to pick up snippets of conversation.

Annie would, with well-timed charm, enter the kitchen with her beguiling smile.

"Ouma!"

"Hello, my dear."

Annie pressed herself against Ouma, hoping that the three women would ignore her presence and continue their gossip. But my mother would gently send her away again, and all she would hear would be Ouma's complaints to her two daughters-in-law about cramps in her innards last night, and Aunt Moya saying she must get to Cape Town, as she really needed some new dresses.

My mother baked a cake every Friday. Sometimes she also made a tart. This was for us, but also for those unexpected week-end visitors. People did not make appointments to come and visit. They simply turned up on a Saturday afternoon or Sunday after church, or in the late afternoon. They did not phone ahead unless they came from afar and wanted to make sure we were at home. Those black wall phones were only used for necessary calls, like Mom phoning through her grocery order to the Co-op or her meat order to the butchery.

Our sheep arrived as a dear fluffy lamb. He grew quickly into a playful young sheep. He was kept, at first, in the Jersey cow's paddock. He had no name because he was destined for the pot, and you can't eat an animal that has a name.

The sheep was so tame that he was later allowed to roam outside the paddock. But due to some hormonal frustration the sheep became crochety. The playful head-knocking he indulged in with us humans became aggressive and caused bruises. He clicked up the steps of the stoep and nibbled my mother's prize pot plants. She stormed out to chase him away angrily, and he put his head down and chased her right back into the house. "Bloody sheep!" she yelled as she slammed the door in his face.

Dad had a *bakkie* which was always parked under some syringa trees. One afternoon the sheep stormed the part-time gardener, old Piet. Piet cursed loudly and blasphemously and made straight for the parked pick-up, the only possible place of safety he could see. Age and stiffness did not prevent him from vaulting on to the back like an athlete. There he had to stay, the sheep belligerently on guard, until my father, in his study, eventually heard Piet's frantic shouts and came with a whip to chase the pugnacious animal away.

The cow's enclosure would now no longer hold Sheep. He broke out. The worst was the way he could hide. He would camouflage himself in Mom's huge garden or somewhere in the vineyards, and no matter how much you reconnoitred, Sheep was nowhere to be seen. Until he spotted you, and came at you from behind a shrub.

The fashion, at the time I was a first year student, was for tight skirts. I was home on holiday when I minced towards the road one day in my very tight skirt and high heels, intent on a quick visit to Ouma. The sheep came out of nowhere, head down for the butting, and chased me. My skirt tore along the seams as I ran. I screamed and took the only refuge I could see: our wide wire farm gate on the tar road. I clambered up and hoisted my backside on to the swaying gate out of the reach of the sheep: to the vast amusement of my family, who rescued me some time later.

Another time he rushed straight at Dad, who was home alone. "There was only one way out; this animal is so big now," Dad explained later, "I had to get on his back and hold his horns. There I was, on the back of the damn woolly sheep, holding him by the horns, and he pranced and danced and tried to throw me. I prayed that no school child would come down the road on a bicycle and see me, the vice-principal, playing buckin' bronco on the back of a bloody sheep!"

We also had a pavement special dachshund mongrel at the time, a large, low-slung fat sausage about three times the size of a real dachshund, with a broad nose. My father had bought him as a puppy, for a ridiculous price, because he was told that

Boesman was a thoroughbred dachshund. My father trusted people too easily.

Boesman was no watchdog. He welcomed all the wrong types and accompanied them to the door, smiling and wagging his tail. But he chased innocent passersby on the street. He also made life hell for the delivery men on bicycles, who brought Mom's groceries and meat. He knew them as well as he knew us, but would never acknowledge the fact. He fetched them way up the road and yapped alongside the bikes all the way to the kitchen door, so of course he caused a few spills, accidents, and angry confrontations.

There was a small primary school in town for the children of farm workers. Early in the morning they came noisily up the road from the farms across the Hex River, laughing and chattering. In time they devised a game with Boesman.

In the afternoon when they jogged home from school they would stop at our gate, which was always open, and call out to Boesman. Boesman would come charging out with his fat body, for all the world like a miniature hippo, and chase the kids down the road. They would scream and yell and laugh, but after a hundred metres Boesman would be winded, stop in his tracks, turn round and puff homewards. Both Boesman and the kids enjoyed this game for ages.

One summer's day the kids stopped at the gate as usual, shoes hanging by the laces around their necks, books in careless bundles under their arms. They called to Boesman again. The shrill soprano cries went something like: "Boesman! Hey, Boesman! *Kom vang ons!* Boesman!"

Maybe Boesman was fast asleep in the summer heat or just not in the mood for chasing. Suddenly Sheep burst out from among

the verdant vineyard rows between our house and the road, where he had been grazing, invisible as usual. He lowered his head and charged through the open gate at the little crowd waiting in the road. Mom, who had come out onto the stoep, heard curses and fervent prayers being screamed into the hot air.

"Ohhh *Jissis*! Today we die! *Jissis, help ons!* It's a monster! Aaaargh …!"

Mother ran to the road, just in time to see shoes, books and schoolbags being wildly discarded all along the way so as not to impede their speed. The little troupe was already almost across the bridge over the Hex River, a few hundred yards down the road, still screaming, running for their lives, the sheep on their heels.

Later, much later, when the sheep was back in our yard, the kids crept fearfully back to pick up the ballast they'd gotten rid of in their headlong flight.

"Poor kids!" Mom laughed. "They expect a lazy brown dog who knows the rules of the game, and instead this huge white animal charges them and chases them right across the bridge! It's time for that sheep to go to other pastures …"

He made excellent eating. But it still felt a bit peculiar to be eating such a well-known adversary.

~

Leg of Lamb the Old-fashioned Way

Coriander seeds, about 3 heaped tablespoons	1 leg of lamb, about 2–2.5 kg
Peeled garlic	Bacon
Thyme (fresh or dried)	Red wine (Tassenberg is fine)
	Pinch cloves

Crush coriander seeds in a pestle and mortar – they simply fly about in a processor. Cut peeled garlic cloves into slivers.

Use a sharp knife point, and make a slit in the leg of lamb. Roll a small piece of bacon in the thyme and insert into the slit, along with a sliver of garlic. Carry on like this – slits about 6 cm apart – all around the leg. Have a non-reacting dish ready, large enough to accommodate the leg: glass or glazed ceramic. Firm plastic containers will also do. Rub crushed coriander all around. Put the leg in the dish, and pour over enough wine to come halfway up the leg. Pat on more coriander, sprinkle a pinch of cloves in the wine, and also add more thyme and chopped garlic to the wine marinade.

Cover lightly with plastic and put in the fridge. Over a period of 1–3 days, turn the leg over periodically. The meat will turn darker due to the wine.

Preheat oven to 180 °C. For roasting the leg of lamb, do not use the marinade, as it can taste slightly bitter when cooked. Rather keep a little back to use in the gravy. Put the marinated leg in an oven roaster. Sprinkle with olive oil or spray well with an olive oil spray. Slices of bacon can also be laid across the top. Add a little water to the roaster. If the leg has a decent layer of fat, it will not dry out and can be roasted without a lid. Otherwise, you can lay a piece of foil loosely over the leg, but remove 30 minutes before you want to take it from the oven, to allow browning.

We normally add enough peeled potatoes to the dish to roast alongside the leg. Roll them in a small bowl in oil before adding them to the roasting tin.

Generally, leg of lamb was roasted for about 25 minutes per 500 g and 20 minutes extra, but lately the fashion is for slightly rare lamb. Roasting times also vary according to the quality of the meat. But never overcook or the meat will dry out.

When ready, move the leg to a serving platter. So far no salt has been used, and the leg can be salted lightly at this stage. Keep warm.

Remove as much of the fat in the roasting tin as possible, but keep the juices which are left. If you used an ordinary metal oven roaster, it can now go straight on to a stove plate or gas flame. You can make a perfectly good gravy with plain Bisto, mixed into 125–250 ml lukewarm water and added to the pan juices. At this stage, add salt, some of the leftover wine marinade and a dash of Worcesterhire sauce to the gravy, and stir until it boils and thickens. Ladle some over the leg of lamb, and serve the rest in a sauce boat. Serve with mint sauce.

This is one of those ultimate comfort foods. You need whole, meaty lamb shanks, preferably the thick ones cut from below a leg of lamb. Ask a butcher to cut them for you.

You need one shank per person. It might look a lot, but the meat does shrink quite a lot while roasting.

Rub the shanks with olive oil, pat on fresh, roughly chopped rosemary, and add a tin of chopped tomatoes or some red wine. Put the shanks in an oven dish which will hold them tightly. I prefer a dish instead of wrapping in aluminium foil, to prevent a reaction between the acidic liquid and the foil. I also like to sprinkle balsamic vinegar over the shanks. And add slivered garlic, or even a whole, unpeeled head of garlic. (Cut off the spiky tops but don't peel at all). On occasion I have wrapped them tightly in aluminium foil with herbs, garlic and water: that works well too; note that an acid such as tomato or wine is not used then.

Cover the dish with foil, tucking in tightly round the edges of the dish, and bake for 3–5 hours at a low 140 °C. They can also be baked overnight, but at an even lower heat, about 100–110 °C.

The trick is to get the shanks butter-soft and just starting to fall off the bone, but they musn't disintegrate completely. So cooking times will very much depend on the meat – size, number of shanks, tenderness or toughness. It's easy enough to check, then shove back into the oven. I do not use salt until after the meat is done.

If you want gravy, mix a little Bisto – we're not going to be unnecessarily upmarket here – with about 150 or 200 ml warm water and add a dash of Worcestershire sauce, and add this mixture three-quarters of the way through the baking time.

This goes well with tender new potatoes and fresh spinach with shavings of parmesan – Parmigiano Reggiano.

CHAPTER 6

~ Mom's Food ~

COME INTO MY KITCHEN, DEAR,

AND HAVE A CUP OF TEA!

SIT DOWN AT MY TABLE, DEAR,

AND TELL ME WHAT YOU SEE!

CAKES AND MUFFINS, SCONES AND PIES,

AN OVEN-READY ROAST!

FLOOR IS SHINY, LAUNDRY'S DONE –

FORGIVE ME IF I BOAST!

Anon. verse

Mom was what is called "a good plain cook". She was not one for fanciful dishes: she seldom used recipes for meals, only for baked goods. Now and then she thumbed through a well-used recipe book for a sweet-sour sauce for tongue, or consulted a frayed newspaper clipping for a new recipe for *frikkadelle*. But most of the time she made meals in her fast, impatient way, with what she had to hand.

She was always up very early. Our breakfasts changed daily, but in a predictable way: it was either cooked oats or maltabella (sorghum) or mealie porridge or Weetbix. Mom considered boxed breakfast cereals to be junk food, which they were in those days. While we ate breakfast, she made us sandwiches to take to school.

Mom had been a primary school teacher, but after she married Dad she never worked outside the house again. In her days it was not the norm for a married woman to work.

When we arrived home from school with Dad, dinner was ready; Mom would whip it from the stove and the oven. Her food might have been plain, but it was delicious, and the vegetables came from Dad's prolific garden. By today's standards the vegetables were somewhat overcooked; that was the way it was supposed to be, way back then. Mom always served cauliflower with a rich cheese sauce, because that's how Dad liked it. But when Dad's green beans were still young and tender, she cooked them very lightly and smothered them with our own Jersey butter. We loved fatty meat and Mum's incomparable roast potatoes: we had not yet heard of cholesterol. And meat was cheap; Mom served platters of chops or steak and thick, dark winter stews. She marinated and roasted huge legs of lamb for Sunday dinner or pot-roasted slabs of beef.

Most meats were what would be called "organic" today. The animals lived on pastures and in coops until the day of their sacrifice, hormones and antibiotics in animal feed were unknown, and the meat was therefore naturally healthy.

Oven-ready poultry was not available in shops during the Fifties. The supermarket itself was an idea still germinating in a city somewhere. So in country places everyone kept a few hens and a rooster, and a chicken for Sunday dinner was a special treat. Dad was the executioner; everyone else ran away. One gets rather too attached to the poultry in one's own yard.

But when that sacrificial fowl lay on its oval porcelain dish, and exuded its wonderful scent, the mourning for the hen or the duck we had known for a while was over. The bird looked fat and round due to the oozing stuffing, and it was roasted to a glistening honey-brown. It had a very different flavour indeed from today's supermarket poultry.

Mom made a very simple poultry stuffing of breadcrumbs, the chopped-up giblets, bacon, onion, garlic, parsley, salt. She moistened it with milk and maybe added an egg. And somehow it was perfect.

She also kept muscovy ducks, the white French ones, for which Dad built a little concrete pool in their coop. So roast duck was also on the Sunday menu sometimes. Muscovy eggs for breakfast were huge, rich and delicious.

Mom baked gorgeous cakes of unsurpassed lightness and taste. Years later when I was married and living in Johannesburg, I was never able to get Mom's cake recipes to work for me as it did for her. The main problem was the altitude I lived at then, which plays havoc with cake recipes devised at low altitudes.

The popular social gathering of the ladies of the Hex Valley were the monthly meetings of the Women's Agricultural Association, held in the inhospitable, high-ceilinged old church hall some way from the town centre. There would always be cakes and biscuits and tea, and sometimes a lady from elsewhere would give demonstrations of flower arranging or talk about "wardrobe planning" or discuss recipes.

Cooking, baking, preserving, knitting and sewing were creative outlets in those days. It was long before pottery, yoga, gyms and painting lessons were part of the life of women in country villages.

"What recipes do you remember best, Ma, from those you used over the years?" I asked her recently over long-distance phone.

She is 85 now, and her eyesight is going bad. This woman, who made her own clothes and curtains, who knitted layettes for our babies, who tenderly handled seeds and tiny plants, who read so widely, now cannot even see the faces of her great-grandchildren.

"I don't remember them by heart. And it's so sad that I can't read recipes any more. So much has changed, and I'm stuck in my old ways." Her voice was rebellious.

She had to give up so many things which were precious to her: her knitting, her sewing, her magazines … My slender mother's grey-green eyes, which never even needed glasses, are going blind.

"If you have to talk about recipes, don't forget my cream puffs," she said.

Of course! Mom's cream puffs: large crispy-fluffy puffs filled with crème patissière. Her cream puffs were legendary in the Valley. She made them for friends' birthdays and our birthdays, for church fêtes and ladies' teas. She was famous for her cream puffs. They were the colour of our kitchen: creamy-yellow. She would dust them with icing sugar before serving. You sunk your teeth into the puff, into the just-right deliciousness of the crème patissière; you always ate too many of them.

"Mom, do you still have your recipe somewhere?"

There was silence at the other end of the phone line. There were regrets and sadness in that silence.

"It's in one of my recipe books. You or Annie must come and get it. It's no use to me any more."

"It's okay, Mom. Just tell me about it."

"You know all about it."

"I don't have your recipe, though. They were always so good, always came out the same! You only ever glanced at the recipe."

"Oh!" She was getting a little tired of the subject; too much probing into her busier, happier past does not sit easily with her these days. "I can't explain it to you. I knew when to beat in the eggs, what the batter should look like. I developed a feel …"

Her cream puffs consisted only of an ordinary roux which she dropped in spoonfuls on a greased tray. In the oven of the Husqvarna they puffed up like golden goslings, and when she slit them, they always had perfect hollows inside for the custard. She would not have known the words "roux" and "crème patissière". She called it a batter and a custard, which of course it was. She made a rich, deeply-flavoured custard of eggs and milk and … I do not yet have her recipe. There are other similar recipes easily available, yet I've never been able to duplicate the perfection of her cream puffs. Something is always missing, but it is not a physical ingredient. It lies in my mother's work-worn hands and her instinctive loving feel for the roux and the custard. It cannot be recreated.

She will never make them again because of her eyes. Their deliciousness, their sexy lusciousness is just a memory, like Ouma's Christmas plum pudding.

∼ MOM'S ROAST POTATOES ∼

This is how Mom made them, and this is the method I use.

Try to find yellow potatoes, not the hard white type. Peel and boil them. Put your oven on 180 or 200 °C. Don't let the potatoes fall apart in the pot, but they must be cooked, and the right sort of potato will flake ever so delicately on the outside. Lift them out with a slotted spoon and let the water drip off.

Put them in an ovenproof dish, and add a drizzle – or use a dessertspoon per potato – of ordinary sunflower oil. Don't salt them. Bake until they are crisp and golden; this might take more than an hour. You can turn them once if you like. The higher heat seems to work best. But it's okay to bake them in the same oven as, for instance, a roasting chicken. But they must be in their own container.

Sour Cream Pastry

This is one of those recipes I call "secret", but I'd love to share it.
It is a recipe from the Hex Valley.
This pastry should be treated like puff pastry: keep it cool
and never overwork it. It needs a very hot oven for the first
10–15 minutes. It cannot be baked blind in a pie plate, as the
sides will fall, so, like puff pastry, it should be baked together with
the pie or tart. It makes superb pastry for small meat pies.

I use a food processor to make it in a few minutes. Mom would
have rubbed in the butter by hand. Please do not even consider
using brick margarine. Only real butter will do.

Strangely enough, even though it's a rich pastry, it doesn't seem
to have the after-effects which might need antacid, like commercial
pastry made with cheaper products. I recommend this "family secret"
wholeheartedly.

625 ml cake flour (2½ cups)

5 ml salt

250 g cold butter

250 ml thick sour cream or, preferably, crème fraîche (1 carton)

Measure the cake flour (no need to sift) and ladle into the processor with the salt. Cut butter into chunks and add. Mix, first at low speed, then faster, until the mixture forms very, very fine crumbs. Add the sour cream/crème fraîche and mix – speed not too high – until a dough ball forms. Should it happen (it should not, actually) that your dough is too dry, add a teaspoon of vinegar. Scrape out with a spatula on to a floured wooden board, and form into a neat ball. Wrap in plastic and chill in fridge, at least 30 minutes and preferably overnight.

I much prefer crème fraîche to sour cream these days. It is widely available in containers similar to cream cheese containers, and you don't have to measure – just use the entire container. It is a lovely thick kind of sour cream, whereas ordinary sour cream can be too watery. Both cost about the same.

When rolling out the pastry (about 800 grams), it is easiest to cut off one third or one half at a time, as the dough will have stiffened. Flatten it somewhat on a floured surface by hitting it with you palms. Roll out thinly, about 3 mm thick.

Whatever you use it for, brush the raw pastry with beaten egg before it goes into the oven. Also use beaten egg to patch the pastry where needed. Always start the pastry at a high temperature and reduce the heat 10–15 minutes later. I heat my fan oven to 250 °C because heat is lost when the oven is opened. Then I put in my pastries, turn heat to 220 °C, and keep it there for 15 minutes. Then lower heat to 180 °C for the duration of the baking time. Try this pastry to make small individual chicken pies … delicious. Bake until your product is golden brown.

Chicken Pie

*This is another of the traditional dishes which has many variations,
but the recipe given here is pretty much the standard one. Buy a good
chicken: those thin blue-tinged, no-name chickens will not give
a good result. Look for plump yellowish flesh or well-fed,
free-range chickens. We're not talking diets here.*

1 chicken, about 1.5 kg
750 ml water
45 ml good granulated
chicken stock , not cubes
(Woolworths or Ina Paarman)
100 ml sago
45 ml cake flour
15 ml "garlic & herb" mixture
(or something similar)
Garlic, fresh or dried, to taste
7 ml grated nutmeg

5–10 ml coarsely ground
black pepper
Pinch ground cloves
Juice of ½ lemon
To taste: you could add thyme,
rosemary, or a little chilli
or Tabasco sauce as well
Seasoning salt like Aromat,
or to your taste
3 eggs

Remove giblets from cavity, if any, and any extra flaps of fat.
Use a large pot, preferably heavy-bottomed. First add the
water, then put in the chicken (this prevents the chicken
skin sticking to the bottom of the pot). Sprinkle the chicken
stock over the chicken and water. Cover pot with lid, bring
to the boil and turn down the heat. If the pot is small and
threatens to boil over, put the lid at an angle to allow steam
to escape.

When chicken is almost tender, soak the sago in a little water for a few seconds, and add to the liquid in the pot. Stir, and let simmer until sago is translucent – another 15 minutes or so. The chicken must be very tender: you want the meat to start falling from the bones.

Take chicken from the stock and place in a dish or bowl to cool, and leave the stock in the pot. When both stock and chicken have cooled so you can handle the meat, remove all bones from the chicken, or cut off the meat. Cut up the meat, and use everything, skin included. Scrape all meat from the carcass and the wings, discarding the wing tips. Make sure no fine bones remain in the meat. Do not chop the meat too finely, because it will affect the texture and taste adversely. Use a slotted spoon to remove all meat and bones which might have remained in the pot of stock. Use the bits of meat and discard all bones.

Add the flour to the stock, and whisk vigorously to prevent lumps forming. Add the seasonings to the stock, except the salt. First taste the stock – it might be salty enough as it is. Add seasoning salt if necessary. Whisk the eggs in a bowl, and add to the sauce.

Stir in the prepared chopped chicken and mix through with a wooden spoon or spatula. Taste again in case you need more seasoning or salt. At this stage the filling can be ladled into another bowl, covered in plastic, and refrigerated until needed.

To make the pie: Preheat oven to 220 °C. Use the sour cream pastry or bought puff pastry, and roll out a "lid" for your pastry on a floured board. Some people like to line their oven dish with pastry, but this could make the pie stodgy, and there is always the risk that the bottom pastry will not brown sufficiently and be "doughy". Serves 6–8.

Ladle the prepared filling into a suitable oven dish. The dish should be quite full and come to about 2 or 3 cm from the top. Brush the edges of the dish with beaten egg to make the pastry adhere. Drape the pastry over the filling – do not stretch; leave some slack in the centre as pastry shrinks when it bakes. Let it overlap some 4 cm. The pastry won't be a perfect fit – cut extra pieces if necessary and patch with beaten egg to the "lid". Pinch the edges of the pastry firmly to the edge of the pie dish with your fingers, brush the entire lid with beaten egg, and put into the hot oven. After about 15 minutes, reduce the heat to 180 °C, and bake for another 45 minutes or until the pie has puffed up well and the pastry is golden brown.

Mom's Chicken Stuffing

About 1 cup day-old white bread, crumbled (or processed
in a blender)

The chicken liver and heart, finely chopped

A few rashers of bacon, cut up

Garlic to taste, chopped

Good pinch dried thyme or 1 tablespoon fresh thyme leaves

½ teaspoon salt or seasoning salt

½ teaspoon white pepper

1 tablespoon soft butter (or olive oil)

1 jumbo egg, beaten

Milk to mix

Mix all ingredients except the milk in a bowl. Add enough milk
to make a soft mix – not too stiff, and not sloppy. Stuff the
chicken. Mom used to do some surgery as well: she used a large
darning needle and some of that thick cotton thread, and sewed
up the bird's backside so the stuffing would not cook out during
roasting. Remember to remove the telltale cotton thread before
the bird goes to the table.

Mom's Herb Dumplings

The word "dumpling" brings to mind a heavy, indigestible lump, reminiscent of old boarding houses, lurking in a soup or stew of a questionable pedigree. This particular recipe, quick and easy, should lay to rest the ghosts of dumplings past. They are featherlight, never flop, and they are comfort food at its best. I can't think of anything more satisfying than a thick, garlicky-fragrant bean or vegetable soup with these dumplings, eaten on a chilly night near a fire. As it's been used countless times by my sister and myself, it's been metricated.

250 ml flour	15 ml finely chopped parsley
10 ml baking powder	15 ml finely chopped onion
3 ml Aromat or Herb Salt	3 ml dried mixed herbs or
A few grinds of black pepper	15 ml chopped fresh herbs
About 45 ml soft butter	1 egg
(2 rounded tablespoons)	Milk

Sift flour, baking powder, salt and pepper into a bowl. Rub the butter and flour between your fingers until flour resembles breadcrumbs. Mix in the parsley, onion and herbs. Beat the egg and stir in with a fork. Now add just enough milk to form a sticky (not sloppy) dough. Drop dessertspoons of this batter into a simmering soup, or a stew with plenty of sauce. Cover the pot. Simmer for 20 minutes. The dumplings rise to the top as they cook, and it's best to take off the lid after 20 minutes and leave barely simmering on the stove for a while, so the tops of the dumplings can dry a little. Makes about 8–10 dumplings.

Granadilla Pudding

It helps to have a granadilla hedge for this one! A typical Fifties pudding, delicious after dinner on a hot day.

1 packet yellow or orange jelly
1 cup boiling water
1 cup cold water
1 tin sweetened condensed milk
Pulp of 10–12 ripe granadillas

Mix jelly into the hot water until dissolved, then add the cold water and mix well. Let the mixture cool until it just starts to set. Whip until foamy. Add the condensed milk and whip well again. Add the granadilla pulp, stir in well, and let the pudding set in the fridge. Makes 4–6 servings.

Banana Pudding

1 packet apricot-flavoured jelly
1 cup boiling water
2 cups cold water
1 cup cream or 1 cup icy-cold evaporated milk*
1 teaspoon vanilla essence
6 fully ripe bananas
1 cup castor sugar

Melt the jelly in the hot water. Add the cold water, and let it reach setting point. Whip well until foamy. Whip the cream (or evaporated milk) separately, and add the vanilla.

Mash the bananas well and mix in the sugar.

Add the whipped cream/evaporated milk and the bananas to the jelly and fold in well. Let the pudding set in the fridge, and serve with custard. Makes 4–6 servings.

*Evaporated milk will not whip unless well chilled.

CHAPTER 7

~ Aunt Ada's Abundant Table ~

SHE HAD A COOK WITH HER WHO STOOD ALONE

FOR MAKING SOUP WITH A MARROW BONE,

DEEP FLAVOURING HERBS AND SPICES FOR SAVOUR.

SHE COULD DISTINGUISH MAYONNAISES BY FLAVOUR,

AND SHE COULD ROAST AND BOIL AND SEETHE AND FRY,

MAKE GOOD RICH STEWS AND BAKE A TASTY PIE ...

AS FOR DESSERTS, SHE MADE IT WITH THE BEST.

with apologies to Geoffrey Chaucer

Ouma Sannie produced six children, a girl and five boys. The girl, Ada, was the eldest. My father was the second child, and four more brothers were born after him. They were beautiful children, evident from the old sepia family photographs. They had large, liquid eyes and secret, naughty smiles. Aunt Ada was later considered a real beauty. She married a young man who had been poor initially, and who had worked for her father. But Uncle Martin was extremely hard-working and shrewd, and he soon bought his own farm. As time went on he became wealthier and wealthier and bought up more land; he became a very rich man indeed.

Aunt Ada had therefore always been a privileged woman. She had been Oupa's favourite child and then her husband's adored wife, for whom she bore five children. Ouma, however, had instructed her daughter well in the old-fashioned virtues she held in such high regard, and Aunt Ada had brought those household skills into her marriage. These were never compromised by her moneyed existence.

She was compulsively, exasperatingly neat, a trait which infuriated her five children. She inspected their rooms and their cupboards for a single piece of underclothing not neatly folded, or a scrap of paper on the carpet. She sniffed through their bathrooms, which had to be shiny clean, always. This led to frequent rebellious feelings against their mother.

Uncle Martin and Aunt Ada were very hospitable people and had a permanently "open house", especially when their children and their cousins were teenagers. It was a lovely place to be over the weekend. At home we only owned one radio, but my cousins had the latest in hi-fi equipment and stacks of long-playing records of the most popular singers of the day. Over weekends music filled their lounge; when I hear the old crooners like Frank Sinatra or Dean Martin sing, I am transported back to that cool, soft lounge.

Aunt Ada liked having us there, as long as we behaved in a well-mannered way. The large American fridges in the pantry were stocked with cold drinks and food, which Aunt Ada sometimes set out on the long table of her breakfast room and then entreated us to eat, eat, eat! She always had a servant on duty; because of her compulsive sense for order and cleanliness, she probably could not bear to be without someone cleaning and washing up.

To me it was a grand house of incredible abundance. How wonderful, I often thought, to be so rich!

Helen, the same age as I, and her elder sister Susan were not spoilt, but with all that money they never wanted for anything either. Their clothes were bought in Cape Town's department stores – this was before the age of boutiques. They wore imported cashmere jerseys in winter with expensive pleated woollen skirts like those I saw in the Vogue advertisements in the town library reading room. They always had the latest fashions, and got enough pocket money to buy the latest hit records and much more.

Throughout my childhood and teenage years Helen and Susan would embarrass me deeply by asking every time we met, without fail, "What a nice dress ... Did you make it yourself?" Much as I loved my cousins, I could kill them for their innocently patronising air. My dresses were mostly home-made by Mom, and when I was older, by myself, but theirs never were. With all my adolescent insecurity, I yearned to be rich enough to buy my clothes at Stuttafords and Garlicks ... Sometimes when they asked their cliché'd question, I lied indignantly: "No, of course not!"

A Coloured lady called Sophie had worked for Aunt Ada from the time my aunt was a young married woman, into her old age. Sophie had worked for Ouma first, but wanted to go with Aunt Ada when she married Uncle Martin. So Sophie and Aunt Ada had practically grown up together. Sophie was generally adored by everyone. She was large and fat and she cooked like a chef. She loved life, and children, and she worshipped Aunt Ada, and when she laughed, which was often, she shook like a jelly. Aunt Ada loved Sophie right back like she loved her own mother. It was a domestic match made in heaven.

Sophie only ever left to have a baby. Aunt Ada would be devastated by her absence, and Sophie never stayed away long. When she came back, my aunt would burst into tears of joy, they would embrace, and the food would suddenly improve.

Sophie had the biggest, most pendulous breasts any of us had ever seen. They were awe-inspiring. You couldn't help it: they drew your eyes like a magnet. When Sophie's babies were small, she carried them around in age-old tradition: strapped to her back with a blanket or sheet. A male cousin joked, "Oh, when it's feeding time, she just tosses a tit over her shoulder for the baby."

Aunt Ada loved to cook, but she was better at baking than cooking. Her dinner table could seat ten or twelve, and at Sunday dinner she liked to see all those chairs filled. Uncle Martin, forever in love with his wife, just smiled indulgently. She and Sophie would both cook, not for ten guests, but for an army. And this created a problem for us, the guests.

Aunt Ada would never allow you to have just one plate of food. Maybe Aunt Ada, in her grand house, born into wealth and married into wealth, must have had it in her head that no one except her own family ever ate enough, and every outsider must be enormously hungry and was lucky to be at her table that day. She meant well: she pressed second helpings on you, then thirds, and would go on like this until you protested physically in some way, like getting up and taking your plate to the kitchen.

I can still hear her voice; still see her next to Uncle Martin, who ate dutifully well, and always with a small smile of contentment. "Come on! Have some more chicken pie!" she would cry. "Yes, yes, you must. You only had a little. And a slice of lamb … Now come on and be a good girl: hand me your plate!"

Unfortunately, once she had your plate, she would also add some more pumpkin, another roast potato, a spoon of green bean bredie …

The first helpings were generous anyway, so it was almost impossible to eat anything more. Aunt Ada's eyes would rove the table to pick out empty spots on dinner plates. "Come, some more …!" was her battle cry at her table, as if she were the reincarnation of Oliver Twist, at last returned to a life of plenty and in need of sharing.

Eventually we just laughed helplessly as she kept pressing food on us, and she did not realise that her very hospitality was the joke. In spite of our good manners we sometimes resorted to holding our empty plates in our laps, out of reach of Aunt Ada, who would be standing up, a spoonful of food held out over the table to tempt us.

Aunt Ada and her alter ego, Sophie, always cooked filling, traditional *boerekos* for these big Sunday dinners. But she loved entertaining, and she had the latest kitchen gadgets available, a privilege I greatly admired. In our kitchen at home, Mom made do with egg beaters, whisks and chopping knives. Aunt Ada had modern *machines*.

She and Uncle Martin entertained many visitors: overseas researchers who came to this valley of grapes on some mission, people they had met on their own travels, friends of their children, their friends in the Valley. Then she hauled out recipe books and scrapbooks. In a later age women with Aunt Ada's means would have called in caterers, but of course there were no such services then. You did your own cooking and baking – with a little help from your "staff", if you had any.

Cucumber Mould

This cucumber dish is easy and quick, and perfect for a summer buffet table. I remember a buffet table in summer, where Aunt Ada and Sophie had made more than one of these moulds and surrounded them with big, fat prawns and mayonnaise on the side.

625 ml grated cucumber	2 x 175 ml containers full-cream Greek or Bulgarian yoghurt
salt	
250 ml chicken stock	Pinch grated nutmeg
30 ml gelatine	To taste: seasoning salt
15 ml finely grated onion	
15 ml finely chopped chives	

Put the grated cucumber in a sieve over a bowl, sprinkle with salt (not too heavily) and let drain for about 30 minutes. Unless you have home-made stock, use Ina Paarman's or Woolworths' stock powder and mix with hot water according to the instructions.

Sprinkle the gelatine over the cooled stock, stir well, and bring to simmering point. Keep warm while you prepare the onions and press the liquid from the grated cucumber with the back a spoon. Mix the cucumber, onion, seasonings and yoghurt in a bowl and add the stock. Mix well and taste for seasoning. You can add a squeeze of lemon juice too.

Pour into a greased mould. Let set overnight in the fridge. Serve with meats, as a salad, or with seafood. Roughly 6 portions.

Mustard Ring

*Attractive and very nice with ham and any meat which
takes kindly to mustards. You can use a fairly
small glass mixing bowl as a mould.*

4 eggs	15 ml mustard powder
250 ml water	2 ml turmeric
125 ml cider vinegar	3 ml salt
175 ml castor sugar	250 ml fresh cream
15 ml gelatine	

Use a double boiler for this, unless you are an experienced cook, in which case a thick-bottomed pot will do. Bring water to boiling in the bottom of the double boiler. Beat the eggs in the top part, preferably with an electric mixer. Whip in the water and vinegar. Separately, mix the sugar, gelatine, mustard powder, turmeric and salt. Stir into the hot egg mixture and whisk until mixture thickens. Do not boil; you don't want cooked eggs. When thickened, take off heat (and off the boiling water) and let cool. Stir frequently while it cools.

Beat cream until thick and firm and fold into the mustard mixture. Spray your mould with nonstick spray, and let it chill in the fridge.

Unmould on a plate, and garnish with thin cucumber slices and parsley. As suggested, it goes with almost all meats, especially ham. It also complements a potato salad.

Corned Tongue with Sultana Sauce

This dish is made ahead of time, which is always helpful when entertaining guests. It only needs to be gently heated before serving.

Buy a salted beef tongue from a reputable butcher or supermarket. It is often best to soak a salted tongue in cold water for a few hours; a too-salty tongue is a disaster.

Boil the tongue in enough water to cover. Mom and Aunt Ada believed it should be boiled until marrow-soft: a saté or sosatie stick should slide easily through the thickest part. People put spices in the water in which the tongue is boiled, but this is a waste, because the skin is removed later so spices cannot possibly have any effect on the taste of the meat. A large tongue might have to simmer for 3–4 hours. Cool tongue in the pot.

When cool, the tough skin of the tongue should be removed, and all loose and suspicious-looking bits cut away. The tongue is then sliced fairly thinly and arranged neatly in a dish. You can moisten the meat with a little of the cooking water.

SULTANA SAUCE

125 ml yellow sugar	30 ml lemon juice
10 ml mustard powder	10 ml grated lemon rind
15 ml flour	About 375 ml beef stock
30 ml grape vinegar	125 ml plump sultanas

Mix the sugar, mustard powder and flour well in a small bowl. Put the rest of the ingredients except the sultanas in a pot, and stir in the dry mixture. Using a whisk to stir, bring the sauce to a boil and let simmer for a few minutes. Add the sultanas. Do taste for seasoning.

Ladle warm sauce over the sliced tongue. The dish can be cooled, covered and kept in the fridge. Cover with foil and heat in the oven before serving.

Serve with white or traditional yellow rice and a selection of vegetables. Portions will depend on size of the tongue, but normally should yield about 6–8 servings.

Sophie's Rich Cheese Sauce for Beef Fillet

Well, it doesn't have a proper name. Sophie served it on thick slices of beautifully rare fillet or rump or T-bone steaks, which she would hurry from the kitchen on hot serving dishes. I halved and metricated the recipe for greater ease.

375 ml grated mature Cheddar

30 ml tomato sauce

30 ml sour cream

3 ml Tabasco

Freshly ground black pepper

10 ml good quality table mustard of your choice

15 ml Worcestershire sauce

30 ml grated Parmesan (Parmigiano Reggiano) or Pecorino

Mix all ingredients except Parmesan with a fork. Prepare the meat until still rare, spread the sauce over each piece, sprinkle over the Parmesan or Pecorino, grill quickly until cheese melts. Serve immediately.

Orange rings: To counteract the rich sauce, orange rings (rind and all) can be poached in a mixture of water and Van der Hum liqueur until just soft. Drain and keep warm, and serve with the meat.

Moulded Chocolate Mousse

Cholesterol hadn't been invented yet, and Aunt Ada's often extravagant and luscious cooking did not prevent her from reaching the age of 85.

63 ml thick cream	5 ml vanilla essence
500 g Bournville chocolate, broken into small blocks	15 ml gelatine, softened in 60 ml water
6 jumbo eggs, separated	250 g butter, soft (not margarine)
15 ml of any orange liqueur (Grand Marnier or Van der Hum) or brandy	About 1 ml salt
	63 ml castor sugar

Using a double boiler is safest: bring water to a simmer in the bottom part. Put the cream in the top and add the chocolate, and let it melt. If you are experienced you can do this in a microwave or in a pot over low heat.

When the chocolate has melted, stir, and then beat in the egg yolks one at a time, beating until thick. Do not boil at any stage. Using an electric beater is easiest. Then stir in the liqueur and vanilla.

Remove from the heat and stir the softened gelatine into the hot mixture. Add the butter bit by bit and whip in.

Beat the egg whites until stiff. Add about 1 ml salt, and add the sugar 15 ml at a time. Beat until sugar is incorporated and egg whites are glossy. Gently fold the chocolate mixture into the meringue.

Pour into a greased mould and chill overnight. A medium bread tin works well, and the chocolate mousse can then be turned out on a rectangular plate. Decorate with cream, cherries and nuts, and serve with a cream liqueur as a sauce. Serves 8–10.

Carrot Coconut Cake

Aunt Ada said she'd been given this recipe in America. It's probably the best carrot cake I've ever tasted. Over the years I metricated the original recipe but otherwise it's unchanged. The finished batter always looks as if the entire thing is going to flop, but so far it's always been a success for me, and hopefully it will work as well for you too. It's not at all difficult or involved to make, but do assemble all the bits and pieces before starting, which makes it all go quicker.

500 ml cake flour	10 ml vanilla essence
20 ml baking powder	500 ml sugar
10 ml cinnamon	About 250 g crushed
5 ml ground mixed spice	pineapple, lightly drained*
5 ml salt	500 ml finely grated carrot
250 ml sunflower oil**	325 ml dessicated coconut
3 jumbo eggs	100 ml walnuts, broken up

Preheat oven to 190 °C. Grease a square baking tin (22 cm x 22 cm x 7 cm) or a large round one. Butter is the best greaser. Line bottom only with nonstick paper, and grease the paper again. Add a little flour and shake it to coat bottom and sides lightly.

Use a 440 g tin of crushed pineapple: let it drain in a coarse sieve, and do not press it at all. Leave until needed.

You could grate the carrot with the aid of a fine processor grater blade, which is quick. The nuts are optional, but such a nice addition that I wouldn't leave them out.

Mix the flour, baking powder and seasonings in a bowl. I don't sift the flour. Beat the oil, eggs, vanilla and sugar very well in a roomy bowl – an electric beater is best. The sugar will not dissolve completely.

Stir in the flour alternately with the rest of the ingredients: pineapple, carrot, coconut and walnuts. Beat well with a wooden spoon or an electric mixer.

The batter is runny. Pour into the prepared tin and bake for 1 hour 10 minutes or until a skewer inserted comes out clean. Do test it first, as ovens differ and it might need more baking time. If using a square tin, it's a good idea to cover the corners with pieces of foil to prevent them burning.

Topping: Mix 500 ml icing sugar with about 125 g cream cheese or creamed cottage cheese and 5 ml vanilla essence. Whip until smooth. Add only half the amount of cream cheese to start with, as it's easy to add too much. Add more as needed, to get a spread-able topping.

* You do not have to weigh the pineappple to be exactly 250 g: the 440 g tin works well. The trick is to drain off most of the liquid, but the crushed pineapple should still be fairly juicy, therefore do not press it down in the sieve.

** Sunflower oil is specified as canola oil is thinner and lighter.

Aunt Ada's Fruit Cake

Not even Aunt Ada could ever replicate her mother's Christmas plum pudding. But eventually most of us used her fruit cake recipe, because it is easy and quick, contains no eggs, and does not have the heaviness of the usual fruit cakes. Needless to say, the dried fruits should be of top quality, and spices should be fresh and strong-smelling.

250 ml yellow sugar
250 ml seedless raisins
250 ml currants
250 ml sultanas
250 ml cut mixed peel
(4 x 250 ml "cake mixture"
will also do if you cannot find
these four ingredients)

60 g, about ¼ package, pitted
dates, chopped
30 ml lemon juice
300 ml boiling water

In a very large pot – I use an enamel basin! – stir everything together. Bring to boiling and simmer 5 minutes without a lid. Remove from heat, cool (it doesn't have to reach room temperature) and add:

250 g room temperature butter
10 ml bicarbonate of soda

When this mixture has cooled down well, scrape into a mixing bowl and add the following, in the order given, and stir through very well. If using an electric mixer, use lowest speed:

10 ml vanilla essence	750 ml self-raising flour (just
10 ml ground cinnamon	less than 1.5 kg packet)
10 ml ground allspice	10 ml salt
10 ml grated nutmeg	100 ml sunflower oil
	125 ml good quality brandy

Then fold in very well with wooden spoon:

2–3 whole bottled figs, chopped into chunks
250 ml whole red maraschino or glacé cherries
150 g (1½ packets) walnuts or pecans, roughly broken

Use a large square or round cake tin. You will need the largest size you can get, not the shallow type you use for layer cakes. Grease well and line with nonstick paper, and grease the paper again. This is fiddly, but worth it. Preheat oven to 190 °C.

Spread the batter evenly in the prepared pan or tin. To prevent the edges burning if using a square tin, cover the corners with pieces of foil. Bake for 2 hours, but after the first hour reduce oven heat, to 180 °C, and place a double thickness of heavy-weight foil over the cake.

Test for doneness by inserting a wooden skewer into the centre. It should come out clean or with a few dry crumbs adhering.

Let cake cool somewhat, then turn out carefully on a cake rack. Sprinkle with 125 ml good brandy.

When cool, store in an airtight tin and sprinkle at least twice more with brandy. As usual, the cake should be baked about a month before using.

CHAPTER 8

～ THE LIFE OF MISS THOMAS ～

... THUS LET ME LIVE, UNSEEN, UNKNOWN;
THUS UNLAMENTED LET ME DIE;
STEAL FROM THE WORLD, AND NOT A STONE
TELL WHERE I LIE.

Alexander Pope

Miss Thomas was the Standard Two schoolteacher in our town in the Valley. She lived in a small thatched bungalow in someone's back yard. She spent her entire working life in the Valley, never applying, to my knowledge, for a post elsewhere. Her possessions were meagre. In each tiny bedroom was a narrow iron bed, the hollow mattresses covered with white counterpanes. Each also had a small dark wardrobe and bedside table. In the living room with its kitchenette at one end, unmatched furniture stood around uneasily: straight-backed wooden chairs with *riempie* seats, a table, bookshelves with few books in them, the empty spaces padded with curling stacks of old magazines, some flower vases. Thin, colourless curtains and a worn piece of carpet on the wooden floor completed the décor.

Maybe she didn't care much about her living space. Maybe to her it was perfectly adequate, a place of her own. I don't know whether she minded being so apparently poor, or whether she simply accepted that schoolteachers never really had money. Did she long to have her own house or flat? Did she ever desire beautiful things? Did she have money squirreled away?

I asked my mother recently, during a phone conversation, where Miss Thomas had come from; was anything known about her background?

"Why ask, after all these years?"

"Because I realise I know nothing about her."

There was silence on the phone line. Then Mom sighed. "I have no idea … How sad. I must have known, once, long ago."

"What was her first name, Mom?"

Mom was quiet again, and then said, "Do you know, I can't for the life of me remember. I think it was … something like … Esta or Bessie. Or was it Hester?"

Miss Thomas did not really belong to the concept of kitchen. A kitchen implies warmth, the aromas of food, the gathering of women, a sleeping cat, children. None of these images fit Miss Thomas.

Everyone called her "Thomas": only "Thomas". Her surname had become, a long time ago, the only name by which she was ever known.

"Thomas, do come for Sunday dinner," Mom would say on the phone. "We haven't seen you for a while."

Miss Thomas did not have a car, but she did have a driver's licence, which Mom did not. So when Dad did not feel like driving Mom to Worcester to do shopping, he asked Thomas to take Mom in his car.

Miss Thomas was a bad driver. I know this, because my sister and I usually went with them. I hated it when she drove Dad's Chevrolet. I would cringe on the back seat. She made the car squeal, she scratched the gears, she tended to brake sharply whenever she spoke more than two words, as if she had to slow down because she could not talk and drive at the same time.

Today I cannot recall Miss Thomas's face. I cannot remember what her hair or eyes or nose looked like. But I do remember her tall angularity: her sharp, large elbows and knees and jaw. We children feared her as a teacher. Her voice was loud and harsh and she was permanently irritated with us. I think she disliked children intensely. She never spoke nicely to any child, not even with the parents present; there was always a brusqueness, an impatience in her voice. She probably became a teacher only because the choice of careers for women then was so limited. You became either a teacher or a nurse, or you went to work in a shop or the bank.

The year that I was in Standard Two, in her class, I remember well how the class would listen for her footfall along the school stoep in the mornings. We marched in neat rows to our class-rooms after assembly. We sat down, never as rowdy as we would have been in another teacher's class; we were almost depressed by the thought of the school day ahead.

She stomped towards the classroom: measured and heavy, elephantine. Her legs and ankles were thick and shapeless, and she wore the kind of shoes nurses wear.

Not even the passing of nearly five decades has dimmed the memory of her schoolteacher voice. To us it was a terrible voice, a pitiless voice which could pour wrath upon your nine-year-old head for the tiniest reason. It reverberated in our ears, frightened us and exhausted us.

She believed that she could sing well. In those days we still had "singing class" and she made us sing rousing patriotic songs from the *F.A.K. Sangbundel*, her own voice booming over our reedy sounds. She also sang in the church choir. But her voice, although strong and true, was like a stone, hard and unmelodious.

Because of the singing classes I remember her upper arms. She loved to conduct us. There was something military in the vigorous swinging of her arms, her imperious gestures. And under her energetic upper arms swung loose fatty skin. I forgot to sing, sometimes, and just stared in wonderment at those upper arms, having brief fantasies of Miss Thomas flying off the podium with those wing-like flaps.

However unlikely it sounds, Thomas was the Valley's milk tart champion.

Had she been pretty, they probably would have called her the milk tart queen. She could be relied upon to cover entire table-tops and trestle tables with milk tarts – for birthday parties and fêtes and church bazaars and funerals. She was heavily depended on for those milk tarts, whatever the occasion.

Store-bought flaky pastry was not yet available, so Thomas made the flaky, buttery pastry herself – that most finicky of pastries. She scorned shortcrust pastry. For real, old-fashioned milk tart, she believed, one must use a top-class flaky pastry. To ensure the quality of her pastry, she would work in the night, in the coolness, alone in her bungalow. She was very proud of her milk tarts.

Of course there was jealousy. Other women's milk tarts were compared to those of Thomas: sometimes Thomas would be found wanting. There was always an insidious undercurrent of jealousy among the cooks and bakers of the Valley. Country women did not often work outside their homes then: they were mostly housewives. So they competed when it came to cooking and baking: secretively, furtively. But Thomas earned her milk tart fame because nobody could turn out as many at one time as she could.

In her lifetime Thomas was asked, bullied perhaps, to churn out milk tarts by the hundreds, maybe thousands: a huge accomplishment. It was such hard work, the making of so much difficult pastry, so much filling. Many things could go wrong, and sometimes it did. But Thomas soldiered on. It must have made her happy, to be so counted on, so needed at times.

It was the single thing at which she excelled; something of her very own creation which was pretty and good and sweet and praised.

Thomas never had a boyfriend. The idea was unthinkable. Her only connection with a presumably marriageable man was a Dutch penfriend with whom she'd been corresponding for years. She mentioned him sometimes, when she came to our house for Sunday dinner. He was a bachelor; she said she only had one hazy photograph of him. She shrugged her shoulders: he was not important, this penfriend, she said. But she quite liked writing the letters and receiving ones in return, with their Dutch stamps, which she saved.

Then, one day, the news spread through town and valley. Thomas's penfriend was coming for a visit! And Thomas herself was furious, because he was already on a boat bound for Cape Town by the time she received his letter. What, she asked my mother, was she going to do with him? Here? In this town where nothing ever happens? She would have put him off, she said, had she known in time that he was planning a visit! For the first time in her life this tall, raw-boned woman was bewildered, almost agitated.

The Dutchman got off the ship in Cape Town, caught a train, and got off in due course at De Doorns station. In those days the station was still at the top end of the town, there was a small café, and a fat stationmaster. Teo Koopmans stood on the platform amid his myriad of suitcases, lost and uncertain.

He wanted a taxi, he told the station master. Could someone please summon a taxi?

The stationmaster laughed and shook his head. There was no taxi here; this town had no taxis!

"Why isn't someone fetching you, sir? Taxis!" The station-master shook with laughter.

The Dutchman threw a tantrum: he hadn't known that this country was also Darkest Africa, with no modern conveniences! There was now no way he could reach his love, Miss Thomas, because he could not possibly carry this mound of luggage down into town …

The stationmaster realised that this was a small crisis, and he would have to act. He could not phone Miss Thomas because she didn't have a phone. There was but one solution. He called out to his workers. "Bring the wagon: the one we use to transport heavy stuff! Inspan the horses! We must help this man ..."

So the Dutchman was installed in solitary glory on the bench beside the driver, on the enormous open wooden transport wagon dating back to the early days of the century, the two huge Percherons clip-clopping him down the streets to his love. To Miss Thomas. His suitcases danced a jig behind him to the rhythm of the horses' hoofs, much like matchboxes on a very large wooden tray. Teo Koopmans arrived at Thomas's bungalow in a style wholly unknown in our little town and it caused a lot of mirth.

The visit did not go well and came to a speedy end. Who knows what really happened? Thomas's explanation was she had caught him on the second morning shaving with a hand mirror over her kitchen sink instead of in her little bathroom. He could not understand her fury just because he was shaving in her *keuken*. They did that in Holland all the time! But this was not Holland, she said. There was a bathroom! They had words. He had said unpleasant things, she said, and pursed her mouth, and told nothing more.

She sent him packing. She phoned the stationmaster on the Co-op's phone and asked him to inspan the wagon again, and to have the driver fetch Teo Koopmans immediately. There would be a passenger train in an hour or so. The Dutchman left the way he had come.

That was her story, and that was all anyone ever knew about her and the Dutchman. The correspondence stopped, of course.

A child has to grow up and move away, become an adult, and then look back at things from a distance to see clearly.

To imagine that a man had ever been attracted to this lonely old maid was impossible. Miss Thomas was possibly the least feminine woman I had ever known. She might have been a lesbian, who would have had to rigorously suppress her sexuality in that narrow-minded society of the Fifties. She was probably a deeply unhappy person: how can you be happy if the only name you were ever called in all your years in the Valley was "Thomas"? Or did she grow used to that, and after a while it didn't matter any more?

No man ever flirted with her, in the way the rotund farmers did with other men's wives, in fun. No one remembers whether she had relatives, or that she went away on holidays.

Years later, when I was married with children, Mom told me that Thomas had retired to an old age home in a nearby town.

It sounded incredibly sad to me. After a lifetime of being a Standard Two teacher in a featureless town she was not retiring to a seaside cottage or a city flat, but leaving that cheerless bungalow in a back yard for an old age home. So she didn't have any money squirreled away.

Might she have been able to make her famous milk tarts for the old folks there? Or would her one sweet talent have been forbidden: "We have cooks, dear, we can't allow you in our kitchens ..."

I wonder if anyone in the Valley still remembers her milk tarts.

The isolation of South Africa and our possible overestimation of homespun, very conventional little "traditions" were brought home to me sharply in the middle Seventies. Swiss colleagues of my husband were visiting his firm, and I was having them to dinner at our house. I had made milk tart for dessert.

"This is a traditional South African recipe," I told them proudly – a young wife who had not yet set a foot on foreign shores.

They tasted it eagerly. Then their faces fell. "But … this is a custard pie," one ventured.

They had been expecting a new, different taste. And of course: it was only a custard pie.

Years later Daniel and I walked down a street in Nancy, Lorraine, in northeastern France, and I came to my usual dead stop in front of a pâtisserie. As always in France the window was a feast of delectable pastries. My eye fell on a fat, sunny yellow slice of pie. "I want to taste *that*," I said. We went in, and I was handed an enormous golden slice of the unfamiliar pie on a white paper napkin. Outside, I bit eagerly into it. "My God," I said, "this is milk tart!"

It was. It was an exact duplicate of our "traditional" milk tart, except that it was double the thickness of ours, slightly more spongy; they'd used real vanilla seeds for flavour, and there was no cinnamon in it. I'm sorry to say this – it was by far the best milk tart I've ever tasted.

"So much for traditional foods." I was as deflated as on that day years ago when the Swiss guy said that our milk tart was only a custard pie.

"So many of our forefathers came from France," my husband consoled. "So maybe milk tart had its origins with the French Huguenots."

"I thought is was more of a Cape Malay recipe."

"It could still have been influenced by the Huguenots or the Dutch," he persisted. Who knows for certain? I'm pleased Miss Thomas never knew that milk tart was not truly our heritage to claim.

Thomas never shared her recipe with anyone, but here is one for an old-fashioned milk tart. A crumb crust filled with a meagre custard filling, that concoction often found at home industries, is not milk tart. It is the humblest of custard pies, and as you try to slice it, it falls apart.

~

Milk Tart

*This is the old-fashioned milk tart I make. There are many slight
variations on this theme. The recipe makes one quite large tart,
but I would rather not reduce the quantities. You could make
two small ones (the size of foil plates). But it is nicer to rather build
up the puff pastry edges with the leftover pastry to make more room,
and to fill the shell to within 1 cm of the top with the custard.
It will rise high and will not spill over.*

Good ready-made puff pastry (Woolworths has an excellent one)	1 litre full-cream milk
	3 sticks cinnamon*
	10 ml vanilla essence
200 ml cake flour	4 eggs, separated **
200 ml sugar	45 ml butter
2.5 ml salt	Sugar and cinnamon

Roll out the puff pastry on a floured board until thinner. Beat
an extra egg in a small bowl. Line your biggest tart plate or tin
with pastry. Do not stretch the pastry, as it will then shrink in
the oven and spoil your efforts. Cut off the extra pastry all along
the edges. Brush the edges with beaten egg. Roll out the off-cuts
of the pastry and cut narrow strips. Join these strips to the pastry
edge with your fingers: the egg will make it adhere. Cut more
strips, using beaten egg to join them to the tart pastry, and build
up the edges. Pinch neatly all along the edge. Finally, brush the
edges and the "walls" with the beaten egg. Put the tart plate in
the fridge to stay cool.

Preheat oven to 210 °C. Mix the flour, sugar and salt in a fairly big heavy-bottomed pot. Mix well, then add some of the litre of milk while whisking well, to make a smooth batter. A wire whisk is indispensable here. Heat the rest of the milk with the cinnamon sticks and vanilla, until bubbles begin to form. Stir often to prevent burning. Remove the cinnamon sticks with a slotted spoon and discard. Add the hot milk slowly to the flour mixture while whisking vigorously (it helps if someone else adds the milk for you!). Whisk while bringing mixture to the boil; make sure there are no lumps.

Let mixture simmer just a few minutes: stir with a whisk to prevent burning at the bottom. Then pull off the heat.

Using electric beaters, beat the egg whites until stiff and firm. Beat the egg yolks. Add the butter to the custard. Stir the custard with the whisk to cool it down and prevent a skin forming on top. When sufficiently cooled not to cook the eggs, stir in the yolks. Use a spatula to make sure all the custard around the bottom edges of the pot is incorporated and the egg is well mixed in. Then whisk in the egg whites slowly. Folding it in, as many recipes say, can be quite difficult; a whisk works better and the results are the same.

Pour the custard into the cold pie shell, to about 1.5 cm from the top edges. Put into the preheated oven. The heat will drop when you open the oven, and now you keep the heat at 200 °C for about 12–15 minutes to give the pastry time to expand and puff. Then reduce to 180 °C. Baking times will vary a bit, but another 40 minutes should do it. The tart should be brown and very puffy all over.

When you take it from the oven, it will fall. This is normal. Cool. Mix ground cinnamon with sugar, and sprinkle over the filling. Always serve milk tart warm or at room temperature, but keep, covered with clingfilm, in the fridge.

* If you do not have cinnamon sticks, add 3 ml ground cinnamon to the milk.

** Some people do not separate the eggs, but add them merely one by one to the custard and whip well. The beaten egg whites make the final result somewhat lighter and airier: it's your choice.

CHAPTER 9

~ THE CHURCH BAZAAR ~

WE LOOK BEFORE AND AFTER,
AND PINE FOR WHAT IS NOT:
OUR SINCEREST LAUGHTER
WITH SOME PAIN IS FRAUGHT;
OUR SWEETEST SONGS ARE THOSE
THAT TELL OF SADDEST THOUGHT.

Percy Bysshe Shelley

The Church Thanksgiving fête, or bazaar, as it was called, was a clone of all such fêtes in the Western world. Months before the great day regular meetings were held; convenors of "tables" were appointed, more noisy meetings were held. Should we have a sweets table again? Remember how the dreadful Visser kids stole from that table last year? And the pudding table must include a wider variety this year … Do you think old Paul will help out at the pancake table again? Will Dawie offer us a nice pig to be auctioned off, you think? And we must discuss the dishes for the lunch …

In those days long ago this feast of Thanksgiving was always held in the old church hall. A new one has long since been built next to the church in town. The Old Hall was a gloomy, cavern-ous space where all plays and choir festivals and rousing speeches floundered and sank because of the atrocious acoustics. But for one day in the year, somewhere in August, the church bazaar turned it into a merry and colourful place.

Inside, the women swarmed like ants preparing for the rainy season. Around the old hall sparse trees battled to cling to life in the dry gravelly soil. Here the men hung out, smoking and laughing and watching the pigs and a few sheep in their pens, to be auctioned off later.

For us children, the bazaar was a great occasion. Mom and Dad had to give you enough money, because it was for the church.

You dressed up in your nicest dress for the church bazaar, you put your money in your little handbag, and you went off with friends and cousins. There you weaved through the noisy, laugh-ing crowds in the hall, and went from table to table to gawk at the riches. There would be a toy table piled with colourful soft toys, lovely home-dressed dolls and wooden lorries and cars carved by gnarled, loving old hands. There was a "small cakes" table laden with delectable cupcakes strewn with hundreds-and-thousands, small sweet tartlets, larger cakes sliced up so a child could buy one slice of chocolate or cream cake. The sweets table had fudge and toffee and shop-bought sweets done up in little bags of cellophane paper tied with thin, coloured ribbons.

The adults came with baskets to fill, and bought home-made sausage and *beskuit*, biltong and, of course, Thomas's milk tarts. They bought knitted baby bootees and tiny jackets, soft sheepskin slippers or a crocheted knee blanket for winter. They chose cakes to take home: for this bazaar the women baked only their best; their reputations were at stake.

At home the produce would be critically examined and tasted: "If old Mary thinks *this* is what grape jam should be like, she'd better have another think!" or "Oh no, this is not Paula's chocolate cake! This must be Molly's; hers is always dry! Oh, how could I have made such a mistake!"

The best feature of the old-time church bazaar in the Valley was the lunch, a lavish affair, which started at 1 p.m. The sale tables were cleared, because by then just about everything had been sold anyway. Now these trestle tables were lined up and pushed into service as two long dining tables which could accommodate dozens of people. Ever-energetic women worked quickly and covered the trestles in white sheets and set places.

Children were not discriminated against. You bought a ticket, and when the time came, you and your friends took any places you liked at the table and sat down on the old folding hall chairs. The only person we did not want to sit next to was "uncle" Robert Rednose, because "uncle" Robert had the unfortunate habit of taking his set of false teeth from his mouth before he ate, and putting it in the top pocket of his khaki shirt. It was hard not to glance sideways at his very unpretty face as he masticated noisily. It rather put you off your chicken pie.

When the people were seated, a line of ladies brought in the most amazing array of *boerekos*, real farm food, from the primitive kitchen of the old hall. These delicious traditional dishes had been prepared at home, but heated again laboriously on paraffin and gas burners, or on the ancient old stove in the kitchen.

Down the table they were passed: chicken pies covered in golden puff pastry, sliced legs of lamb and pork with gravy, sliced beef tongue, more gravies, beef stews, stewed beans, sweet pumpkin, white rice, yellow rice, roast potatoes, mashed potatoes, gem squash, baked sweet potatoes, peas, carrots … It was marvellous. I never saw anyone "dieting". Everyone at the long table ladled out and tucked in. After the main dishes came the desserts. Not much new here – usually cold puddings – but the unconstrained pleasure of picking and choosing among the bowls and dishes that were sent down along the table was a highlight.

Fortunately not nearly everyone who came to the fête stayed for the dinner, as that would have overwhelmed even the efforts of the tireless women who worked behind the scenes.

A classmate, Amara, a quiet brown-haired girl, lived with her parents in one of the neat red-brick station houses. Her mother was a bright and beautiful woman. Donna Meinert yearned to be fully accepted by the women of the town. But Mrs Meinert drank. Much as she wanted to conceal this fact, alcoholism can never stay a secret. Amara never invited friends to her home. We, the children, did not quite know why, but our finely-tuned antennae had long ago picked up from the adults that there was something wrong in the red-brick Meinert house.

Mrs Meinert's real name was Donatella, and she was Italian. She'd come to South Africa as a high school girl, part of a Catholic church choir. Nobody knows the exact details, but during their trip the choir was treated to a weekend seaside holiday where, during an evening beach party on a perfect, warm night, Donatella – a sweet Italian Catholic girl – did the unthinkable. She made love behind the sand dunes to a young South African guy. After she returned to Italy, she was found to be pregnant. The young man sent her money for a plane ticket. Her parents disowned her anyway. She fled to South Africa where she married her lover, Koos Meinert. It must have been intense love at first sight, or perhaps simply lust, or maybe drink had played a role that night on the warm beach. Young people far away from home sometimes do impulsive things. After his marriage Koos Meinert, for reasons unknown, left a more promising future and started working for the then South African Railways and Harbours.

So the dark-haired, sloe-eyed Donatella from the hills of Tuscany eventually found herself living in the red-brick, no-hope house in the neat but dull rows of railway houses of our town. Cheap drink became, possibly, her only escape from her circumstances and her longing for Tuscany and her family.

The year Amara and I were in Standard Four, Mrs Meinert pledged a cake for the Thanksgiving bazaar. "My mom bakes the most wonderful cakes!" Amara said one day during recess. We were discussing the coming church bazaar in a tight little huddle. "She used to bake wedding cakes for people, you know, in the town where we lived before we came here. People paid a lot of money for those cakes!"

"Wow!" We were impressed. Wedding cakes, we knew, stood on little pillars, and were decorated with flowers and ribbons made with icing. Sometimes there were a tiny bride and groom atop the cake. So Mrs Meinert had hidden talents we knew nothing about.

On the day of the bazaar that year the Large Cake table was delightful to look at. There were cakes covered in smooth chocolate, or in pale yellow or white or pink frosting. Some cakes were feathery with roasted flaked almonds, others had masses of thin chocolate shavings scattered over snowy white meringue frosting. One cake, smooth as white silk, was decorated all around with little marzipan roses in palest pastels. I wondered if this was the one made by Amara Meinert's mother.

In the middle of these gorgeous confections stood a strange, dark green cake. It drew the eye immediately because it looked hideous, even poisonous. Someone must have had an accident with a bottle of food colouring, people sniggered. But why bring the awful thing to the fête? Who brought it? No one knew. It was pointed out and giggled at. The violently green icing had been smeared carefully over and around, so it resembled a dark green haystack.

The tables were eventually needed for the dinner, by which time they had been stripped of their riches. In the centre of the empty cake table, on the paper tablecloth which had been white but was now blotched and smeared with bits of frosting and cake crumbs, the dark green cake still stood, unwanted and untouched.

Some women were cleaning up the hall now; Mom was also helping. Amara Meinert sidled from a back door towards the cake table. I saw one lady bending down and whispering to Amara. Amara blushed, and reluctantly stretched her thin arms across the dirty paper covers. She lifted up the green cake and disappeared with it towards the kitchen of the old church hall.

I followed, curious. She threaded her way through the throng of women in the old kitchen.

She went out the back door, and I followed. Some of the women cleaning up watched us curiously.

"Amara …" I said outside, uncertain, uncomfortable. She turned to me and her face was defiant.

"Mom couldn't … Mom was too ill to bake the cake so I did … Everyone laughed at it. And I thought … I thought the cake was so beautiful …"

"It is, it is!"

"You're lying. But it's a good cake, it's just that the icing is a little too green …" She looked at the cake in her two hands. "I know what I'm going to do with it. I'm going up there …" she gestured with her head, "to give it to Nellie. Nellie has five children. They," she said to me, "will love my cake." I knew Nellie: she did part-time housework in town.

And she started trudging towards the narrow gravel road which ran on one side of the Old Hall up a steep hill. Beyond the hill were the humble houses of some Coloured labourers. I wanted to go with Amara, but her stiff back told me to keep away.

"Nellie will be so pleased!" I yelled after Amara, but she kept on walking and didn't answer.

I hope that Amara found a good husband, that she had lovely children, and that she forgot about the green cake incident. Amara, I discovered later, is the Italian word for *bitter*.

Yellow Rice

A traditional meal is not complete without yellow rice. But there are still people who think it means simply rice coloured yellow with turmeric. This is a legacy of the Malays, as are most of our tastiest traditional dishes. Yellow rice goes well with all pickled tongue dishes, with bobotie and with chicken pie.

250 ml long-grain rice
5 ml salt
5 ml turmeric
30 ml yellow sugar
A few cinnamon sticks OR 2.5 ml ground cinnamon
625 ml water
125 ml seedless raisins or sultanas

Stir everything together and bring to the boil, reduce heat, put lid on, but slanted so that steam can escape. Simmer until all liquid has been absorbed. About 4–6 portions.

Stewed Green Beans

About 500 g green beans

5 ml salt

5 ml sugar

1 medium onion, sliced

2 medium potatoes, sliced

About 125 ml water

Butter

Grated nutmeg

Tail the beans and cut thinly crosswise into little rounds. Using a wooden board is easiest. Put in a pot, and add the salt and sugar, then the sliced onion and potatoes. Pour in enough water so it does not burn. Simmer slowly, covered, until vegetables are soft. Mash with a potato masher – this is a mashed kind of dish. If it is at all watery, leave off the lid and simmer for a while to allow the excess liquid to evaporate. Then add a knob of butter and sprinkle generously with the nutmeg. Serves 4–6.

Pumpkin Fritters

Without sugar it is a side dish. With cinnamon sugar,
it's a dessert – an old recipe everyone likes.

500 ml mashed or puréed cooked pumpkin, firm, not watery
60 ml flour, or enough to thicken the purée
10 ml baking powder
3 ml salt
1 egg

Using a whisk, mix the pumpkin purée, flour, baking powder and salt. It should be a soft mixture. Beat the egg well, add to the pumpkin mixture, and whisk in well.

Heat oil in a pan (or a mixture of oil and butter). When fairly hot, drop tablespoons of the mixture into the pan. Fry until light brown on both sides. If necessary, drain on kitchen paper as you remove them from the pan. Keep warm, and serve with cinnamon-sugar. Alternatively, serve with lemon wedges as a side dish with baked fish or meat. Makes about 10 fritters.

Cinnamon sugar: made by mixing about 3 tablespoons sugar with 1 tablespoon ground cinnamon, or to taste.

Pancakes

Yes, a worldwide fast food of sorts, but if you do not have a trusty recipe, here's one. It's the only one I use, and it works for both savoury and sweet fillings.

250 g cake flour
15 ml sugar (leave this out if using savoury fillings)
3 ml salt
3 eggs
200 ml full-cream milk
30 ml melted butter
30 ml good brandy

Sift the flour and add the sugar and salt. Beat the eggs, and add to the dry ingredients. Mix in the milk, butter and brandy, and whisk with a wire whisk or electric beater to prevent lumps forming. (If they do, strain the mixture through a sieve.) You can, of course, simply throw everything into your food processor, and whizz until smooth.

Pour the mixture into a jug, and let stand for at least 1 hour before using. When you start cooking the pancakes, the batter should be about the consistency of cream. If the batter has thickened, stir in a little water.

It's easiest to use a small nonstick pan: there are special crêpe pans available. Heat the pan and grease with a little butter. I prefer butter for its nonstick qualities and better taste, but you can use oil if preferred.

Use about 2–3 tablespoons batter per pancake – it will depend on the size of your pan, and how thin you want them. Cook until the batter firms and little bubbles form on top, then flip over with a teflon-coated egg lifter or something similar. Put the finished pancakes or crêpes on a plate and cover lightly with a piece of foil, and keep warm in the oven. Repeat until you have used up all the batter. The pancakes should be golden, not brown – they take less than a minute per side. Again depending on your pan size and how thick your crêpes are, you should get anything from 12 to 20.

Waterblommetjie Stew

The waterblommetjie *is a water plant which grows wild (now also cultivated) on the dams and vleis of the Boland in late winter and in spring. The flower heads are harvested, and they are often available in season in supermarkets, in plastic punnets. I see shoppers staring at them doubtfully, then passing by. Do try this unique "vegetable". Its flavour is vaguely reminiscent of young green beans.*

For 4 people you need the following, although I'd prefer more waterblommetjies *than I specify here. Please note that accurate weights are not important. No cook way back when would have even used a recipe for this.*

1 deep punnet *waterblommetjies*, firm, fresh
Salt, pepper, flour, juice of 1 lemon
oil for frying
1–1.5 kg lamb or mutton chops, or good stewing lamb
About 300 ml water
1 chilli, or pinch cayenne, or Tabasco (optional)
Peeled, chopped potatoes or baby potatoes (optional)

Rinse the *waterblommetjies* and remove the stems, if any. Mix salt and pepper into flour in a small bowl. Heat oil in a heavy-bottomed pot. Roll the pieces of meat in the seasoned flour, and add to the pot, a few at a time. Brown on all sides, remove, and do the next batch, until all the meat has been browned. Put it all back into the pot, season with salt and pepper, and add water and lemon juice. Simmer, covered, for about 45 minutes.

Add the *waterblommetjies*. Simply pack them on top of the meat. At this stage you can also add peeled chopped potatoes or baby potatoes if you choose.

Simmer until everything is tender. Do not stir too much, as you do not want to break up the vegetables completely. Check for liquid – add a little more if necessary.

The addition of chilli is a matter of taste. Add as much or as little as you like, or leave it out.

Serve with rice and salad.

Snow pudding

Also an oldie ...

25 ml gelatine
60 ml cold water
250 ml boiling water
250 ml sugar
60 ml lemon juice
Finely grated zest of about ½ lemon
2 eggs, separated

Soak the gelatine in the cold water, then add to the boiling water and stir until dissolved. Add the sugar, lemon juice and zest. Pour the mixture through a sieve into a bowl, and cool.

When the mixture starts to set, whisk well with either a whisk or electric beater until light and foamy. Beat the egg whites until stiff and fold in. At this point you can pour the pudding into a mould, or simply chill it in a pudding bowl.

You could use the leftover egg yolks to make a custard for the pudding. Serves about 8.

CHAPTER 10

~ LITTLE WHITE HOUSES ~

O, TO HAVE A LITTLE HOUSE!
TO OWN THE HEARTH AND STOOL AND ALL!
THE HEAPED-UP SODS UPON THE FIRE,
THE PILE OF TURF AGAINST THE WALL!
TO HAVE A CLOCK WITH WEIGHTS AND CHAINS
AND PENDULUM SWINGING UP AND DOWN!
A DRESSER FILLED WITH SHINING DELPH,
SPECKLED AND WHITE AND BLUE AND BROWN!

Padraic Colum

For years I have had a desire to take my camera and go on a sentimental journey through the old Cape Province, to photograph old-fashioned farm labourers' cottages. This, I felt, might be a historic as well as an architectural record of a way of life that was passing. These small white-washed dwellings used to be a distinctive feature of our country landscape, though many people probably never gave them a second look.

I knew they were disappearing fast, as farmers modernised their workers' quarters and built new houses equipped with electricity and running water. I wanted these pictures of labourers' cottages under old oak trees, huddled under milkwoods, against barren hills, next to streams, or crouching in neglected desolation among the low hills and dusty veld of the empty Karoo.

These little houses for farm workers had often been built in unintentionally picturesque locations. This was not because the original providers were particularly munificent, but because the houses needed the shade of trees, or hilly ground to keep rainwater out; or a stream to provide water. In the Hex Valley where I grew up, they were often surrounded by vineyards; the farmer needed his labourers close to their workplace.

To the unobservant eye these dwellings might all have seemed alike: rectangular in shape, whitewashed, extremely modest, always with the distinctive protuberance of the hearth and chimney on one side.

But there were, in fact, many small variations in this traditional cottage architecture.

It is not my intention to romanticise these dwellings. They were small and barely serviceable, and often had to shelter a large family. They had no electricity, running water or bathrooms. The occupants were very rarely provided with any but the most basic needs: walls, a roof, a hearth.

Still I cannot deny that I am sentimentally attracted to these little houses. They are reminders of a simpler time, when life for all of us was far less complicated than today. They had a certain atmosphere and warmth and a picturesque presence which the newer, modern houses do not have.

Some had been built of stone, roughly plastered over, so that the contours of the original stone showed through. Sometimes they

had corrugated iron roofs, which leaked when it rained. Others were thatched, a much cosier roofing material than any other.

As a child I got to know these little white houses intimately; they had a seductive quality which lured us to peek in. On my Uncle Uli's farm there were four or six in a row, among the vineyards. Sometimes, when we were kids, we showed up at their doors with a gift of fruit or a few potatoes, hoping in turn that there might be some cold *roosterkoek* ...

Some dwellings had stunted trees in their "yards", and other people liked to sweep their yards clean with reed brooms – neat, swirled Zen-like patterns in the dust. Some had flower or vegetable gardens.

"A swept yard deters the snakes," old Aunt Sanna told me as she swish-swished rhythmically with her reed broom.

The doors were low, and the small windows inadequate for letting out all the smokiness and the human odours. As you entered at the only door, there would be a small table covered with a flowered plastic cloth, and a few unmatched, rickety chairs. There was a cupboard or a "dresser" where basic supplies were kept. A few precious possessions like pretty *breekborde* would be on display. In fact, a real display cabinet was a prized possession, where all kinds of knick-knacks were kept behind its glass doors. Somewhere against the wall near the hearth an oval tin bath would hang on a thick nail – the family's bath. On a wooden trestle or a narrow table near the hearth clean water for drinking and washing dishes would be kept in battered enamel pails or old oak wine barrels, covered with cheesecloth or netting against flies and dirt.

There would be one or two bedrooms, iron beds with coir mattresses neatly made and covered with candlewick bedspreads or *lappieskomberse* smoothed down, showing the hollows in the middle. There might be worn bits of carpets or mats on the uneven floor. A little table next to the bed, an oil lamp, a Bible. Always, somewhere in the room, a Bible, stuffed with little keepsakes: cards, dried leaves and flowers, old tattered photographs, Sunday School cards with a picture and a verse. There would be a clothes cupboard and a chest of drawers; in poorer houses only a faded curtain drawn across a corner of the room, with clothes hidden behind it.

These houses, where people lived a basic and simple life, had a modest sufficiency which shamed me, a White girl with so many more privileges.

Of course there were also awful cottages, where the inhabitants drank and cursed and abused one another. Such houses would be filthy and unpleasant. But those were not the ones we visited as children.

We went to the nice ones, like that of *Antie* Sanna. She was old and did not work any more. Her daughter and son-in-law worked for my Uncle Uli. *Antie* Sanna was rather fat, and she sat in a chair outside under a tree, and knitted jerseys, with her feet stretched out to the sun. She was there when the kids came home from school, and she baked bread daily. She was the head of the household. She made the rules, and they were strict. Her house was neat, and she didn't suffer drinking at weekends or the taking of God's name in vain.

The heart of the cottages was the hearth. It might have been only a built-up cement slab set into a deep, broad niche, with a chimney. The fire would be made there; the hearth blackened with the smoke of many years. A flat-bottomed iron pot set on a home-made contraption to hold it above the coals emitted a fragrance of onions and meat. It might be the plainest of stews, but it always had a particularly enticing smell. Open fires do that – they make food taste better than the sum of its parts.

Most of the hearths, however, had a black coal stove tucked into the niche. The stove started humming with life as day's end drew near, when it was made up to cook the day's main meal and heat water for washing up and bathing.

It crackled and hissed, and the smells of food mingled with the fragrance of woodsmoke. The black stove and the plain hearth had an insatiable appetite for wood. This caused hardship and back-breaking labour: the daily gathering of wood. Some farmers provided loads of wood from time to time. But it was an appetite that could never be satisfied.

Usually coal and wood were kept in wooden boxes next to the stove. Large, dented aluminium kettles hissed and twittered in the shadows at the back of the stove, their bellies full of hot water. On a cold day there was no better place to be than near the hearth – as long as you stayed out of the cook's way.

Antie Sanna could do wonders with food. She could turn the cheapest and meanest ingredients into a flavourful and filling pot of food. She would, for instance, buy a bag of chicken feet for a few cents, and sit down at the kitchen table to clean them, slowly, patiently. She singed the hard skin over a candle flame, then peeled it off. She cut off the nails. At this point I can sense the shudders of readers. I would remind the sophisticates that the world's greatest cuisines all developed from poor man's food.

Antie would then take one or two onions, slice them thinly, and fry them in fat: good, genuine, rendered mutton or pork fat. To that she added the cleaned feet – about five per person, I'd guess, with water, salt, sago – always a handful of sago. To this she added a good splash of vinegar; she said it "drew out the good-ness from the bones". On went the lid, slanted to keep a chink open for the steam to escape. This pot simmered slowly for … how long? Maybe an hour, maybe much longer; I don't remember. But when it was ready, the ugly, humble chicken feet had turned into a nutritious, gelatinous stew. If she had any, *Antie* might cook rice to go with it, because the "long sauce", as she called it, needed something to soak into. If there was no rice, there were always thick slices of *Antie's* home-baked bread to dunk into that sauce. It was, naturally, not a dish eaten with delicacy. You took one chicken foot at a time, and you sucked on it; the sucking made noises; you didn't care because this was not Ouma Sannie's Victorian table …

Offal, potatoes, sweet potatoes, pumpkin, coffee, bread … those were often the mainstays of the labourers' diets, depending on where they lived. I would still gladly exchange a restaurant meal for just one more chance to eat *Antie's* sheep offal, to dunk her bread in that gluey khaki-coloured "long sauce".

My cousins and I would sometimes go with *Antie's* grandchildren into the scrubby hills where the train tracks ran, where the dry Karoo invaded the green Hex Valley, and hunt for wood. Nothing much grew there except typical Karoo shrubs, and we only found pathetic, thin sticks which we tied in bundles with old rags.

Sometimes someone would come round to the little houses with wood to sell, but this threw out the precarious budget of the people of the cottages. "Look for wood," the people always said to us children whenever we went off on one of our forages or picnics in Groothoek, the dark craggy kloof in the Hex River mountains.

Even now, at the same age as *Antie* Sanna was then, I find it difficult to walk past driftwood thrown up by the tides. It is so plentiful here. I gather it up until my arms are full; the sticks scratch my skin but I carry the bundle home like a baby, to add to our braai wood. Sometimes I wish that I could slip back in time for a minute or two, and tip the bleached, tangled stack into *Antie's* woodbox next to the stove. She would have beamed, top teeth missing, her eyes narrowing as she smiled her pleased, dimpled smile. And later, feeding the ocean-washed sticks into the open firedoor I know she would have said, "How lovely it smells! Must be the sea in the wood ..."

Roosterkoek. That was what we were always hoping for, when we peered into the cottages we visited. *Roosterkoek* is bread dough shaped into flattish patty shapes and baked on a metal grid over the smouldering coals of an open fire in the yard. It was delicious:

smokey and somehow more than just bread. Sometimes it was spread with rendered fat: beef or pork or tail-fat from a sheep.

On some chilly winter afternoons we crowded into a cottage with our Coloured playmates. The snow clouds hung over the Hex River Mountains, pallid cloaks with tattered edges, which slipped like ghostly shrouds into the shadows of Groothoek Kloof. The vineyards were bare and lifeless. The dented kettles sang on the stove, food smells filled the air as usual, and the northwester tore around the corners. In here, in this cottage, it was warm, if a little close with human bodies and not enough fresh air. But we didn't care.

And this was always the sort of weather when ghost stories would be told. The people of the cottages loved to tell ghost stories, which really came into their own on those sombre winter evenings. Dusk came early and the winds cut to the marrow outside; sometimes the rain slanted down. It added just the right touches to good ghost stories. We listened avidly and shivered in horrified delight.

"There's this little black dog," old Chris said, as he thoughtfully rolled a cigarette with bits of newspaper and rough tobacco, "which runs around on the farmyard some nights. I've seen him again, just two nights ago. Just a little black dog … And then there's old Petrus … On moonlit nights when the snow lies on the peaks of the Matroosberg you can see him sitting on the wall of the cement dam. And his eyes follow you. And there's this chill down your spine, like icy flakes of snow would feel on the warm skin of your back …"

Reverent silence as we looked at old Chris, wide-eyed. The wind moaned. The day drew in and the clouds crept lower down the mountain slopes. It was time to go home, but the lure of the stories were great, and we had no particular desire to leave this warm nest and run home in the chilly half-darkness.

"And then there's old Chris," someone would say. "Shame. He's not resting. Not at all at rest … Mavis says she went to O'Miss Sannie the other night, and she saw Chris again near the packing shed. All grey and transparent, just those eyes alive in his skeleton head … You remember how thin he was from the Tuberculosis? And how just his eyes seemed to grow bigger on his deathbed …?"

"O'Miss Sannie" was Ouma.

The scariest story of all was the one of the murdered woman who haunted the streets of the town by night. We used to walk everywhere in those days; it was quite safe, and we often found ourselves on the streets after dark. I regularly walked alone to the library on Wednesday nights when it was open, and on my way back home, when it was very dark in the side streets and the weak yellow street lights offered no reassurance, my back grew hollow and cold … I was always too terrified to glance back to see whether the ghost was behind me. She probably was.

This woman had been seen by so many people, White and Coloured, that the story must have been true. Many years ago, in a lovers' quarrel, a man murdered his wife in a drunken rage in a street near the railway station. The story went that she often simply appeared behind you if you happened to be walking in the streets at night, no matter which street you chose. She would follow behind you until you got to the road which divided Uncle Uli's farm from our property and which ran down into the Valley, the very road to our house lower down. There she would disappear.

There were many ghosts to talk about, the stories told and retold, because the Valley is ancient and many farms date back a few hundred years. But back then that was all we had to fear: ghosts. Otherwise, we were still safe anywhere in the dark.

Another stove-corner evening topic was superstitions. I have forgotten almost all of them now, but they put the fear of God into us as children. There was a worm which put in a rare appearance in the vineyards. It was large and fat and green and hairy, with spots like eyes on its body. If you ever, ever had the bad luck to see this worm after the sun had set, you would die before sunrise – when the cocks started crowing. This worm was therefore known as the *Cockcrow* worm …

A man-woman lived down among the willows and reeds of the Hex River – *Doekvoet*. No one knew whether this apparition was a man or a woman or something in-between. Its feet were swaddled in rags, to prevent people from hearing it approach. Of course this man-woman also only walked at night. And if *Doekvoet* found you alone, perhaps near the river in a vineyard, he-she would kill you …

One superstition lives on into this present day. If a boy contracted a sore of any kind on his feet, it was said to be "simply a *pisvoet*". He peed, the explanation went, and some drops fell on his foot. Or maybe some other boy's urine "infected" him by splashing on him.

I never did get that photographic record. We probably never explored far enough, for recently, by the merest chance, I did come across a most picturesque cottage nestled in the folds of a hill, nasturtiums blooming around its walls and chickens clucking in the shady yard. I did not have a camera with me. So perhaps we simply missed those still tucked away on farms not seen from the roads.

But it does seem as if most of these cottages have disappeared, replaced by mass-produced rows of square, upright houses of brick and mortar with corrugated iron roofs. They have electricity, running water and flush toilets. In the Hex Valley some of these clusters of homes are very pretty, with neatly tended and squared-off gardens, and young saplings which are growing into shady trees.

One still finds neglected corners, however, where miserable dwellings huddle in messy yards; not the same thing at all as *Antie* Sanna's house.

The labourers' babies and toddlers now often have crèches where staff look after them while their parents work. The older children go to school in neat navy or black uniforms. No doubt many lives have improved immeasurably since the early Nineties.

Here and there the ruins of the old cottages can be seen, their white paint dull and blotchy on crumbling clay walls. They are slowly disintegrating and merging with their mother earth as if they had never existed.

∽ ROOSTERKOEK (GRIDDLE BREAD) ∽

This is bread dough shaped into hand-size patties and cooked over the low coals of a wood fire. Bread dough, ready risen in plastic bags, can be bought at many supermarkets, but home-made bread is always best. The dough must not be too soft, because it will sag through the griddle or fall apart: it must be firm enough to hold its shape.

Grease the griddle with fat or butter to prevent sticking. Grill until crisp on both sides. Break open and eat hot with butter.

∼ STONE SOUP ∼

There was an old children's fairy tale called "Stone Soup". It told of a poor, but clever old woman, who put a pot of water on the fire next to a roadside. Then she put a clean stone in the water. Everyone who passed by peered into the pot and asked what on earth she was doing cooking a stone, and she replied that she was making Stone Soup. "But," she would say to the astonished wayfarer, "it would be greatly improved by the addition of an onion."

Invariably the passer-by would provide the onion. To the next person she would tell the same story, adding, "but it would be so much nicer if I had a potato." And so it went on. Her Stone Soup was improved continuously by her suggestions to inquisitive passers-by: perhaps parsley, one carrot, some salt, a tomato …

And in the end she had a filling pot of "Stone Soup".

It reminds me of the nourishing soups of the women in the little white houses.

There is no recipe for this winter broth, and neither would the women of the little white houses have had one. They soaked dried sugar beans in water. They bought or begged soup bones from the butcher; these were given away or cost only a few pennies. At the back of the stove, in a large pot, the beans and the bones, with an onion or two, became the basis for a winter soup which never seemed to run out.

The soup simmered, the beans softened, the bones yielded their flavour and also bits of meat and fat. Vinegar was added; it drew nourishment from the bones. A little sugar was indispensable: it aided the flavour. Anything else that could be used went into this soup: carrots, cabbage, beet leaves, potatoes, tomatoes, and any leftovers.

This soup could take on a myriad incarnations, and yield different tastes, depending on what was available. It became more flavourful as it grew older on the stove. It poisoned no one, because if it cooled, it was always cooked again. With thick doorstops of home-made bread it filled any hungry stomach. "If you're clever," *Antie* Sanna said, "you can be poor, but you needn't go hungry."

Antie Sanna's Sugar Loaf

Some time during my high school years I did scribble down this recipe at Antie *Sanna's table. Like all women with coal and wood stoves, she felt the oven temperature with her hand and knew exactly when it was right. I'd say use a moderate oven, 180 °C or even slightly less. Eggs used to be plentiful, because most of the farm folk kept a few hens and a rooster.*

½ cup soft butter

2 cups light brown sugar

4 egg yolks

1 egg white

About 2⅔ cup flour (about 670 ml)

1 teaspoon salt

5 teaspoons baking powder

1 rounded teaspoon ground cinnamon

½ teaspoon ground cloves

1 cup milk + 1 teaspoon vanilla essence

Lightly cream the butter and the sugar. Add the yolks one at a time, beating in each one. Then beat in the egg white. Mix the dry ingredients in a bowl, then add alternately with the vanilla milk, beating well after each addition.

If the batter is too thick, add a little water. Bake in a well-greased bread tin for 45–60 minutes. Yields roughly 8 slices.

CHAPTER 11

~ GRAND HOTEL ~

OH LOVELY DAY! WE'RE GOING TO STAY
IN A FANCY GRAND HOTEL!
WE'LL DRESS TO THE NINES AND DRINK FANCY WINES
IN THE WONDERFUL GRAND HOTEL!
WE'LL ORDER POTAGE AND MEATS AND BLANCMANGE,
WE'LL ALSO ATTEND HIGH TEA
WITH SCONES FOR MUM AND CAKES FOR ME
IN THAT FANCY GRAND HOTEL!

Anon.

Today, looking back, it remains a little surprising to me that my father, a teacher, could once in a blue moon afford to take us off for a weekend to Cape Town, sometimes further afield. We always stayed in a good hotel, because my parents abhorred "shabby places".

Such an excursion was always extremely exciting to me and my sister Annie. My brother was born seven years after Annie and twelve years after me, so he missed most of the fun.

Even the way Dad would curse the busy Cape Town traffic was

exciting to us, but of course, his kind of cursing never included the rude words we were waiting for. He hated driving in city traffic, and by the time he had safely parked the green 1948 Chevrolet Fleetmaster in the hotel parking area, he would be hot and bothered.

"When we go downtown, we will take the bus!" he would say as he hauled out suitcases. "I shall not do battle again with the traffic in Adderley Street!"

Of course, in those days, porters were standing ready with trolleys to relieve us of the task of schlepping anything ourselves. My sister, five years younger than me, would carry her small pink handbag clutched in both hands, her little chin lifted haughtily as she followed the retinue of retainers. She would pretend to be a princess for a weekend instead of the daughter of a fairly poor schoolteacher. And from a very young age she knew how to put on the style.

We were, for forty-eight magical hours, in a hotel! Instead of being home washing dishes or churning butter, we were being served! Things were *fetched* and *carried* for us!

Mealtimes were the biggest thrill for the two of us. All meals were included in the price in those days, so we ate in our hotel.

In the Fifties hotel dining rooms were huge, gloomy spaces with high ceilings, devoid of any atmosphere. Sometimes there was a bowl of flowers on a buffet, but they might have been artificial. The colour schemes, if they could be called that, were pure utility: cream and brown, cream and dark green, cream and dark blue. In the Fifties there was no escaping shiny cream wall paint.

Dining room tables were covered in starched white cloths, with stiff napkins artfully folded into shapes on your bread plate or standing to attention in your dinner plate. Wine was not normally drunk with meals; it was still reserved for festive occasions.

Hotel food was mediocre in those days. The menus were *table d'hôte* and consisted mostly of predictable British-style food. But oh, the thrill for us two kids when a waiter in a black suit with a funny little black bolero handed each of us a menu, as if we were grown-up! Oh, how grand it all was! So the food, as far as we were concerned, was infused with a profound magic before we had even tasted it.

While we "perused" the menus, bread was set upon the table, with small ice-cold butter curls in little silver dishes. The serrated little curls were so cold that dew pearled on them and there was no way you could spread it without breaking the bread.

The bread was plentiful: a mound of thin slices of white and brown, cut in neat triangles and arranged on a white napkin in a basket. It was terribly ordinary bread, just bakery bread, and dryish, as my mother always pointed out. It could never in our wildest dreams be compared to her home-baked bread, she told us.

But to us, only faintly acquainted with bakery bread, this was as special as the croissants and brioches would be to me many years later in Paris.

And these baskets were the bane of my parents' lives on such a weekend, because Annie was a breadoholic. She could not resist bread. And this was *special*, it was *hotel* bread!

Faced with the prospect of a weekend away and the excitement of being in a hotel, Annie always promised Dad beforehand to leave the bread alone and eat more from the menu at all meals. She could never keep that promise. However enchanted she might have been by the idea of the menu, she would be full before she had even tasted the soup. This annoyed my parents enormously, as it was seen as a great waste of money not to eat well from the menu.

But it was impossible to stop Annie from eating bread, because when my parents tried to, she created a noisy fuss, like a drunken alcoholic refused another drink by the bartender. And that was something my proper parents tried to prevent at all costs. You did not attract attention to yourself in a public dining room!

Annie's standard main meal at hotels stayed the same: lots of bread; half a chicken drumstick and a roast potato; a second helping of roast potato; (no veggies please) and ice cream. Potatoes in any form were fine with her. Dad considered her attitude towards hotel meals a personal insult. Annie, a saucy and cutely impudent child, couldn't care less.

A hotel dinner in the Fifties usually began with some incongruous little "starter" in a stemmed glass bowl, which was set before you without preamble. This could be canned fruit salad: if you were extremely lucky you might find a red fragment of glacé cherry in yours. Sometimes it consisted of a few grapefruit segments, sour and bitter. Once it was a goblet filled with enough acidic shop-bought mayonnaise for twenty large prawns – but only four tiny ones clung precariously to the rim, as if terrified of drowning in all that mayo.

There would be two soups: a consommé and a potage, without fail. My father explained patiently to his two kids that "potage" was fairly thick, and "consommé" was thin. It didn't matter, really, as both would be equally insipid, regardless of what grand names they might have on the thick white paper of the menu.

Then there were two or three fish dishes to choose from, of which one was usually, in Cape Town, cold curried snoek or pickled fish in the Cape Malay style but, alas, seldom as good as the real thing can be. In those days it was also nothing out of the ordinary to find fresh lobster on the menu.

Then came a short list of dishes of indeterminate purpose, like sweetcorn on toast, mince on toast, or my favourite, marrow bones on toast.

Meats were generously provided but their preparation was run-of-the-mill: roast chicken, roast lamb, roast pork. Roast lamb was always served with mint sauce, pork always came with apple sauce, and ham with some fruit jelly. The mint sauce was bright green, jellied, and tasted medicinal, totally unlike the mint sauce Mom made with her garden mint, grape vinegar and sugar.

The desserts were disappointing. It seemed as if all hotels way back then had "Queen's Pudding" as a permanent menu feature: a concoction of bread crumbs, apricot jam and meringue, which never quite lived up to its name. They must have had a mountain of leftover bread daily. The second choice was usually ice cream with, if we were lucky, chocolate sauce.

The seaside town of Hermanus, meandering along miles of coast-line with rugged mountains behind it, has several hotels. But some decades back none could compete, as far as food was concerned, with the astonishing menus of the Birkenhead Hotel. This hotel has long ceased to exist, which is sad, because it had a stunning aspect on the sea with a beach to either side and a wonderful view over Walker Bay.[1]

If you didn't stay in the hotel, you definitely went there to dine. The dinner menu was one of incredible abundance, if uneven

---

[1] Recently a boutique hotel opened in the same spot.

quality. We loved those Birkenhead dinners, however, for their cheerful excess, for their ridiculous over-the-top superfluity. This was long before nouvelle cuisine hit our foodie shores ...

In the good old heydays of the Birkenhead Hotel we had riotous family dinners there in December, with uncles, aunts, cousins, Ouma, all of us seated at a long, pre-booked table. The food and wine came in endless profusion, there was much laughing and retelling of family jokes and family memories. That was one hotel meal when my parents had no trouble with the fact that other people were staring at us, at this large, raucous family continually raising glasses in toasts and shouting with laughter. Those were fun times.

I still have a Birkenhead Hotel dinner menu of February 1973 (see opposite). Unfortunately no meal price is indicated.

I don't know what would have been presented if one had ordered the Fillets of Anchovy: would it really have been a few salty, canned anchovy fillets? And what exactly were Spiced Sprats? Do we have sprats in South Africa, or was this a small mistake of fish identification? Why weren't all the hot meats listed together, but some of them separated by stars? Ah, well ... it's not important any more, for we shall not see such a menu ever again.

Times have changed, and now we eat *á la carte* unless we turn off the highways to look for small hotels where we might still get a *table d'hôte* menu.

Menu

**TYYY

BIRKENHEAD HOTEL, HERMANUS

GUAVA JUICE
TOMATO COCKTAIL
GRAPEFRUIT SEGMENTS
• • •
CREAM OF ASPARAGUS
• • •
FRIED SOLE WITH SAUCE TARTARE
STEWED PERLEMOEN WITH RICE AND LEMON
HOMEMADE CURRIED YELLOWTAIL
MIDDLECUT IN CHILLI SAUCE
DUTCH ROLLMOP HERRING
MARRINATED ANGEL FISH
SEAFOOD MAYONNAISE
FILLETS OF ANCHOVY
KING KLIP SALAD
SPICED SPRATS
SMOKED SNOEK
• • •
EGG MAYONNAISE
CREAMED MUSHROOMS ON TOAST
• • •
BOILED CORNED OX TONGUE ON MASHED POTATOES WITH PICCALILLI PICKLES
• • •
GRILLED RUMPSTEAK WITH CREOLE SAUCE
• • •
ROAST DUCKLING WITH ORANGE SALAD AND GARDEN PEAS
• • •
ROAST STUFFED SPRING CHICKEN WITH FRENCH SALAD
ROAST SUCKING PIG AND APPLE JELLY
ROAST LEG OF LAMB AND MINT SAUCE
CHILLED ESCOURT HAM WITH PINEAPPLE CHUNKS
• • •
VEGETABLES IN SEASON
• • •
COLD BUFFET
HOMEMADE CHICKEN BRAWN AND SALADS
• • •
BOILED CORNED SILVERSIDE OF BEEF AND SAUERKRAUT
• • •
BIERWURST, SWISS SALAMI, CERVALAT, HOLSTEINER, FRENCH AND GARLIC POLONY
SELECTED SALADS   PICKLES VARIOUS
• • •
STEAMED PLUM PUDDING WITH WINE SAUCE
BAKED MARSHMALLOW PUDDING AND CUSTARD
TIPSY TRIFLE AND CREAM
LOGANBERRIES AND CREAM
FRUIT SALAD AND CREAM
SWEETMELON CHUNKS
CHOCOLATE MOCHA
FRESH APPLES
ASSORTED ICE CREAMS

NEAPOLITAN	MARASCHINO	RUM & RAISIN	BANANA	CHOCOLATE
PEPPERMINT	VANILLA	STRAWBERRY		RASPBERRY
WITH CHOCOLATE,	CHERRY,	GRANADILLA,	BUTTERSCOTCH,	PINEAPPLE,
	COCONUT OR HONEY TOPPINGS			

CHEESE BOARD   BISCUIT
COFFEE IS SERVED IN THE FOYER

Menu from the Birkenhead Hotel

Marrow Bones on Toast

Recently, we were pleasantly surprised to see this unassuming little dish again on a restaurant's menu. It is also a "comfort food", if you are not too worried about eating fats.

4 beef marrow bones, about 4–5 cm long, for each slice of toast.
Oil, salt, white pepper, water or stock
Fairly thick slices of bread

Heat a thick-bottomed pot and add a little oil, just enough to prevent sticking. You can use a pan, but it will splatter a bit. With tongs, pack in the marrow bones, marrow end on the bottom. Fry for a minute, then add just a tiny bit of water or stock. You want it to boil away gradually. Season the marrow bones with salt and pepper, but do not stir. Cover the pot and simmer for about 15–20 minutes depending on thickness and size.

Make toast but do not butter. Have warm plates ready. Lift the marrow bones out carefully. In some cases the marrow might fall out: try not to let this happen, or cook a few extra bones. You want to get the entire bone with its marrow on the toast, and there must be no watery liquid to spoil the toast. Have extra salt ready. Each person removes the marrow with a small spoon and eats as they like: spread on their toast, or eaten in chunks. And they may want to suck the bones as well! The flavour is usually excellent and it does not need tarting up.

Mint Sauce

*Ordinary garden mint grows so easily, and this is so easy to make
that there is little need to buy bottled mint sauce, which invariably
has preservatives and colourings added to it.*

Pick and rinse a good bunch of mint. Strip the leaves off the hard
stems and use the tops whole. Chop up finely to make about
1 cup, pushing it in slightly: you want enough mint in the sauce.

Put the mint in a clean bottle which has a good screw top.
Add about 175 ml cider vinegar and 150 ml castor sugar. (Castor
sugar melts more easily than granulated sugar, but either can be
used.) You can add a tiny pinch of salt if you like, or vary the
quantities given.

Screw on the top, and shake the bottle well. The sugar will take
time to dissolve, and the flavour will improve upon standing.
Taste the mint sauce when all the sugar has dissolved – the acidity is a matter of taste. Keeps forever in the fridge.

~ FRUIT SALAD ~

This is just a note on fruit salad, which needs no recipe. My
Ouma and Mom believed that only soft fruits should be used in
fruit salad. No apples, ever, because they are too hard and spoil
the texture. Also, don't put orange segments in fruit salad which
is going to stand awhile before serving, because the white pith
causes a bitter taste.

The basis of a good fruit salad is ripe, but firm, papaya. The best
fruits to add are sweet melon, drained canned peaches, drained
bottled or canned pears, drained canned guava, grapes, pineapple

(but not the hard centre), gooseberries. Of course all the fruits used can be fresh, but any less-than-perfect fruits, e.g. unripe cling peaches, will spoil the end result, therefore the canned variety might be better. Don't cut any fruit into small pieces: it should be bite-sized chunks.

Bananas are almost indispensable in fruit salad, if you don't mind the fact that they tend to discolour slightly.

Use some of the drained syrups to pour over the salad. The fruit punches available in boxes these days are also delicious. Adding vanilla essence to fruit salad – not less than 10 ml for a large quantity – gives it a certain *je ne sais quoi* … And if children are not partaking, a shot of Van der Hum or Grand Marnier will not go amiss.

Malva Pudding

This is a pudding you must have in your recipe collection.
It is sinfully delicious. It's an oldie but definitely a keeper.
Do try this on the first cold day you meet.

200 g sugar	3 ml salt
2 eggs	15 ml butter
15 ml apricot jam	5 ml cider or grape vinegar
150 g flour	100 ml milk
5 ml bicarbonate of soda	5 ml vanilla essence

FOR THE SAUCE
200 ml cream
100 g butter
150 g sugar
100 ml hot water

Preheat oven to 180 °C. Beat the sugar and eggs well in a food processor (or with an electric mixer) until thick and lemon-coloured, and add the jam, beating in.

Sift together the flour, soda and salt. Melt the butter and add the vinegar. Add this mixture and the milk and vanilla to the egg mixture alternately with the flour. Beat well and bake in a covered ovenproof dish for 45 minutes.

Melt together the ingredients for the sauce, stirring well, and pour it over the pudding as it comes out of the oven. Serves 4.

CHAPTER 12

~ OUMA GRETA ~

I WILL HAVE A FEW COOKING-POTS,
THEY SHALL BE BRIGHT;
THEY SHALL REFLECT TO BLINDING
GOD'S STRAIGHT LIGHT.
I WILL HAVE FOUR GARMENTS,
THEY SHALL BE CLEAN;
MY SERVICE SHALL BE GOOD,
THOUGH MY DIET BE MEAN.
THEN I SHALL HAVE EXCESS TO GIVE TO THE POOR,
AND RIGHT TO COUNSEL BEGGARS AT THE DOOR.
Anna Wickham

During the winter school holidays in June, we visited Mom's mother, Ouma Greta. She lived in the Eastern Cape, in a small town in a valley famous for its apples and pears: the Langkloof. Ouma Greta had been a widow since my mother was sixteen-years-old.

Ouma Greta was short and plump and soft and unfailingly sweet. She was probably the kindest person I had ever known.

She wore the simplest clothes, knitted her own jerseys, and kept us kids supplied with beautiful socks which she knitted with crochet yarn. Children wore white socks and black shoes then, and we had the prettiest socks of all.

Her life was vastly different compared to that of my Hex Valley Ouma. Ouma Greta lived in a typical small-town South African house: square and plain. She was not profoundly poor, but she had been used to a modest lifestyle all her life. I think if someone gave her a million rand she would have refused it; she would have had no idea what to do with it.

Our family always looked forward to trips of any kind. In the Fifties straight highways had not yet been built and any trip could have wholly unexpected and surprising twists and turns, not least because my father had no sense of direction. He got lost even on journeys he had made dozens of times. My mother recounts how, during World War II, with strict petrol rationing, he even took a wrong turn on the well-known route to Kleinmond – a near-disaster because of the petrol problem. You could probably turn Dad around a few times in his own garden and he would be disoriented and unable to point out where east or west was.

Once, on one of those surprise outings Dad liked to plan, we took off to the West Coast. Dad was especially keen on visiting the little fishermen's village of Paternoster on this trip. We spent a night at a hotel in Velddrift, which was then a prosperous town with a lively fisheries industry. So Dad took us on a tour through a fish canning factory there: he saw it as educational. Surprisingly enough, it was enjoyable. The fishing trawlers came up the river and decanted tons of slippery silver fish onto conveyer belts which ran into the factory. We watched, amazed, how the fish

– pilchards – were cleaned, beheaded, canned and labelled, without much interference by human hands.

Then it was off to Paternoster, a short tangle of gravel roads further on. The road was rather endless. Annie threatened to get carsick. We stopped so that she could breathe in sea air: surely the sea must be just over the next hill.

It wasn't. We started complaining. Then we came upon that well-known feature of the African landscape: an old Coloured man sitting on a stone beside the road in the middle of nowhere. Dad stopped, and he and the old man exchanged greetings.

"*Oupa*," Dad asked, "is this the road to Paternoster?"

The old man frowned, perplexed. He took off his battered felt hat and scratched his head while he pondered the question.

Then he shook his head regretfully. "No, boss. Sorry. Never heard of him."

On the empty flatlands of the West Coast, its towns within a few miles of one another, we had become hopelessly lost.

My mother, on the other hand, had the peculiar conviction that all journeys longer than an hour were best started not long after midnight. That was another exciting part for Annie and me: to be roused in the pitch dark at 2.30 a.m. and given a good shot of caffeine-rich coffee to wake us up properly. It was winter, and cold, when we travelled to Ouma Greta, and we shivered as we dressed, but then adrenaline joined the caffeine in our veins, and we giggled happily as we helped to load the last bits into the car in the icy dark. We already thought ahead to the delicious *padkos* that Mom had prepared.

We sat in the back of Dad's green Chev under a blanket against the chill (where our little brother Georgie joined us in later years), and peered ahead in awe as the headlights picked out the road in that deeper blackness before dawn. After a while the steady drone of the car engine made us drop off to sleep again. When the sun had climbed frostily over unknown hills and naked thorn trees, Dad pulled off the road and stopped the car under some pepper trees. We climbed out stiffly, shivered, stretched out. Mom would open tins and hand out egg-and-mayonnaise or sardine sandwiches, boiled eggs, hot coffee. Later on, we would stop again for lunch and eat flavourful cold *frikkadelle* or cold chicken joints.

This was before prepackaged cold meats, before take-away foods, farm stalls and roadside cafés. All Dad bought en route was petrol, and petrol stations only had petrol, cans of oil, water, and sometimes a chest fridge with cold drinks.

We always arrived at Ouma's house in a bad-tempered and dishevelled state. This was due to my sister's unfailing and dramatic bouts of carsickness, which would develop soon after we turned off the main tarred road and hit the gravelly, dusty and corrugated back roads. Whatever precautions Mom took – water, towels – they were too late to prevent the inevitable. Annie never warned us in time. She would sit in her corner in the back and, when asked, deny feeling nauseous at all. Then, unexpectedly, she'd shoot forward, grab hold of her mouth with one hand and thump Dad on the shoulder to stop, stop …

Always, always too late. She would vomit over whatever was closest: Mom's shoulders in front of her, or on me, or in later years, over poor Georgie, the toddler. The volume she managed to emit after all that *padkos* was impressive. The mess was incredible. Mom would make futile efforts to clean us up at the side of the road. By that time we were always in a godforsaken semi-desert, dusty and inhospitable, where nothing grew except hardy Karoo bushes. After this unpleasant and slightly hysterical interlude I would watch Annie closely and suspiciously for the tell-tale blanching of her normally pink cheeks, which would signal the next bout. By the time we got to Ouma's home town we stank of sulphurous eggs and old sardines.

In Ouma Greta's kitchen was a deep hearth where her black Welcome Dover stood, the same type of hearth found in old farmhouses and labourers' cottages. Next to the stove were battered wooden boxes, one containing wood and dried corncobs, the other one coal. It was a small kitchen, with a scrubbed yellow-wood table and chairs, some cupboards, and an old leather sofa.

There was, like in all old houses, a pantry. It smelled of fresh bread and spices. The cupboards had wire gauze windows, and sometimes she hung a fat sausage – *boerewors* – over a nail, to dry slightly in the cool gloom. She didn't have a fridge. Tin boxes with pictures on them stood on the counter below the cupboards and held cookies and *beskuit*.

Ouma cooked whatever was in season; she was a plain cook, but somehow the old black stove and her deft hand made everything taste good.

There was no electricity in town then. We used lamps and candles; even now the smell of paraffin and candlewax remind me of Ouma Greta's house. At dusk she would fetch her oil lamps, inspect them, trim their wicks, clean and fill them if necessary, and light them. They had porcelain shades, and they created warm pools of yellow light. You carried yours carefully to your bedroom by its tin handle. There were candles, too, in wide tin candle-holders, with a box of matches, for extra light; for lighting at night if you needed it.

Hot water for washing was heated on the stove, just like in *Antie* Sanna's and other humble homes. Ouma had a bathroom with a bath and a basin, but it had only cold water from a rainwater tank. There was an outside lavatory, a bucket toilet, emptied once a week by the municipal "night cart".

Ouma Greta never wore make-up or dolled up like Ouma Sannie: that was not in her frame of reference at all. She lived by the tenets of the Bible without ever preaching or telling us how to behave. When she laughed, she shook. We loved her laugh; just listening to her laugh could set you off on a bout of giggles. She had a stock of harmless platitudes and trotted them out at the appropriate times, like "A stitch in time saves nine", "Easy come, easy go", or "Red sky at night is the shepherd's delight, red sky in the morning, sailor's warning". Her little sayings were the nearest she ever came to admonishments. I never heard her say anything bad about anyone, but she loved to relate funny or amusing things which had happened to people in the town, and then that delicious laughter would bubble up and her eyes would squeeze shut with mirth.

The town exuded a fragrance all its own. It smelled of pine needles and dust, of woodsmoke and herby mountain shrubs. The streets were gravel, and it was a very tranquil town, where old women leaned on the lower half of their front doors and watched intently as you walked by: not many strangers visited. The town has a beautiful sandstone Dutch Reformed Church and a large school where Mom was a teacher before she married Dad. We played tennis on the school courts, which were open during the holidays and even had the nets up.

Sometimes we climbed some way up the bristly mountain behind the town to reach the white-painted stones which spelled out the name of the town: JOUBERTINA.

We ate our main meal in the afternoons, in the kitchen with its sweet woodsmoke scent. Ouma cooked traditional South African foods. Lamb, a chicken stew or a pie, sizzling baked potatoes from that dark hot oven, sweet potatoes sliced in rounds, flavoured with brown sugar and a cinnamon stick, stewed green beans, sweet little carrots. She cooked foods which came straight from the earth. Neighbours all had enormous well-watered back gardens from which came slews of potatoes and carrots and onions and beets and sweet potatoes, the wonderful yellow kind called *borriepatats*. These sweet potatoes were heavenly when baked in their skins in the oven, and you dug in a knife and fork to break them open and get at the steaming golden, tender flesh.

The French would later have a name for Ouma's kind of cooking: cooking of the *terroir*, of the soil and climate of your area.

Years later my husband and our two sons – the youngest was eight-months-old – went to see Ouma Greta while on a trip to my parents. It was a long detour, but worth it because she hadn't yet seen her great-grandsons. Later I was so glad we had made that detour in pouring weather, because a year later Ouma Greta died.

Ouma Greta made banana bread and sugar loaf and wonderful little half-moon jam tarts with a short pastry. Like Ouma Sannie's Christmas pudding, like my mother's cream puffs, this short pastry can not be duplicated: I think she probably used something like sheep tail fat. It was meltingly tender and contained her own apricot jam.

Ouma also made a kind of noodles-in-milk – a favourite supper meal when we were little, known as *melkkos*. It was utterly simple: a dough, rolled out and cut into strips, and boiled in milk with sugar and cinnamon, just the sort of heartwarming dish children love.

I would have enjoyed these visits much more, but Ouma Greta's little house had a ghost.

Through all the years of winter visits I drove my parents mad with my nightly anxieties and insistence that there was a ghost in the house. He – it was definitely a man, an older man, I said – was there at night, in the bedroom where Annie and I slept.

"You are crazy," Mom said every year. "It's all your imagination. Stop the nonsense."

My fear recurred nightly as murky twilight settled over the town. I hated nighttime there. After the ritual of washing and brushing teeth – we used the old-fashioned enamel jug which stood in its enamel basin – I jumped into bed and, when the lamp was blown out, I closed my eyes immediately. I knew that if I opened them in the dark, I would see the ghost …

The only place where I never felt his ethereal presence was in the cosy kitchen.

Mom steadfastly denied, all those years, that there could possibly be a ghost in her mother's house; she and Dad did not believe in such nonsense anyway.

"Nobody else has ever lived here! Your Ouma had this house built after your grandfather died! Nobody ever died in this house! You are neurotic!" she protested.

But I always sensed something in Mom's attitude when the bothersome issue of the ghost was raised. And I wondered what it was. There was a hesitancy, a faltering, about her irritated protestations. I knew with the unerring instinct of a child that there was more to it than my being neurotic.

It was to be years later before I heard the truth, before I became aware of the family skeleton in the cupboard which had been kept from us. And I realised who the ghost had been.

After all I had not been the only one who had known about the ghost. My aunt, the second eldest, as a child, woke up one night to see a man bending over the bed of her younger sister, the third daughter, as if he was having a closer look at her.

A male cousin, some years younger than me, actually saw and described him while on a visit to Ouma Greta.

"There's a tall man in our room every night!" the little boy protested fearfully. He and his sister were twins, and they shared Ouma's third bedroom. "And he has a gun with him!"

My late grandfather had been a school headmaster during the Twenties and Thirties of the previous century. The few photographs which exist of him show a tall, dark and very good-looking man. He was a schoolmaster in the days when the teachers and the *dominee* were looked up to and treated with great reverence. They were the "intellectuals" of their day and they had reputations to maintain.

My grandfather, besides being a headmaster, also owned a farm. He was an outdoorsman with a great love of dogs and horses, and he was a crack shot.

I only know the bare outlines of the story. I will never know more, as I could not ask my mother about it. This episode has negatively coloured and affected her whole life.

The drama which had played out as a profound tragedy for all concerned in the Thirties – seventy long years ago – would have had almost negligible consequences today. But times and mores differed drastically from today's liberal-minded society. Moral judgement was swift and harsh.

At the time, grandfather and Ouma Greta were living in another small village in the Langkloof. They had four daughters, of which the youngest was two and my mother, the eldest, was fifteen or sixteen.

But my grandfather, the headmaster, had an affair – when such a transgression, in that closed and claustrophobic community, was inconceivable. The clandestine love affair must have been carried on very furtively; probably no one knew about it. Greta didn't know her husband's secret.

The girl fell pregnant. This, in modern times, would not be sensational news either. But in the Thirties this was now a calamitous scenario. From the sketchy details I have, it does not seem as if grandfather had the slightest intention of divorcing my gran and marrying this girl. Anyway, divorce would have been as great a scandal as the illegitimate child. Abortion didn't exist, of course.

My handsome grandfather must have been desperate. He needed to tell someone, because confiding becomes a compelling need when you are in deep trouble. He could not go to his local *predikant*. The churchman was a friend; they respected one another; it was unthinkable. There was no way out for the ill-fated lovers, except to face total disgrace and the ostracism of the community.

Then something happened which, at the time, might have seemed to Grandfather like a hand stretched out in empathy if not sympathy.

A travelling revivalist preacher appeared in the Langkloof. He held well-attended services in school or church halls, and he always announced in his sonorous voice that anybody was welcome to come and talk to him about their sins and their troubles. He would listen, and pray with them …

My grandfather went to see this preacher, remote from the life of this valley, but still a man of God who might offer succour. He confessed. It must have been a painful and embarrassing interview.

Was this travelling minister, this man of God, overcome with shock and outrage at the confession he had heard? Or was he just an ordinary *skinderbek* who could not keep a confidence?

For he did not keep the sensational confession to himself. Before he left the valley on his holy mission of spreading the Word, he betrayed my grandfather's trust and told the local *dominee*, my grandfather's friend, all about it.

Within days the story spread across the Langkloof. And, in time-honoured tradition in narrow-minded communities, the people turned their backs on my grandfather and his pregnant mistress. They did so physically and vociferously. The valley sizzled.

Grandfather took his gun and, somewhere on his farm, in the lonely hills, he shot himself. But he did not die immediately. It took him days to die, days in which Greta tended to him and watched him die. He had time to ask his wife's forgiveness before he succumbed to his self-inflicted wound. Did she forgive him? This tender-hearted, soft woman, did she hate him then? I doubt it. Ouma Greta did not have it in her to hate. But she must have been in shock; to add to it all, she herself was ill at the time with thyroid problems.

After grandfather's death and his lonely, scorned funeral Ouma Greta had to go into hospital, far away, in Port Elizabeth. She had to have a goitre removed.

There was almost no money.

My mother, a sensitive teenager, was suddenly the mother of the household where the smallest was two years old. Then Ouma

Greta came out of hospital and tried to take up the shredded pieces of her once tranquil life.

I cannot forgive that long-dead community for this: with the few exceptions of loyal friends, the people turned their backs on Greta and her children. They made them into outcasts: the shattered little family was guilty by association of everything that had come to pass.

My Ouma Greta had a small house built in Joubertina and moved there.

My grandfather obviously did not find release in death by his own hand. He had left too much unfinished business behind.

A half-sister to my mother and her sisters was born in due course, but understandably they didn't want anything to do with her or her mother.

After her matric my mother, on the insistence of Ouma Greta, left the Langkloof to study for her teacher's diploma at a college in the Western Cape. Then she came back to teach in the town where her mother lived. She felt she had to be with her mother and younger sisters.

A couple of years after my mother began teaching she discovered that her father's illegitimate child, her half-sister, was in her class ...

No wonder, then, that Grandfather had haunted the little brown house, built by Ouma Greta so that she and her daughters could try and make a fresh start. No wonder he was seen holding the same gun with which he'd killed himself.

Ouma Greta died in the Seventies. I am sure with her pure and loving heart she would have taken the earth-bound spirit of my grandfather with her to the Heaven which she, at least, so richly deserved.

Stewed Sweet Potatoes

2 or 3 large sweet potatoes
½ cup (or more, to taste) yellow sugar
1 tablespoon flour
Naartjie peel or cinnamon for flavour
Salt
2 tablespoons (or more) butter
1 cup water

Cut the sweet potatoes into slices and layer in a pot. Sprinkle sugar, flour and naartjie peel or cinnamon with a pinch of salt over each layer and dot with butter. Add the water. Simmer this slowly on top of the stove, shaking the pot now and then.

The sweet potatoes are ready when soft when pierced and the water has cooked away. This recipe yields about 6 servings.

Melkkos (Homemade Noodles in Milk)

These old recipes do not have carefully measured ingredients. This is how Ouma wrote it down in the falling-apart printed cookbook I now treasure. She wrote her own recipes on the pages without print, and at the end of chapters.

Flour, salt, egg, milk

Sift flour and add salt. (I'd guess about 2 cups of flour for 4 small servings ...) Break egg in the flour and work into the flour with a rounded knife blade until a stiff dough forms. Sprinkle flour on a wooden board. Roll out very thinly. Leave awhile to dry somewhat. Sprinkle with a little flour. Cut into strips. Boil milk, add a lump of butter, two cinnamon sticks and sugar, add the strips of dough, and simmer until cooked and the milk has thickened slightly, about 4 minutes, or as for fresh pasta. Serve in small bowls.

(I assume one added water if the dough was too dry.)

Meat dishes made by Ouma Greta and her entire generation were so straightforward and simple that there are no recipes. Meat was organic, from local farms. Lamb and mutton, especially, like Karoo lamb today, were very good to begin with because the sheep grazed on herbaceous shrubs which gave the meat an excellent flavour.

Meats were most often made into flavourful stews without needing the various herbs and spices we need today. An onion or two was browned in fat. Rendered fat, yes, because it was the general-purpose shortening in those days: pork, mutton and even beef fat.

Chunks of meat were rolled in flour and added to the pot and fried. Then water was added and perhaps a dash of vinegar. The meat braised slowly in black iron pots on a wood stove.

After an hour or so carrots, chopped celery or shelled peas might be added, and always, of course, potatoes. Thickeners for gravy were sago or flour. Sago has to be simmered in the meat stock for quite a while, and stirred, until the little white beads become translucent. Flour or cornflour was beaten into a little water or stock, and added. Then came salt and white pepper. Chopped parsley or thyme were the only well-known herbs, and used if available.

Corn Fritters

Handy, this, as a side dish, or served as part of a substantial breakfast with bacon. Because I like making corn fritters when we tire of potatoes or rice as a starch, I have adapted the measurements for modern ease. Ouma scraped kernels off boiled corn cobs. That is not necessary today. I use canned corn kernels instead.

400 ml drained canned corn kernels, because this is more or less
what you will get from a 340 g tin of kernels

200 ml flour

5 ml baking powder

2.5 ml salt

Good pinch white pepper

2 eggs

60 ml melted butter

Milk

Mix the corn into the dry ingredients. Beat the eggs very well, and add with the butter. Mix in very well. If the mixture is still quite dry add a little milk and stir well again. Fry tablespoons in hot oil on both sides, until puffy and light brown. Will make 4 big "corn burgers" or 6–8 small fritters.

Quick Baked Coconut Pudding

Ouma called it a "milk pudding". Because I have used it often,
I metricated the old recipe.

4 eggs

250 ml sugar

125 ml cake flour

2 ml salt

3 ml baking powder

250 ml desiccated coconut

60 ml melted butter

5 ml vanilla essence

500 ml milk

Preheat oven to 180 °C. Beat the eggs. In a separate bowl, mix the sugar with the flour, salt, baking powder and coconut. Add the eggs, butter, vanilla and milk, and beat well. Grease a pie dish, add the batter, and bake for 45–55 minutes until golden brown and set. Serve warm. It makes 4–6 servings.

Upside-down Caramel-Choc Cake

*This is a no-nonsense, delicious Ouma Greta cake.
It's easy and fairly quick, but read the recipe through
first because it's made in two stages.*

1 tin sweetened condensed milk
100 g milk chocolate with nuts

Grease and fully line a cake tin with nonstick baking paper. Grease the nonstick paper well with butter. This fiddly step is vital.

Melt the condensed milk and chocolate (broken into pieces) in a small heavy-bottomed pot, and stir to mix well. Pour the mixture into the prepared cake tin, spread evenly over the bottom, cool somewhat, then let harden in the fridge or freezer, but it only needs to be cold and set, not frozen. This happens quite quickly.

375 ml cake flour
3 ml salt
15 ml baking powder
180 g soft butter
250 ml castor sugar
lemon or lime juice (optional)
2 eggs, beaten
5 ml vanilla essence
175 ml buttermilk

Preheat oven to 180 °C. Sift flour, salt and baking powder into a bowl. Cream the butter and sugar until light in a roomy mixing bowl with an electric mixer. I like to add a squeeze of fresh lemon or lime juice to this mixture, as it helps the creaming process. Beat the eggs and vanilla in a small bowl. Add beaten eggs to the creamed butter mixture and mix well. Fold in the dry ingredients and the buttermilk. Mix well. The batter should be quite firm.

Ladle the cake batter carefully over the hard caramel layer you now have in the cake tin. Even out the top of the batter.

Bake for about 70 minutes. Test with a skewer after 60 minutes. If it comes out clean, the cake is done. Leave the cake in the tin to cool down for about 30 minutes, then turn it out on a cake plate. Put the cake plate on top of the cake tin, and turn both over. The cake should slide out of the tin with no trouble. Remove the paper. Sometimes there are little air holes in the choc-caramel topping, which is quite normal. You could disguise these with a topping of sour cherries or simply a sprinkle of icing sugar.

Ginger Beer

Anyone for real, old-fashioned, home-made ginger beer? It's one of the greatest thirst quenchers ever. This has been copied directly, with some extra notes, from Ouma Greta's own recipe. No metrication here because it's almost impossible. Please note that her "bottles" were Imperial bottles about the size of our 750 ml wine bottles of today. Exact measurements are not important. My mother tells me that Ouma made this in a big white enamel basin. Cheesecloth was tied over the top. When the raisins rose to the top, the ginger beer was ready to bottle. To do that, put a funnel in the bottlenecks and ladle in the beer. Don't screw the tops shut: ginger beer has been known to expand! In Ouma's days corks were used, inserted lightly, so that expanding gasses could shoot out the cork …

12 bottles (use empty wine bottles) water	1 teaspoon dried yeast
3 lbs sugar (that's about 1.3 kg)	1 packet (15 g) Cream of Tartar
2 very slightly rounded tablespoons ground ginger	12 raisins
	2 lemons, halved

Mix everything except the lemons in a large non-reactive container (enamel or glass). Squeeze the lemons and add the juice. Put the used half lemons in the mixture as well.

Stir well. Cover against dust and flies. Leave in a cool place for 24 hours, by which time the raisins should have risen to the top of the ginger beer. Remove raisins and lemon halves, and bottle.

Buttermilk Rusks

Of course rusks were always at hand to dunk into a cup of coffee. Ouma made two kinds: the type made with yeast, and which required an awful amount of kneading and pummelling and energy, and this classic oldie which is much easier.

2 kg self-raising flour
400 ml yellow sugar (just under 2 cups)
10 ml salt
500 g cold butter
2 eggs
About 750 ml–1 litre buttermilk
15 ml vanilla essence

Preheat oven to 180 °C. Grease 2 baking tins.

Mix the self-raising flour, sugar and salt in a large, fairly shallow bowl. Grate the butter into the dry mixture on the coarse side of a cheese grater. Now put in clean hands and rub in the butter, until the mixture is crumbly and the butter evenly distributed throughout.

Beat the eggs in a bowl and add to it 1 cup buttermilk and the vanilla. Pour over the mixture in the bowl. Now add – slowly – enough buttermilk to make a slightly sticky batter, almost like a scone dough. You could use a wooden spoon to mix, but hands do the job better.

Form balls of about 5 or 6 cm in diameter, and pack them close together in the greased baking tins. Because the batter is fairly sticky, it helps to dip your hands in cooking oil first, and rub it in, before forming the balls.

Bake in the preheated oven. If you have a modern fan oven, or your oven is large enough, the two tins can go in together. Baking time is approximately 1 hour, but depends on many variables, such as size and thickness of the "balls" and your oven.

Be careful not to burn the tops, which can be lightly topped with foil later on in the baking process if necessary. The finished rusks should be golden brown, and will have risen and spread out considerably.

Cool in the tins. Some like to break the balls into rough rusks, but I have found it's better to use a serrated knife and cut them into rusk shapes. There will be a lot of crumbs as you work: do not worry, it always happens, and the garden birds will love them.

Pack the rusks against one another, stacked at an angle, in the same tins. Dry overnight in an 80 °C oven, with the oven door propped open slightly with a folded cloth.

Before you remove the rusks, make sure the centre ones and the thick pieces are completely hard and dry, otherwise leave the whole lot in the oven for a few hours longer. Cool, and store in airtight tins.

CHAPTER 13

~ THE BEST YEARS OF OUR LIVES ~

THERE ARE GAINS FOR ALL OUR LOSSES,
THERE ARE BALMS FOR ALL OUR PAIN,
BUT WHEN YOUTH, THE DREAM, DEPARTS,
IT TAKES SOMETHING FROM OUR HEARTS,
AND IT NEVER COMES AGAIN.

Richard Henry Stoddard

I went off to university, where the social life and personal interactions had far more important implications for my development as a person than my academic achievements. In fact, if it hadn't been for my father's warning that I would have to go back to the Valley and work in the bank if I failed a year, I would have been tempted to ignore classes, never open a book, and spend my days in the cafés and my evenings dancing.

After our insular childhood lives in small towns or in rural areas, university life was like a great golden lotus opening up. So many young people of our own age! Suddenly, so many friends! So much to discuss and discover! So many dates and picnics and *vleisbraai* parties! So many infatuations!

But it was an innocent time. Maybe dagga was smoked by a few daring students, but modern drugs were unknown. The only drugs we knew about were dangerous diet pills like Tenuate, which could be bought over the counter and which took away your appetite. The biggest drug on campus was booze, and its worst relative was brandy. Us girls only ever had a glass of wine at residence dinners or dances, or a beer or two at *braais*. Nice girls didn't get drunk. But, naturally, at least once in the three or four years we spent at university, even the nice ones had a glass too many.

The Pill was available only on prescription to married women, and had lots of side-effects then. Condoms could only be bought at a pharmacy, and that meant the boys had to sidle up the aisles trying to avoid the salesladies, to reach to the white-coated male pharmacist at the prescriptions counter, to whisper their request, red-faced. And more often than not their daring would be rewarded with a sharp, accusatory glance.

We were no angels, but *sleeping together* was still considered *not done* by *nice* girls. But even nice girls did get into temptation, and at the end of my first year, five girls in my residence of 250 young women were pregnant, and disappeared quietly off campus, never to return.

We were terrified of pregnancy. Abortion, even if you could find out where and how, was a dangerous back-street business. So should the unthinkable happen, you would either have to risk death, or spend the last six months of your pregnancy at some "Christian home" as a sinful, repentant, unmarried mother-to-be with a botched future and furious parents, and have to put your baby up for adoption. Hobson's choice …

Yet everything was so much simpler than today. The campus

and town were safe, even at 3 a.m. Most students stayed in residences on-campus, and included in the board and lodging were three meals a day. These tended to be good and generous at the start of a term, but as money started running out, meals became more tasteless and stingy.

It was the Sixties. The Sixties were the best of times in all of history to be young.

Before the Sixties there was the youth rebellion of the Fifties. Up until then there were only two generations: children and adults. You could not aspire to be an adult before you were married and had children of your own.

Then, somewhere in the middle Fifties, a not-so-quiet revolution turned the world on its head. It's hard to pinpoint what set it off, or why. Suddenly, mid-Fifties, Bill Haley and his Comets appeared, a new star system in our universe. *Rock around the Clock* appeared in cinemas, unremarkable except for the music, which shook up a generation of youngsters. James Dean and Natalie Wood became idols overnight with *Rebel without a Cause*. Then Elvis happened, and rock 'n roll was born fully formed and perfect. The kids started rocking and bopping, and these kids became a new generation: teenagers!

Elvis could not keep still and swayed his pelvis in tune with his irresistible numbers ... "I need your love tonight", "Such a night", "Love me Tender", "It's Now or Never".

Parents had a collective seizure. They were horrified, offended, and scandalised. This rock music was wicked and sinful. Their children were being corrupted by the evils of America ... Elvis, some believed, had been sent directly by Satan himself to pervert the youth.

And it was such sweet seduction. Youth grabbed the word *teen-ager*, bit deeply into it, loved the taste, and held on like terriers.

Once you turned thirteen, you were – wonderful word! – a teenager! Now they were *somebodies*, not plain *children* any more! In the cities, ducktails hatched, wearing longish hair combed like a duck's tail in their necks, rode noisy motorbikes and wearing black leather jackets bearing painted slogans like "I am a teenage rebel" on the back. They lounged against walls in white T-shirts and smoked cigarettes like James Dean did, fag held between thumb and index finger. They assumed frowning, narrow-eyed expressions, trying to look tough, but it was just a pose. It was still a long, long time before real gangsterism.

When the boys in the Valley wore their hair in a ducktail style to school they were sent to the principal's office and got a few hard ones on the backside with a cane. It wasn't child abuse then, it was discipline. That afternoon, as the principal had dictated, they sat in the barber's chair with a sore behind, and he cut them a short back-and-sides again, with probably a little sermon thrown into the bargain.

Then came the Sixties. London became known as Swinging London. Jean Shrimpton was the top model who shocked an Australian horserace meeting by turning up in a dress a few centi-metres above her knees. The mini was born, and Mary Quant was the designer of the decade.

The Beach Boys belted out "Swinging Safari" over and over from one of the cafés in Stellenbosch. There we sat around pots of tea – which was the cheapest thing on order – and solved the world's and our own problems. Bop sessions were held every weekend, and Elvis was the King. Life was simply wonderful.

Unfortunately it was also about that time that teenage girls became overly conscious of their figures. Everyone wanted to be as thin as Jean Shrimpton and Twiggy. I could never manage to deprive myself of food, and, like most of my friends, ate three meals a day and never gained an ounce. But my roommate and best friend, Susie, became one of the weight-obsessed, although she was by no means overweight. Susie did tend to go to extremes sometimes. When she studied for test series or exams, she studied for such long hours without any break or relaxation that she became haggard, pale, and broke out in acne. Once she decided to diet, she almost never went to the dining room. Susie drove me up the wall. She would have a piece of dried toast and bitter black tea for breakfast, some overcooked vegetables for lunch, and nothing for dinner. As we were active in sports, she was starving by 9 p.m. when the residence tuckshop opened. She would then buy a clutch of chocolate bars, wolf down the lot, and promptly come down with stomach cramps and nausea. These she would try to soothe with old-fashioned remedies like Lennon's tinctures.

This pattern of starving herself and then gorging on sweets was to repeat itself to the point of insanity – mine. I tried hard to get her to eat sensibly at table, but just being in the dining hall was a transgression of her own ridiculous dieting rules. Susie, on her roller-coaster of starving and overeating, therefore never lost the few pounds she wanted to lose until after she left university.

The dieting obsession, which in Susie's case was more amusing than dangerous, had its dark side. We all became very worried about Margie, who had started seeing food as the deadly enemy, to be avoided at all costs. Margie had a round face, and maybe the shape of her face made her believe she was fat. She became thinner and thinner. Nothing we said about her scary weight loss made any difference to her. Our objections to her scarecrow looks were seen as jealousy. In her mind, she was "almost" thin. She wrote her second year-end exams and went on holiday with her parents. She never returned. Margie died during the holidays. She had starved herself to death.

Mona was the beloved daughter of very rich parents. She grew up in a palatial home in one of Cape Town's snooty southern suburbs. Mona seemed born with a golden – not silver – spoon in her mouth. She was blonde and extremely pretty. But in her first year at university she also fell prey to the dieting obsession. Before she could finish her degree, her parents whisked her off to a sanatorium in Switzerland to save her life. Mona lived, but she could never have children. In later years we heard that she was still anorexic.

Anorexia didn't have a name then. It wasn't really recognised: because thin was suddenly so in, even the mothers often congratulated their daughters on their slender figures: grist for the anorexia mill.

One of the saddest stories is that of Anita. Anita was one of our group of friends, all roommates in the same corridor in the same residence. As a first year student she caused a sensation on campus. She was incredibly beautiful, with thick naturally creamy-blonde hair, blue eyes and a tanned skin. She was tall and slender and aloof. And from the start she was very faddy about food. We were fed well in that residence, but Anita nibbled on cooked carrots one week, on gem squash the next. She was not quite anorexic, but she seemed to hate cooked food. Sometimes she would quite happily eat a chocolate bar or a packet of crisps, yet, in general, her eating habits were extremely unhealthy.

When we were in our second year at university, Anita dropped out and left to get married to a farmer far away, and she exited from our lives.

Some years later a mutual friend told me that Anita was divorced. She had had two children, and both were in a home for the mentally handicapped. Apparently, when she fell pregnant, she was so terrified of "getting fat" that she lived on egg whites and a little gelatine throughout both pregnancies ... Whether that was the cause of these tragic defects, I do not know, but having seen Anita at table staring at a plate of good food as if it were poison, I can well believe that she was able to exist on egg whites during her pregnancies.

I met Daniel at the end of my second year at Stellenbosch University. He was tall, blonde and, to me, captivating. To ask me out on that first, fateful date he turned up at my res on a motorcycle. He wore tight silver stovepipes – then a desirable fashion item for men – and a black leather jacket (borrowed, I later learnt, as was the bike). He leaned casually against the wall of the entrance hall with the requisite tough narrow-eyed look and a cigarette between thumb and index finger. His blond hair was combed ducktail-style. It was an auspicious start ... I was hooked. His look was just right: sort of Elvis Presley meets James Dean ...

He was also a student, also staying in a residence. We went to a bop session that night – somehow Nat King Cole singing "Blueberry Hill" always reminds me of that date, because it was a slow number and we could dance closely. I had no idea then that he was the man I was going to marry, but I certainly found him extremely attractive.

In our last year at university Daniel and his friends moved out of their res to private rooms on the top floor of a huge old Victorian house.

And Maxie entered our lives. Maxie was actually Massimo Mamberti, an Italian student who had come to Stellenbosch for six months to do research for a Master's thesis. Daniel and his friends were asked by Maxie's professor to take him under their wing, as his English was wobbly and his Afrikaans, naturally, non-existent.

Massimo had the dark, alert face of a sweet and handsome rodent. He came from somewhere south of Rome. And it was Maxie, Massimo, who showed us how to make what was to become a staple in our collective cooking repertoire for several years to come, that standby of students and young working people: Spaghetti Bolognese.

There is great controversy about this dish. It is often maintained that there is no genuine Italian dish by this name. Pasta in Bologna is made from a soft-wheat flour and cut differently, some say, and people there eat rice more often than pasta. It is the southern Italians who so dote on hard-wheat pastas. Yet there is a real Bolognese Sauce, which is made rather differently from the student standby, Spag Bol. But, whatever its origin, Spaghetti Bolognaise or Bolognese is alive and well and living in all digs where young people are found.

"Maxie's going to make us a pasta dish at our place," Daniel said. "He misses Italian food."

Our place were the Victorian attic rooms they rented. The house belonged to a young couple with a baby, who lived downstairs. The grounds were huge and had majestic, shadowy oak trees where doves cooed all day long.

On the Saturday night of Maxie's Italian food, there were eight or nine of us, boys and girls. Where it had come from, I don't know any more, but Maxie used two primus stoves and two large, battered tin pots. In fact, he might have borrowed it from the couple downstairs. We were using Frank's big corner room for this occasion.

Maxie chopped things, silently and efficiently, looking up quizzically now and then at the small crowd milling around, laughing, drinking cheap red wine, and speaking in two languages that were both foreign to him. Scents of frying bacon, onion and garlic started filling the room and drifting out the door. Maxie stayed at his post like a good chef, taking sips of red wine every now and then.

Eventually the dish was finished, and Maxie doled out commands to his *sous chefs* in his broken English. He drained the spaghetti at a wash-basin, emptied it into a receptacle, and then added his sauce and forked it in carefully. The receptacle was a nice shape for the process – fat-bellied, with a nice handle on one side for a good grip. The pasta smelled very, very good. We were famished.

Then Mimi yelled, "Oh my God, it's a chamber pot!"

All four of us girls screamed in horror.

Maxie gave us a comical, puzzled look as if to say, "Now what's the fuss about?"

"I'm not eating out of a pisspot!" A girl had her hands in front of her mouth and was retreating from the proffered dish and plate as if it could strike out and bite her.

"Look, calm down, calm down! We have scrubbed out the pot! It's shiny-clean and germ-free," Daniel said. "It hasn't even been used …"

"Like hell it hasn't! You don't even have a bathroom up here!"

"We promise," Emile said. "You don't think we want to eat out of a dirty pisspot, do you?"

Reluctantly, us girls took plates – where did these boys get porcelain plates from? Maxie ladled generous portions. Reluctantly, we tasted Maxie's Spaghetti Bolognese. We polished the lot. We forgot about the dish it came in. I still have a black-and-white photograph of me, in an overstated pose on Daniel's lap, my mouth open so I can be fed another forkful from the chamber-pot.

Massimo shared his delicious recipe with us, of course. In the next couple of years, alone and away from the nurturing campus life, many of us would resort to variations on Maxie's spaghetti dish, but I doubt that we could ever infuse our Spag Bol efforts with the inimitable Italian deliciousness which steamed from the chamber pot that night.

∾

Maxie's Spaghetti Bolognese

Enough for 8–10 people.

2 packets (500 g each)
high-quality spaghetti
Salt
2–3 large onions, chopped
Olive oil and/or butter
2 packets (250 g each)
meaty rindless bacon,
roughly chopped
A little dark grape vinegar
3 tins chopped tomatoes

4–6 (or more, to taste) fat,
flavourful cloves garlic,
crushed and chopped
About 2 teaspoons sugar
Freshly ground black pepper
A bunch of flat-leafed
parsley, rinsed
About 2 cups grated sharp
Cheddar cheese

Bring a very large pot of water, to which you've added a table-spoon of salt, to a rolling boil.

In the meantime, sauté the chopped onion in the olive oil, stirring now and then. When it softens, add the bacon. Keep heat fairly high but don't let it burn. Add a tiny bit of water and vinegar if the oil disappears, and stir well. When the onions are pale brown and the bacon is cooked, add the tomatoes and stir through. Add the garlic. Add about 2 teaspoons sugar and 2 teaspoons salt: you will have to taste and judge this for yourself. Let this mixture bubble for a while to let some of the tomatoey liquid evaporate. You don't want a watery sauce. Make sure it doesn't burn. Finish this with lots of black pepper and finely chopped parsley.

When the water boils, let the spaghetti slide in. When the water comes to the boil again, time it: usually, at a rolling boil, it is perfectly cooked after 11 minutes. Drain well, put into a deep receptacle and fork in the sauce, then fork through the cheese.

Note that it is always better to have the sauce ready before the spaghetti is cooked, because cooked spaghetti easily becomes a solid mass. Some people add olive oil to prevent that, but then the sauce will not adhere to the pasta as it should. Naturally the cheese should be Parmigiano Reggiano – but what student can afford that?

Of course, minced meat or even canned meat – *bullybeef* – are usually used instead of the bacon.

CHAPTER 14

~ LOLA'S PLAN ~

NEVER WEDDING, EVER WOOING,
STILL A LOVE-LORN HEART PURSUING,
READ YOU NOT THE WRONG YOU'RE DOING
IN MY CHEEK'S PALE HUE?
ALL MY LIFE WITH SORROW STREWING,
WED, OR CEASE TO WOO.

Thomas Campbell

When I left Mom's cream-coloured kitchen behind to attend university, I could not cook at all. My mother dropped haphazard hints and rules about cooking, but she never taught Annie and me to cook. She did not have the patience; she was swift of movement and nimble on her feet in her kitchen. We washed up and put things away, but as much as she loved us, Mom found us sloppy and clumsy when we did things in the kitchen. She preferred doing things herself; she never made a mess.

Cooking and recipe collecting for Annie and me came much later. During the years of study and fun and love affairs kitchens played a very minor role in our lives. However, in our university residences my friends and I did learn a few basic truths about food: if your mother sends you cookies, a cake, rusks or biltong, you'd better hide it well or share it freely, otherwise it will be pinched, snitched, filched.

Whether hotplates were not allowed or not available I cannot recall, but we didn't have them. Fast food in your room when you got peckish was a problem.

You cannot toast bread successfully on a one-bar heater, we discovered, but an upturned, hot iron is good for the job. It becomes somewhat more complicated when you crave toast with melted cheese on top.

Not all of us had electric kettles, but we did have those curled immersion heaters, with which you boil water in a jug. This was perfect for boiling eggs as well.

To satisfy that late-night sweet tooth you could keep a bar of chocolate under your undies in your wardrobe, or you could cook a tin of sweetened condensed milk on a primus stove in a pot of water for three hours, and you'd get a delicious tin of caramel. But you should not attend a two-hour residence meeting and leave the condensed milk boiling away in its water bath. You might come back and find, like two roommates did, that the water had boiled dry, and the tin had exploded. There is much more sweetened condensed milk outside an exploded tin than there was inside the intact tin. It will spatter everything in the room, including your beds, books, the clothes you left lying around, the floor, the walls. And sticky caramel stalactites will drip from the ceiling.

Our lack of cooking skills became a small problem when we left the protected world of residences and dining halls to brave the real world for the first time. For eighteen months Susie and I shared a flat in Parow and lived on not much more than polluted air and bread. Susie's obsession with dieting was forgotten: we hardly ever had enough to eat now.

We earned ridiculous pittances as young teachers. In our seedy, sparsely-furnished flat we grew thin on meagre diets of bread and tea. Sometimes we bought greasy fish and chips at the corner café. On dates, we sometimes got to eat a more substantial dinner; even a hamburger was hog heaven. What little money we had we spent on clothes – naturally – and bus fares to our schools.

Flats in Cape Town didn't come complete with stoves. You had to buy your own, and what girl of twenty-one would dream of buying a stove on the never-never for what is, at best, a very temporary dwelling-place? It was simply a roof over your head where you prepared lessons and marked books and kept your few belongings and slept on a second-hand bed with a lumpy coir mattress.

I brought two old paraffin cooking contraptions from home, called "blueflame stoves". Each could handle one small pot or pan. One day, in hungry desperation and with no money, we discovered that, in the snoek season, snoek roe was the cheapest source of protein. It cost 15 cents a pound (500 g) at the local butchery-cum-fish shop. I fried onion, added chopped snoek roe, seasoned it with salt and pepper, and we ate it on toast. Almost a gourmet meal, for a few cents!

After the teaching spell in Cape Town, I moved to Johannesburg to be closer to Daniel, who was working during the day and studying at Wits University at night. Teaching, I had decided by then, was not for me. I wanted to be a journalist – which was easier to dream about than to realise. I found a job in the publications department of a large firm concerned with cars and travel, in De Villiers Street. When I walked in there I didn't know a soul. But within a few days I had at least five good friends.

Even on my miniscule salary – but a king's ransom compared to what I earned as a teacher (less than R200 a month in those days!) – I managed to find a flat for rent in Braamfontein. Braamfontein then was a quiet area of apartment and office buildings. It was tiny, but it was mine alone and I loved it. It didn't need much in the way of furnishings because space was limited to one single room and a tiny bathroom. I bought two second-hand beds and a table. I bought cheap hessian and made curtains on Daniel's mother's sewing machine over a weekend. It was still safe to walk almost anywhere alone. Only Mary, my senior at work, had a ramshackle VW bug. Lola and I and the others either took a bus to work in the CBD, or we walked.

As happens when you are young, I met many new friends, so I stopped being homesick altogether. I did miss the sea and the green Boland with a passion, but I wasn't unhappy. I had no phone and no money to pay for calls anyway, so I wrote letters to my old university friends and to my family. My dearest possessions were a small transistor radio and a red Olivetti Lettera 22 typewriter.

Fortunately our firm had a cafeteria, where a well-rounded white woman surrounded by well-rounded black women cooked delicious homey food, *boerekos*: a large plate plus dessert cost about 75 cents. Sometimes Daniel, the elusive boyfriend, took me to his upmarket Saxonwold home for a meal with his parents, or to use his mother's washing machine for my laundry. He was living at home but was penniless as I was. Fancy restaurants were out of the question.

Daniel's parents had one of those white Thirties double-storey mansions on a large stand in Saxonwold. They lived rather grandly. Mrs Roos had a cook. On Sundays they usually had guests for dinner, and the gardener and cook donned white jackets with red sashes and served at the round stinkwood dining room table. This impressed me no end.

Sometimes I went out with other male friends – Daniel and I were at a stage where we were not all that certain of a future together any more.

"I'm so pleased you enjoy your food!" one of them told me. "I'm glad you're not a nibbler! So many girls are always on diet. It's a waste to take them to a restaurant like this …"

Well, thank *you*, kind sir: with lobster and prawns on the menu a poverty-stricken girl would be a fool not to indulge.

Those were also the last years of my life during which I would have no obligations to others as far as food preparation was concerned; no cares about where my food came from, or whether, in fact, I even had food in my flat.

Eventually Daniel and I discovered that we were, after all, in love, and gourmet food was not high on our list of priorities.

Now and then I invited Daniel over for a meal. It usually consisted of T-bone steak, boiled potatoes and *petit pois* from a tin. I could do a T-bone, and I could boil potatoes. Sometimes I made Maxie's Spaghetti Bolognese. And we might have a glass of wine each.

Lola was one of my friends at work. Lola also had a problem which she was inclined to share with us regularly over a wet hanky when she had PMS.

Mary and Laura had on-off boyfriends, and I had Daniel. But

Lola – Lola was desperate for a date, desperate for male friends. She had no one.

"You're pretty, and you're always going somewhere. Me," she cried in a corner of the cafeteria, "I have nobody! I spend every weekend alone! I'm bored and lonely! I never meet any men! I'm going to be an old maid!"

We would commiserate, and pat her hand, not sure how we could help.

Lola invited me, Laura and Mary for Sunday lunch at her flat in Hillbrow. We accepted, but with no great enthusiasm. On Sunday afternoons Daniel and I usually played tennis with pals. Mary had a new man in sight, and she wanted to be home in case he rang. Laura wanted to visit her parents. But we had always told Lola how much we cared about her, so we owed it to her to attend this hen lunch. Lola was pleased. She had recently "done up" her flat, she said, and she wanted us to see it. She would cook a nice meal, she promised.

Hillbrow was a clean, safe area then, with an Exclusive Books, film theatres, small restaurants, and the Fontana supermarket which was open twenty-four hours a day.

Lola had "done up" her small flat in the fashionable colour combo of the day: black and red. But Lola had been over-enthusiastic. She had a black sofa with red cushions. There were two chairs with red loose covers. The curtains had black and red stripes. The black carpet had red dots. Even the single print against one bare wall was an abstract in red and black. The small table in a corner of the living room was neatly laid with black table mats, red napkins, and glasses.

Lola, a big girl, was a fluttery, disorganised cook in her tiny kitchenette. She grabbed this and that, put it down again, took up something else. She was nervous and over-excited at playing hostess. So the meal took a long time to prepare. We sat at her kitchenette counter and chatted and laughed and drank her cheap, acidic white wine while Lola kept faffing around ineffectually, refusing help.

"Lola, do you have cheese or peanuts?" Mary pleaded. "I'm getting drunk."

She made a small distressed sound, swung round, opened her small fridge.

"No," she said in a small, sad voice. She opened a plastic bread-bin, but the bread in there had green fuzzy spots. "Should I go and get some bread?"

"No, Lola, we'll never eat if you go anywhere now," Laura giggled, rather desperately.

"Crispbread?" I suggested, knowing it was hopeless.

Lola was boiling a chicken. It made us apprehensive, and Mary threw a furtive glance in my direction. We might not have known much about cooking, but a chicken swimming in a pot of plain boiling water was not promising. She also cooked rice, and she opened the predictable tin of peas. She sliced tomatoes.

At long last we were served. Lola hadn't added anything to the chicken except (too little) salt. After its long time in the pot of water it had no taste at all. We ate, because our stomachs were crying out for something except sour wine. Her rice was badly over-salted.

But Lola was our friend, and we ate with as much pretended appetite as we could muster. Over this meal – and no doubt also due to the wine – she became maudlin again and told us, tearfully as usual, sniffling, how much she wanted "a nice boyfriend" and how she had no idea where she could meet men anyway.

We considered Lola's problem. Privately I thought that, if the way to a man's heart is through his stomach, Lola needed serious cooking lessons. But then, anyway, so did I.

Then Lola really did meet someone. She went to one of those free cocktail parties for the opening of an art exhibition. There she sipped at a glass of warm, cheap wine in a milling crowd. A man knocked the glass out of her hand by accident, apologised profusely, and got her another. They exchanged the kind of small talk strangers indulge in. Where do you stay? Do you know the artist?

He was a pleasant-looking, tall guy in jeans and a T-shirt, and he was friendly and laughed easily. He seemed interested in what she told him, which was not much more than her name, and where she lived and worked.

Over lunch in our cafeteria she told us about Leo. She thought he was wonderful; her eyes shone. Being Lola, she already equated chatting over a glass of plonk with a total stranger as the momentous prelude to a love affair.

"Lola, you don't know the man at all!" Laura warned.

"Oh ... but he was so sweet!" She dug dreamily into her plate of farmhouse food.

"Yes, but don't read things into a short conversation at a cocktail party," Mary cautioned.

"I've already invited him to come to my flat and pick some of my books to read," she said, with sudden awe, as if she only realised at that moment what a rash thing she had done.

Perhaps it was rash. We others had already discussed Lola's books. She had a decent glass-fronted bookcase in her small lounge, and although she could afford only paperbacks, the titles impressed. She had concentrated on the classics. They were all there: *Madame Bovary, The Old Man and the Sea, The Sea Wolf, Nausea, Our Man in Havana*, the *Alexandria Quartet*. Dickens, Salinger, Steinbeck, Hemingway. Ayn Rand. Shakespeare. John Updike. Five shelves of good books.

But one detail did not escape our scrutiny. Not one of those books had been read. Their spines were as smooth as baby's bottoms. Lola had bought those books, one by one, only to impress visitors. We hoped that Leo Hayes, being a man, would not notice; would only think that this woman, Lola, was something of an intellectual.

A week later in the cafeteria she burbled happily, "You'll never believe it, I've invited Leo Hayes to supper on Friday, and he accepted! I can't believe it myself! He was going through my books, and I … I couldn't help myself; I was making tea for us, and I suddenly asked him, "Would you like to come to supper?" I couldn't believe I said it! And he said, "Yes, that would be nice", without even looking round!"

We thought of the disastrous meal she'd cooked us. "What are you going to cook?" Laura asked.

"Oh … the usual …" she waved dreamily in the air with one plump arm. "I thought … chicken and rice … and …"

"No!" we shouted almost as one. "No, Lola! Not that!"

She came down to earth and widened her prominent eyes. "Was it that bad …?"

"Yes," Mary said with no preamble. "Go to Fontana and buy a whole rotisserie chicken …"

We worked out what else she could buy and pass off as homemade, and I suggested she get some good chocolate cake at the Café Wien for dessert, which she could serve with ice-cream as dessert.

"But I can't be so … so deceitful! It's like make-up: you make the guy think you're pretty, and it's all just paint! I want him to see I can cook!"

Mary, decisive as always, spelled out the unpalatable truth to her. "Lola, you can't cook. None of us can. Buying food in Hillbrow, which is overflowing with good stuff, is no more deceitful than you having bought all those books and never having read them. I hope your Leo didn't ask you your opinion of *Franny and Zooey*."

I thought Mary was being cruel, but Lola shrugged her shoulders and said resignedly, "I only want people to think I'm well-read. That's all."

"A paperback which has been read has a creased spine, Lola …"

"Do you have time for a cup of tea after work? At my place?" The voice was thick with tears.

It was a Monday afternoon, and Lola stood in my office door. She looked terrible. She'd obviously been crying, on and off, all day. Her face was puffy and blotchy with crying and her eyelids were red and swollen.

"Of course I do. I'll walk home with you after work. I'll take a bus back to Braamfontein."

We sat at the counter of her kitchenette while the rush-hour tumult screeched and hooted past in the street below.

"I'm so in love …" She started crying again, softly and hopelessly. Lola was very good at crying. "He seemed so nice. I took him cookies at his flat; he doesn't stay very far from me…" She sniffled into a handful of tissues. "And now … it's *awful*!"

Around me I could see the efforts she had been making. Nearby on the counter lay a new edition of *The Joy of Cooking*, in hardcover. There were other signs that she'd been spending what little money she had on improving her cooking skills. Brand new slotted spoons, an egg-lifter, wooden spoons of differing sizes and a whisk were stuck artfully in a ceramic container. On the windowsill fresh thyme and parsley had been put in tall glasses of water: they were just beginning to wilt and yellow. Ripe tomatoes, two avocados and a pineapple were arranged on a white platter.

"Lola," I asked gently and put a hand on her arm, "just tell me what happened. I have to get home."

"I ... I thought we had something going ... He is exactly the kind of man I want. He's so intelligent ... so informed. He has a science degree and a great job. I ..." she indicated her new kitchen acquisitions with a wave of an arm, "I studied recipes ... I baked him brownies! I think I can now roast a chicken myself. But ..."

"Did you sleep with him?"

That was still the $64,000 question.

"No!" she cried. "We never got that far! I love him so much! I made plans ... " She stopped, sniffed, and wiped her eyes yet again. "I tried something and it went awfully wrong. Oh. I'm so humiliated!"

Yesterday afternoon, Sunday, at about five, she had carried out what she thought was her *coup d'etat*.

She dressed herself in virginal white from top to toe. She put on an ankle-length, floaty white dress, white stockings, white shoes. She pulled on elbow-length white gloves. Then she donned a broad-brimmed white hat and rounded it all off with a small white clutch bag, and set off for Leo's apartment on foot. She must have drawn curious glances, but she didn't mention it. She was too intent on her purpose. At his apartment she rang the bell.

When he opened the door there was a woman with him. This woman had long blonde hair, wore, according to Lola's muffled confession, "masses of make-up", and her slim figure was poured into a black cat suit. "She was lovely, lovely …" Lola sobbed.

Lola just stood there, speechless, and felt a deep flush creep over her face. She was mortified. For a while nobody moved: the two people in the doorway faced Lola with stunned expressions. Then Leo told Lola, none too gently, to go home and please forget about him. This woman, he told Lola, was Fiona. They'd just become engaged.

I put my arm around Lola's hunched shoulders. "But why," I asked as I handed her another tissue and glanced at my watch, "did you dress up all in white to go and see him?"

Lola's head was now flat on her arms on her counter and her words were indistinct.

"I wanted him … to see me, in his mind's eye, as a bride …! I thought … if he saw me all in white, like that, he might think … I thought he'd be alone and …" She could not finish the sentence through her tears.

I cringed inside; I felt myself shrink with horror for Lola's sake. How could she be so silly, so naïve?

"Lola dear … men's minds do not work like that." I tried other useless, consoling words.

Shortly afterwards Lola found another job and another flat, in a faraway suburb. We lost contact.

Years later I heard by chance that Lola's story had a happy ending after all. She did eventually meet her nice young man. They got married, and I was told she had three children: two little girls and a boy.

Roast Chicken and Vegetables

This is the kind of dish which was unknown when Lola made her boiled chicken and salty rice. As South Africa moved into the international arena again, we became more aware of new food trends. One of the nicest ideas ever must be roasted veggies. So this dish is perfect for when your best friends are coming and you're dying to spend time with them instead of labouring in the kitchen. Prepare everything ahead of time and put it in one of those large, square oven dishes, like the ones which usually come with the oven anyway.

1 plump chicken – 1.5 kg will feed 4 generously
Seasoning: Some chilli preparation like peri-peri oil, chilli-garlic sauce, or Tabasco, plus thyme or rosemary
Salt, like a herbed sea salt, black pepper, nutmeg
Lots of garlic

6 peeled potatoes
Butternut rounds or squares (ready-prepared in a prepack)
Bell peppers, preferably in different colours
Ripe tomatoes
Honey
Olive oil, water, chicken stock powder

Prepare the chicken by removing loose flaps of fat, and take out any giblets. Season inside and rub the chicken all over, with your hands, with whatever sauce or oil you prefer. A chilli preparation gives a nice colour, but if the sauce is thick, it could burn a little. Once you have the sauce/oil rubbed in, season with salt. Put the chicken in one corner of the oven pan. (If there were giblets, put them in too. Many people love them).

Wash the sweet peppers, cut off the tops and remove the seeds. They have to stand on their bottoms, so test that, and slice off thin pieces if necessary, to prevent them toppling when baking. Try not to cut through the bottoms. Peel and insert a small tomato in each pepper, and season.

Arrange the potatoes, butternut and stuffed peppers neatly next to the chicken. The butternut, if sliced, can overlap a little. Do not salt the potatoes, but season the butternut with nutmeg. (A salted potato will not crisp properly.)

Insert sliced garlic everywhere – inside the chicken and between the vegetables. Use more herbs if you like. Drizzle honey over the tomatoes in the peppers – about a teaspoon or so per tomato. Add a little water – half a cup will do – to the baking tin. Sprinkle chicken stock powder very lightly over everything. Drizzle the vegetables with olive oil, or, best of all, spray with garlic-scented olive oil spray, which is much easier. This ensures that your veggies have a thin layer of olive oil all over their tops.

Now the dish can safely wait until you're ready, either in a fridge, if yours is large enough, or covered on the kitchen counter – not longer than a couple of hours, though.

To roast, preheat your oven to 180 °C, wait for the indication that it's reached that heat, and pop the pan into the oven. That's your entire main meal. The flavours complement each other beautifully. Do check later, and if you notice that the sauce on the chicken is darkening rather fast, place a loose piece of foil lightly over the chicken, but not over the vegetables. This simple dish needs no more attention and will be ready in less than 2 hours.

The starter is up to you, but a cold seafood thingy can also be done a day ahead. And, of course, you need a very big bowl of mixed green salad leaves. Plus cold white wine.

CHAPTER 15

~ A HOME AT LAST ~

OUR PORTION IS NOT LARGE, INDEED;
BUT THEN HOW LITTLE DO WE NEED,
FOR NATURE'S CALLS ARE FEW;
IN THIS THE ART OF LIVING LIES,
TO WANT NO MORE THAN MAY SUFFICE,
AND MAKE THAT LITTLE DO.
Nathaniel Cotton

I stand in my kitchenette in the seaside house with the few ingredients needed for the pastry I am about to make. It is so easy, so delicious, so rich: butter, crème fraîche, flour, salt, the pastry recipe from the Hex Valley.

I am making chicken pie. The chicken is cooling in its fragrant, thickened stock.

When working with food my hands are quick and sure now; I've had decades of practice. The processor quickly fashions the pastry into a ball. I remove it to a floured wooden board; it is slightly sticky. I knead it briefly to form it into a ball, wrap it in plastic, and put it in the fridge to rest.

The chicken, its flesh falling from its bones, must be deboned. It's a messy but satisfying task. As I put the bones and bits of cartilage in a plastic bowl, the first seagulls land screeching on the lawn.

Do they have second sight? Because how, otherwise, do they always know I am about to throw something on the lawn which they might find edible?

A kelp gull is a lovely bird when it glides on the air currents, a streamlined silhouette caught on many photographs and sketches. It is a neat bird, its feathers always smooth and clean. It is a much larger bird than the smaller grey-headed gull of the Atlantic coastline.

But the kelp gull has sly, beady eyes and the body language of a crooked salesman. It moves towards scraps in a sidelong manner, glancing this way and that, like a thief waiting to grab cheap sunglasses from a pavement display.

They are not the birds romanticised in yearning love songs. They are the scavengers of the coasts, with an awful repertoire of sounds: nails scratching on metal, mad cawings, miaows like cats. They wake us in the pink dawn, far too early, reconnoitring in case bits of food had magically appeared on the lawn during the night.

As I go out with the bowl of bones, they scatter noisily. I toss it out, and they approach like famine-ravaged buzzards to fight over the few bits of edibles.

Beyond them the sea is endlessly blue and calm, and two chokka boats drift by, painted boats on a painted sea except for the chugging of their diesel engines.

Today, thirty-five years ago, Daniel and I got married in Stellenbosch. We did it the old-fashioned way: a church wedding, with family, friends, a sit-down dinner, a dance. Our wedding gift from Daniel's parents was a white Ford Corsair, which soon developed every problem known to car mechanics. My parents gave me an electric sewing machine, which might not have been a glam present, but which would prove to be worth its weight in gold in the years to come.

We went on honeymoon to my uncle's seaside cottage in Keurboomstrand, where Daniel promptly caught a tummy bug and was very ill. As soon as he recovered, I got tonsillitis. Then we returned to Johannesburg to live in my bachelor flat. It was cheap, and it was centrally situated in Braamfontein – more of a residential suburb then, and fairly quiet at night. Except for the damn traffic lights far below our thirteenth floor: here cars screeched to a halt and pulled away noisily, twenty-four hours a day. But we were young and we slept through the traffic noises. We got used to them.

The minute entrance "hall" contained an ancient gas stove with an almost useless oven, our new fridge, a few cupboards and a sink.

My new husband worked in the Johannesburg CBD. Before our wedding I had resigned from my old job because I needed a few months off, with so much to organise. The firm would not give me unpaid leave, so I left.

After our honeymoon I found another badly-paid job in the library of an oil company, where I battled with translations of geological reports from English to Afrikaans and vice versa. Long rows of grey files containing folded reams of squiggly seismic surveys stood on endless grey industrial shelving. But the job had the perk of being two blocks from our flat.

After work I raced to the little supermarket across the street, to buy groceries and dinner. Life was quite affordable then, even on our meagre income. We were saving my salary for a deposit on a house somewhere in the future, and Daniel gave me the princely sum of R50 per month to provide all our food, groceries and toiletries. On that R50 we had steak or fried chicken pieces almost every night. As I worked until 5 p.m., there was no time for long-simmered stews – not that I knew how to cook them anyway.

A bottle of sunflower oil cost 28 cents. A tin of the best tiny Norwegian sild sardines in sardine oil cost 8 cents. I sometimes bought a tin of smoked oysters for 25 cents to put on cream crackers as hors d'oeuvres when Daniel came home: a small delusion of grandeur.

When I pushed that trolley through the narrow aisles of the tiny supermarket it was the best moment of my entire day. I was wearing a gold wedding band, and I was pushing a trolley: I had a husband now; I was no longer the archetypal single girl throwing two chops and an iceberg lettuce into a basket. I had my man now to look after! The ring and the trolley were trophies of triumph. It didn't take much to make me happy.

Inadvertently I also started married life with a set of unwritten rules which had been handed down by my grannies and my mother. These I was to regret in later years, when the concept of "Superwoman" added a career to those domestic tenets and stretched you to your limit.

In earlier times a married woman's place was in the home. A wife looked after her husband, they stated with firm lips and serious eyes. That meant you shopped and cooked and cleaned, changed the bed linen and towels at precise intervals, and kept your oven clean. You prepared "decent meals", preferably three per day, which was fortunately impossible in my frantic city life.

But I did happily prepare a not-always-decent meal every night. I would rush home with my purchases, light the flickering flame of the recalcitrant gas oven, lay the small table, and get stuck in. Well, as stuck in as you can get when you only fry steak or chicken, cook two potatoes, cut up tomatoes – and not much else. I was always ecstatic when I heard Daniel's footsteps approaching at 6.30. We could have lived on cold water because we had love.

With our simple dinner we had a glass of wine each. This came from a dinky containing 375 ml of red or white plonk. That was all we drank – a dinky with dinner every night. We felt very adult and sophisticated.

One day I went into the Portuguese greengrocer, and decided to try cooking spinach. I looked at the huge swiss chard leaves and bought three. This, I reckoned, was more than enough for us. They were washed and boiled in water. I could not believe my eyes when I opened the pot: there lay a tiny green blob the size of a newborn baby's palm.

Once I tried doing a whole roast chicken. This, to me, had always been a comfort food, for which I got a craving as urgent as that sugar craving when PMS hit. I rushed home in my lunch hour, heated the ghastly gas oven to Gas mark 7, and shoved in the chicken which I had prepared with no more than salt and pepper. I had scant knowledge of herbs or marinades. The oven hissed asthmatically as I rushed back to the office.

All afternoon I dreamily contemplated that roasting chicken. I'd cook potatoes … realising too late that I could have put peeled potatoes alongside the chicken.

"Gas mark 7?!" screeched someone. "Are you crazy? Your chicken will be burnt to a cinder! Do you realise it's going to be in that oven for more than three-and-a-half-hours?"

"You don't know my oven!" I was cocky and confident as I calmly drew neat black letters to stick on the back of yet another file. "At Mark 7 it's probably no more than 100 °C …"

The chicken, when I opened the oven breathlessly, seemed fine, if a little pale. I cut open a tin of mixed vegetables and hastily peeled potatoes. I sliced tomatoes for a salad. And after Daniel and I had exchanged long, deep kisses, and he'd washed his hands and face, I brought the much-anticipated dinner triumphantly to the table.

"You carve …" I indicated grandly and handed him a blunt carving knife.

As he started cutting off the leg, which I was salivating for, blood seeped out. It was quite raw. The chicken was done only on the extreme outside after its interminable hours in the oven. I burst into tears.

One morning, almost exactly a year after our marriage, I got up as usual to make tea before the mad rush to get ready for the office. And a small, but strange thing happened, which was entirely contrary to my normal robust reaction to all food. I opened it to get milk, and as I got a whiff of smoky cheese my stomach curdled. There was a wedge of smoked Cheddar in the fridge. A faint nausea swept over me.

With the unerring instinct that only women possess I thought, "My God, I'm pregnant!" and then, "But I can't be! It's too soon!" And I hadn't even skipped a period.

But I was. The pregnancy spelled the end of the year-long honeymoon and called for a more serious look at our lifestyle. We'd been saving up my salary. Now we urgently needed to look for a house.

Life in a one-room apartment was footloose and fancy-free.

Daniel and I took off on impromptu weekends by simply lock-ing the apartment door. Once we decided within a few hours to go to Lourenço Marques. (This was before Independence and before it became Maputo.) It was the 27th of December. We hired camping equipment, grabbed our passports, packed the car, and spent three days in Lourenço Marques' camping and caravan park. I hated the camping, the grey sand which got into everything, and the primitive ablution block, but we loved the Laurentina beer and the palm trees. We ate piles of that immortal speciality of Lourenço Marques: peri-peri prawns. We were strapped for cash but prawns came cheaply and in tall red heaps on white rice. They were juicy and indescribably delicious. We drank immoderate amounts of cold, crisp Casal Garçia.

On another occasion, when I was two-and-a-half months pregnant and the house search was on in earnest, we went off on a whim to the Natal North Coast without once thinking about malaria and prophylactic pills. It was high summer, very hot, and exceedingly humid. My guardian angel must have been working overtime.

All this came to a halt as my pregnancy progressed. The days of wine and roses were over.

The house-hunting was discouraging. We discovered we had barely enough money for a small deposit on what would be a very humble dwelling.

Daniel, with a dispirited agent in tow, made a fortuitous discov-ery one day. The agent had shown him yet another white-painted dog kennel-sized houselet, which he vetoed, in an unknown little suburb. He asked the agent to drive him through a few streets, intrigued. This forgotten enclave perched on what was then the edges of Johannesburg's northwest outposts, next door to some decidedly scruffy and rundown suburbs. He found it on the first street corner: the house that would be our first real home.

A finicky German builder had built a house for his daughter who was getting married. Only she never did – and as luck would have it, the simple but pretty little house was still empty. The agent didn't even know it was on the market.

It turned out to be R1 000 more than our budget would allow. R1 000 was a lot of money in those days. But the house was perfect for us. Across the street from the front door was open municipal ground, lying fallow, and to me irresistible: wide open space at last for a country girl.

The house had one bathroom, three small bedrooms, an L-shaped lounge and dining room, and parquet floors. Once upon a time the ground it was built on had been part of a farm. A quince hedge grew along the pavement. On the other side of the

house was a peach tree, gnarled and neglected like a starving old man, with a sturdy apricot tree nearby, and in a corner grew a tall mulberry tree.

Outside the main bedroom a fig tree draped ancient sculptural branches over the remnants of an even older stone wall. So all around us we saw riches beyond price. We could prune and fertilise; we had a veritable orchard of fruit trees!

But what clinched the deal were the two huge pear trees flanking the short driveway. In spring, in full bloom, they would be two glorious sentinels.

When my parents came to visit, much later, my mother identified them as saffron pears: a type of heirloom pear of which our two trees might have been some of the last living examples in the country ...

The German owner-builder, a difficult and intransigent character, insisted quite strenuously that I, pregnancy and all, should get down on all fours and shine up the parquet floors with floor polish. I refused point blank, and we had the floors sanded and varnished professionally. In fact, cleaning the house, washing down walls and scrubbing out all cupboards after that sanding was probably a harder job than if I had simply polished the damn floors myself!

The kitchen was a delight after the peevish old gas monster of the flat. The stove was electric, and brand new. There was a breakfast nook, for which we bought a pine table and two benches. We were in heaven – all that room to move about after the cramped one-room flat!

I made all the curtains on the sewing machine which had been the wedding present from my parents. Suddenly nothing was too much trouble, and I went many miles to find well-priced materials. To my first home help's consternation, I also hung the curtains myself, one by one as I finished them. This, she said, was looking for trouble: baby would be born with the umbilical cord around its neck, what with me standing on chairs, up and down all day …

It was in this house that I had the first tentative stirrings of foodie aspirations. I had a decent stove, a large fridge, and once I stopped working, I also had time on my hands.

Everyone we knew came to see the house. They all liked it, but they were doubtful about the neighborhood. The suburb was definitely not "in". But even Daniel's rather grand parents fell under the spell of the little suburb which smacked of the Thirties, and the cosy house looking out on all that open veld.

Later, in spring, after the baby's birth, our two saffron pear trees, like I expected, burst into glorious bloom like old-maid brides in masses of white lace. It was a joy and pleasure to us and to everyone passing by. The pity was that, like old maids who marry in over-the-top glory at last but are nearly barren, we never harvested many of the big, juicy pears. The trees were too high and too spreading for us to spray, and they fell prey to the pests who like pears. And the mousebirds had a feast, which they unfortunately continued in the fig tree.

There were practical day to day problems in the beginning. We had no phone, and were told no lines were available for the foreseeable future. We still had the wedding present car but in this outpost one car was inadequate. Supermarkets were many kilometres away in other suburbs; we only had a small café and a butchery within walking distance. Daniel had to get to work and every morning he sprinted for the bus, several blocks away, leaving the car for me. We managed somehow.

Daniel was hopeless when it came to timekeeping, and was always late, like Dagwood; he was fussed and harrassed by time, tearing off with his briefcase. Some days when I was sure I wouldn't need the car, he'd take it. On those days I'd take leisurely walks to the café and the butchery several blocks away and uphill. I was young and fit and I liked the quiet streets and the absence of traffic.

We had good neighbours and bad neighbours. Most of them were old and had lived their entire lives in that suburb. We adopted the old-fashioned way of addressing older people as uncle and aunt, which in Afrikaans often has no connotation to family ties.

Two houses from us down the road "Uncle" Koos sat on the front porch of his ancient dirty hovel, day after day. He never read a newspaper or fiddled with a small job like whittling wood or mending a shoe. He preferred lounging half-hidden in the shadow of the creeper-encrusted little porch in summer, or sitting on the cracked steps in the sun in winter. He passed his daylight hours watching the street, where during weekdays only sniffing dogs, a languorous cat, a blue-overalled workman or a lone car passed by during office hours. When he was in his cups, which was often, he would shout remarks – not necessarily pleasant or polite – at passersby. He disliked me with a passion, since the day we moved in. If I passed by on my way to the café for bread or milk, he would sneer, half-hidden by his untrimmed shrubs and creepers, "There she goes again! On her way to spend money! The rich people! Ha!" This was followed by a revolting hawking and spitting sound.

Was I, a young woman whose husband wore business suits to the office, to him a symbol of the rich proletariat? Because we had moved into the only new house in the area? Who knows? He himself almost never set a foot outside this forgotten little suburb except to buy booze. We were unwelcome intruders as far as he was concerned.

An old couple lived just across from us on the side street on a big plot. The old man kept a vegetable garden going and had a borehole, and "Aunt" Mavis would sometimes arrive at our front door with a basket full of carrots, beets or onions. I loved Aunt Mavis and Uncle Tom. They were sweet, kind, old-fashioned people. I loved sitting in her kitchen, where she kept a large black stove burning, although she had an electric stove as well. Her simple house with its cream walls and dark woodwork made me think of Ouma Greta's house, unreachably far away in the Langkloof. She had the same serene aura about her as Ouma Greta. I would sit at her kitchen table and watch her placidly peeling potatoes and scraping carrots, and I would experience a sense of deep peace. The pulsing city fifteen kilometres away never intruded into this house.

Lower down in the side street lived "Aunt" Anna with her extremely shy old brother, "Uncle" Sam, who never looked me in the eye and blushed when I greeted him. Neither of them had ever married. Their gloomy, sparsely furnished living room was forever shuttered against sunlight. Ancient kitschy pictures hung from high black-painted picture rails on black string: a gaudy drawing of the Voortrekker Monument in Pretoria outlined in silver paper, a bleached print of a boy with abnormally wide eyes with an arm around his fat puppy, and that ancient pointer to the sinner, *De Breede en de Smalle Weg*, showing the broad way full of happy, dancing people on their way into the maws of Hell. On the narrow way towards the gates of Heaven black-garbed, bowed, sad people struggled up a steep and rocky trail.

I recalled seeing this picture in dark hallways in old houses in the valley where I grew up. How dismaying it was always to be reminded that the way to heaven was so creepy and depressing, while the happy road to hell was so much more attractive!

Aunt Anna had a nasty little mongrel dog who barked at me and on occasion nipped my ankles. She told me why he sometimes attacked me and at other times did not. "He bites women in trousers," she said firmly, and added self-righteously, "he dislikes women who wear trousers, like you do." Good grief, a dog and his mistress who had decided that a woman in slacks or jeans was on her way to Hell! Dancing along the Broad Way!

Yet I really liked Aunt Anna. She was a practical, energetic woman who baked cakes and rusks and cookies and whose little kitchen was permanently scented with vanilla and spices. She presented me with herbs, chives, and advice about babies although she'd never had any.

Then there was Aunt Billy, the bane of Aunt Anna's life … happily caterwauling along the Broad Way and not to be diverted by any amount of sermonising.

Aunt Billy and Uncle Joe's shabby old house with its peeling gutters, dirty walls, sun-bleached square of lawn, and deep, shadowy front porch was directly opposite Aunt Anna and Uncle Sam. Here Aunt Billy and Uncle Joe lived in a permanent fume of alcohol and cigarettes. He was gaunt and hollow-cheeked and she was as rotund as a whale. On one extremely hot and memorable day, when the poor bashful old bachelor, Uncle Sam, was in his front garden watering some precious shrubs,

Aunt Billy strode into the middle of the street, stood defiantly on the hot tar in her torn sandals, and lifted her tent of a dress to well above her naked, enormous, droopy breasts and fat stomach, and fanned her face vigorously with her bundled skirts. She wore dingy, loose cotton bloomers.

"It's too bloody hot today!" she screamed at no one in particular.

"It's not the first time she's done that," Aunt Anna told me, darkly furious. "She does it on purpose … Poor Sam …"

It was difficult to know how to interpret that remark.

We held a housewarming. The week before I had spent hours perusing my few cookery books. Daniel had recently bought me a much-desired paperback, Robert Carrier's *Great Dishes of the World*. At the time, Carrier was the chef of the decade. Here was a man who told you how to make all those dishes you'd only heard the names of, and more. It was the kind of book I took to bed with me to read instead of actually cooking from it. Most of the recipes were a bit daunting. But I'd tried a few: French onion soup, coq au vin and his crêpe recipe. In my South African cookbook, *Cook and Enjoy It* by Mrs de Villiers – the standby cookbook of all South African brides – were perfectly adequate pancake recipes. But "crêpes" sounded so much grander than "pancakes".

The party started off well. We played Elvis long-playing records and the cheap plonk flowed, although I was abstemious due to being heavily pregnant by now.

It was only when I helped myself to my own food at last, that the horrible truth dawned. Every single dish I had made – except for the roast potatoes – was swimming in a sour liquid of some sort.

I'd made chicken pieces in a barbecue-type sauce which was too sour. There was too much vinegar in the dressing I'd used on the potato salad instead of mayonnaise. There were coleslaw and overcooked green beans and a green salad. Everything had some sort of lemony or vinegary marinade or dressing. What had I been thinking? I tried not to see the puckering mouths around me … Hadn't I tasted the dishes? I had – but only one at a time, so it didn't register that I had a combination of too many acidic tastes.

Big lesson to me: plan the tastes! Don't overwhelm food with sauces! Oh, there was so much to learn …

Fortunately I'd kept to canned fruits and ice cream for dessert. I had given Carrier's "Rum Baba" a fleeting thought and decided it was too difficult to attempt. When I did make it, a year or so later when my parents came to visit, I overdid the rum, and my young brother got tiddly on the pudding.

From now on, until I got a better grip on cookery know-how, I would stay with traditional foods as Mom made them. I would not, I decided, start whisking up peculiar marinades and alien sauces again.

Cream Cheese Dip

It was a time of chips and dips. It went out of fashion for a long time, but a dip in the fridge is still handy. Haul it out and serve with crackers. It should reach room temperature, otherwise it might need thinning with a little with milk.

250 g cream cheese or creamed cottage cheese
15 ml finely grated onion
About 30 ml finely chopped green pepper
3 ml salt or Aromat
5 ml castor sugar
60 ml thick, tangy mayonnaise
5 ml chilli-garlic sauce

Mix everything well together, scrape into a small bowl, cover, and leave in the fridge for an hour, or overnight, to develop the flavour. Yields about 250 ml dip.

Bacon-Cheese Cocktail Pastries

Use defrosted puff pastry, and roll it out thinly on a floured surface.
Use it to line shallow patty pan hollows. Usually you'll find the top
of a small bowl or soup cup cuts the perfect rounds. This recipe
makes about 18–24 small pastries.

2 rolls of puffy pastry, 400 g each, defrosted
250 g rindless bacon
375 ml milk
3 eggs
375 ml grated Cheddar cheese
5 ml salt

Preheat oven to 200 °C. Grill the bacon until really crisp and, when slightly cooled, cut or chop into tiny pieces. Put the milk in a good-sized bowl, and break the eggs into the milk. Beat well with a whisk or electric beater. Stir in the cheese with a fork and add the salt.

Divide the bacon bits among the patty cases, then fill each case not more than two-thirds full. Bake in preheated oven for about 15 minutes or until the custard has set.

Prawns in Cheese Sauce

An ambitious starter, rich and delicious. Don't use cottage cheese for this one, as cream cheese handles heat better than cottage cheese.

1 kg fresh prawns (not cooked), shelled and deveined	2 cloves garlic, crushed
Butter and olive oil	15 ml finely grated onion
250 g blue cheese (any good quality will do)	15 ml finely chopped parsley
	15 ml finely chopped chives
250 g cream cheese	180 ml dry or semi-dry white wine

Dry the cleaned and rinsed prawns – use a clean kitchen cloth as kitchen paper tends to stick. Put some butter and olive oil in a pan or wok, heat until hot, and fry the prawns in batches – very quickly, just until they turn pink and curl up. Drain them on scrunched-up kitchen paper.

Grate the blue cheese coarsely. Now mix all the ingredients together except the prawns. Melt the cheese mixture over low heat in a saucepan, stirring with a whisk all the time. Remove immediately once it melts; do not boil. Stir in the prawns.

Taste for seasoning: the blue cheese is salty, but the dish might still need extra salt.

This dish should be served as soon as it's ready. You can prepare the cheese mixture ahead and put it in a pot, ready for heating. You can do the prawns ahead as well, but keep in mind that you want hot or warm prawns to go into the cheese sauce, and they should not be overcooked. As a starter, this should serve 6–8.

Trout Pâté

250 g smoked trout
45 ml butter
100 g fresh breadcrumbs (best made in a processor/blender)
Finely grated rind and juice of 1 lemon
Freshly ground black pepper
2 ml grated nutmeg
5 ml anchovy essence or anchovy paste
125 ml fresh cream
Salt if necessary

Remove skin and bones from the trout, if any, and mash the flesh. Melt the butter and pour over the breadcrumbs. Add the lemon rind and juice to the crumbs. Season it with pepper, nutmeg and anchovy essence or paste. Add the mashed fish, fold in well, then fold in the cream. Taste whether it needs salt. Spoon into a small bowl, cover, and keep in the fridge. Serve with thin slices of wholewheat bread. As a snack or starter, this will serve 4–6.

Quick Apple Pie

This is a really heavenly dessert and a favourite with everyone who tastes it. It's quick and easy to make, and tastes as if you'd gone to enormous trouble. Serve it with vanilla ice cream or thick custard.

In a pie dish, arrange:
4–5 Granny Smith apples, peeled and sliced

Sprinkle apples with:
15 ml sugar mixed with

15 ml cinnamon

In a bowl, combine and spread over the apples:
200 ml sugar

250 ml flour

10 ml baking powder

1 jumbo egg, beaten

185–190 g butter, barely-melted

125–250 ml broken pecans or walnuts (optional)

5 ml vanilla essence

3 ml salt

Preheat oven to 180 °C. Bake pie for 45 minutes or until golden brown. Serves 4–6.

CHAPTER 16

~ THE SUPERWOMAN DILEMMA ~

OUR BIRTH IS BUT A SLEEP AND A FORGETTING:
THE SOUL THAT RISES WITH US, OUR LIFE'S STAR,
HATH HAD ELSEWHERE ITS SETTING,
AND COMETH FROM AFAR;
NOT IN ENTIRE FORGETFULNESS,
AND NOT IN UTTER NAKEDNESS,
BUT TRAILING CLOUDS OF GLORY DO WE COME
FROM GOD, WHO IS OUR HOME.
HEAVEN LIES ABOUT US IN OUR INFANCY...

William Wordsworth

Our little boy was born on a cold, late July day after a long labour. There wasn't much available for pain relief in labour then; epidurals were rarely used and were not considered very safe. It was a protracted, exhausting labour, and I didn't think I was dying. I was certain that I was dying, and I didn't mind much.

So although I saw the blueish little thing being born, I had little interest in him. I was wiped out. In a time before ultrasound we didn't know the sex of our babies before birth. During my pregnancy I had felt quite detached from the little rugby ball growing inside me and ruining my slim waist. It was amusing, later, to feel it kick and push up some part of itself under my ribcage, but he/she remained a stranger to me. I could never summon up the wet cow eyes, hand-on-the-tummy pose of a tenderly expectant mother.

After the birth, from which poor Daniel was excluded, to his chagrin, I slept for a long time. I was woken by a sister to a room full of flowers and cards. She had a tiny, blue-swaddled bundle in her arms. She handed him to me, instructing me to feed him.

She left. I opened up the soft cloth around the face of this little stranger, and peculiar things happened. The tiny face with the huge eyes looked up into mine quizzically, not like a baby, not grizzling for a breast, not with vague and unfocused eyes. His expression was bright, curious and serene as he studied my face.

Various thoughts flitted through my bemused mind. One: this baby can see me and the stories of how babies see things out of focus were nonsense. Two: this little soul is scanning my face because he wants to see what his mom looks like in this life. He's curious to see whether he got the right mommy … And my third thought, incongruous, anomalous, was directed at the baby: *you have been on this earth before. I know you. You're a wise old soul and I have met you somewhere in time before.*

And then, instantaneously, I fell in love. They don't tell you that in the baby books. They tell you everything about babies, but not that you could fall hopelessly in love with your baby.

This one wasn't even pretty, not then. Big bright eyes, yes, but also a funny small blob for a nose and a receding chin. "You might not be pretty," I told my new love, "but welcome, my darling, welcome to the world!"

He prospered and grew quickly. He drank my milk eagerly, and what a miracle it was to think that I, me, had grown this new person inside me, and the milk I was producing was making him gain weight by the day. He almost never cried. The only fly in this ointment of love and baby smells was that baby would not sleep much more than two or three hours at a time. Daniel slept through all the broken nights because little Danny didn't go "Waahhh…!" in the night like other babies. He slept in his pram next to my side of the bed, and he had a habit of making small noises and little questioning grunts to let me know he was awake and ready for another drink. The bar had to be open twenty-four hours a day.

It was very tiring. House and home, in a sense, collapsed around me as I sleepwalked during the day and tried to get Dannyboy to stick to some kind of schedule. But babies make their own rules.

He grew more and more beautiful. His chin appeared; he wasn't going to be a chinless wonder after all. His nose assumed the correct snub baby shape. He grew lovely hair with streaks of different browns and golds. He filled out to become a deliciously firm, plump baby. For months poor Daniel felt a bit superfluous, neglected … It is impossible to be a sexy, sparkling wife as well as a new mother. You act exactly like a hen with chickens. All your concentration and attention is on your chicken, and the rest of the flock should please leave you alone while you cluck-cluck and spread your wings protectively over your baby.

Eventually, after several months, Danny settled into some sort of schedule, and he was eating solids. I put his cooked vegetables through a baby mouli – a nifty little contraption into which you put the veggies, turned a handle, and a soft purée fell into a bowl. Sometimes he ate bottled food. He was the most contented baby I ever had the pleasure to meet. He was even-tempered and laid-back – a chilled-out baby. He let strangers pick him up and hand him around to be admired. He stayed happily with mother-in-law or sister-in-law, Hayley, when I needed to do serious shopping or a translation or write an article.

Except that he still didn't sleep through the night. He woke several times for attention or a dry nappy or milk. Daniel still slept peacefully right through, and I was still so sleep-deprived that it sometimes drove me to silent tears.

Life goes through stages. We were now at the stage where most of our friends were married and having babies. While the men talked sports and male stuff, we women talked babies, pregnancies, baby handbooks, baby habits and baby food. And contraceptives. None of us could see our way clear to having half-a-dozen children, like Ouma Sannie had.

Contraceptives were a problem. Some women were okay with the Pill, but I couldn't take it because it made me depressed and caused other physical side-effects. The men disliked condoms. There was the Loop, which also hadn't been perfected yet. There was a foam-type contraceptive on the market then, which seemed like a good option.

But Danny was a "foam baby" so we already knew it was far from foolproof. One of my best friends had twins, and got such a fright that she had the loop inserted as well as going on the Pill: double indemnity.

Danny had his first birthday. Ma-in-law came with cynical Aunt Betta. Hayley came with her two toddlers and her new baby, and a few neighbours turned up with little gifts. He was too young, we had decided, for one of those silly, chaotic parties where all your friends came with their babies, who smeared icing into the carpets. Parties for one-year-olds seemed to cause nothing but problems. The living room would be a mess and all the babies would end up either hysterical, exhausted or nauseous from eating too much ice cream.

After his birthday, our small family left for a week's holiday in the Kruger Park. We were still relying (the wrong word) on that contraceptive foam. My period was late, which it often was, but a week late…? It was in the Kruger Park, in a hut at Pretoriuskop while Daniel was outside making a fire for a braai and I was giving Danny a bath, that it hit me: I was pregnant again.

I put Danny into the faithful ancient pram which had been my brother's as a baby, weaved towards Daniel in shock and burst into tears. I could not face having a baby again so soon. We hadn't planned on a second child until Danny was at least three years old. In fact, I was quietly planning on having no more children. I needed nothing more than Daniel and my precious Danny.

But it seemed the celestial powers, who probably decide when to send souls to earth and when to fetch them again, knew what they were doing.

So within less than twenty-two months we had two little boys. Stephen was, however, no laid-back Danny. Stephen came into the world screaming in protest at being born. After I had had a rest, he was put into my arms still screaming. As we would find out, Stephen was going to scream and complain a lot during the next three months. He was a colicky baby with a big temper.

But eventually we all slept through the night, and we were the proud parents of two genuinely beautiful children. Danny had eyes the colour of sweet sherry. Stephen had two orbs of clearest blue. Danny's blond baby curls became a shiny brown mop with sun stripes, and Stephen was a true blond with pink cheeks. They were sturdy, bright kids. Danny was the calm, wise one and Stephen the noisy, short-tempered one. Danny was untidy, and grew into a tough, adventurous little boy – but with a sensitive side which made him sometimes run to his mommy in tears when he was upset. Stephen of the quick temper was neat and tidy, more fearful, and much more careful of life and limb than his older brother.

While Danny and Stephen were still babies, I kept up the freelance translating for the extra bit of money. I was, like most housebound mothers, frustrated and lonely at home. Somewhere during this baby time I bought a few American food magazines for the first time. I was fascinated by the colour pictures, the travel articles, the recipes, the entire foodie culture about which I knew nothing.

I read, even studied, cookbooks and overseas food magazines, as we had no such magazines in South Africa then. There was a creative side to me which needed an outlet. The kitchen became that outlet.

Even with the kids around my feet, I could experiment. Daniel became used, bemusedly, to coming home to a house redolent with herbs and garlic or curry and spices. In our local library I discovered a treasure trove of cookery books, which I took to bed at night and read like novels.

Slowly our life became more ordered again. But my husband was a bit player in those years of doggy-paddling: he was working on his own career and felt that he was doing it all for us. In later years he would regret not delegating more, not allowing himself to relax or take time off sometimes. But he was also a victim of the times: young white men who aspired to a solid career still said to their senior, "Yes, sir!", "Sure, sir" and "No, I don't mind working late, sir" … It was what was expected.

Money was still in short supply. Daniel taught law classes at night at a technikon: it was an extra income. Twice a year he spent weeks at a time in Zurich for his firm, and I was left on my own with the children.

Although we had friends scattered all over Greater Johannesburg, there wasn't a support system I could turn to. Friends and family were too busy with their own lives to add babysitting to their schedules.

It was the time of the cruel concept of Superwoman. We strove to be Her. We desperately wanted to be perfect wives, wonderful mothers, keep an exemplary home – and build successful careers. Apparently, through good management, women should have been able to do all that. I was failing miserably on all counts, regardless of my improving cooking skills. I simply did not have the temperament to be Superwoman. I was an over-anxious mother who would have been best off with a farmer husband on a quiet farm somewhere, with a placid older woman at hand to help me with the kids and calm my anxieties … Ah, fate! I was failing the Superwoman class dismally.

Although domestic help came and went, I was useless as a "madam". I could not summon up the air of authority necessary to spell out firmly to another woman what her duties and chores entailed. Most simply loafed around. But they always loved the children, and made reliable occasional babysitters.

Daniel acquired a very old, very crotchety diesel Mercedes because we badly needed a second car. This jalopy had to be parked on the incline in the side street, because the car had to be push-started every morning. It spewed out clouds of foul diesel fumes and there was always something wrong with it. If the oil didn't leak, the water did. The wipers stopped working in hard rain. It blew up things in its engine. Sometimes Daniel would have to stop his early-morning efforts at starting the heap, and run down the street to catch a late bus down on the main road.

With the two young kids I now needed the other car, the wedding gift Ford, almost daily, being so far away from all amenities. There was the shopping to do. The kids contracted childhood illnesses with terrifying rapidity. Stephen was prone to croup. In their toddler years, both of them under the age of six, they lived lives of such foolhardy and unpredictable recklessness that I often found myself negotiating the traffic like a racing driver to get to the doctor with, yet again, a bleeding, crying child needing stitches – or a brain scan because he fell on his head.

Stephen was two years old when I could bear the relative lack of communication with the world of working women no longer. Even if being Superwoman was not for me, I was ready for some outside stimulation. Mary, my friend and senior at the Publications Department some years ago, was now the editor of a woman's magazine, *Darling*. Laura was the same magazine's fashion editor. Mary had had twin daughters only four months before Danny was born.

One day I drove to town in the unreliable white Ford. The offices of Republican Press, which had several magazines in their stable, were in an office block in End Street, in the industrial parts of the city.

Mary had a large office of her own, with an impressive view over the city.

"Mary, I'm going mad with nothing to do. I mean, hardly nothing, but you know what I mean. No outside interest. I know you have a food editor. But when she leaves, if she leaves, can I have her job?"

Mary, more sophisticated than ever, regarded me doubtfully.

"*Food?* You want to be a *food* editor?"

"I've come a long way, Mary!"

Mary considered for a while, tapping a pen on her blotter.

"It's strange you should turn up today. My food editor is leaving for overseas in six weeks' time, and I have no one to replace her. Look ..." she sat forward and she was very serious, "you can have the job. But although you're my friend I must warn you: I'll have to see how it goes. You're on probation. If it doesn't work, if your work doesn't come up to scratch, you're out. The world of journalism is a tough world."

I was ecstatic; it seemed like good karma to me that I had chosen the right time to ask for that job! I hadn't expected to get a foot in the door so quickly.

"It's two pages every two weeks. Our target group is young – think under 35 – and with-it. So far we've gone with black and white line drawings. But I want more colour, so we'll need one colour tranny at least, with each article. We don't have much of a budget. You'll have to learn how to style food yourself for the camera."

"What's a tranny?"

"Transparency. We don't work with photo's."

Oh God. How was I going to manage all that? But I said nothing except "Thank you".

"It's a freelance job and it doesn't pay much."

"Ingredients are paid for?"

"Afraid not. I have to work within a very tight budget. But you can use our photographers for the pics."

Good grief, what have I done, I wondered afterwards on my way back home. *Trannies.* Food styling. I don't even know the jargon. How appropriate: fools rush in where angels fear to tread …

These are the real kitchen chronicles: I test recipes madly, weigh, measure, write it all down in minute detail, I change other people's recipes, taste, add things, taste again, make notes. I worry about the grocery money I spend on ingredients, money I cannot claim back. Most of the time Daniel and I eat my efforts.

How ridiculous all this testing is, I think: other women have their own tastes. How can I prescribe to them? How much salt would they want in this soup? Would anyone be willing to try and serve fruit with fried fish? Will anybody still be interested in my mother's whipped-up jelly-like puddings?

What is a recipe? I myself have never used a single recipe that I did not tweak to my taste. Why would anyone want to read my painfully meticulous measurements and actually try the dish? Can I trust what I'm doing here?

I am not a career woman. I do not have the self-confidence. I do not possess the serenity, the calm approach, the firm dis-cipline needed to be all things to all people. This is the nearest I can come to Superwoman: baby on hip, stirring a sauce with right hand, pushing a cat out of way with one foot. Make notes on messy little pad on kitchen counter: so much cheese, so much Tabasco, so much salt. Taste yet again.

Oh no! Stephen squirming on my hip needs a fresh nappy; when will I get this child out of nappies? Pull sauce off heat, rush Stephen to bedroom, perform the toilet ceremony, scrub hands, put Stephen in his walking ring. Rush back to kitchen. Stove plate is redhot, sauce has formed a thick skin. The maid, the one who goes off to sleep when she feels like it, has disappeared shortly after 1 p.m. I can't be bothered; I do everything for the kids myself anyway.

Time: 4.30 p.m. Leave the sauce for now. Throw a pre-pack of chicken pieces from freezer in a bowl of hot water: forgot again to take meat from freezer this morning for Daniel and me. Prayer: please, dear Lord, keep Aunt Betta away this afternoon. I need to make the kids' evening meal, and I must use the chicken, half-frozen or not, to try out that chicken-with-sweet-peppers recipe I saw somewhere, then lost, and will now have to re-invent and scribble down as I cook ...

Danny comes in the back door, filthy. He shows me a bleeding knee, which must be washed and disinfected. Being Danny, he does not cry, he is proud of the wound because he earned it through bravery: falling out of the mulberry tree.

The days were becoming hotter as I prepared to hand my first effort at an article to Mary; we'd had our first thundershowers. I started off hesitantly with salad recipes, because I imagined them to be a safer bet than fancier dishes. Mary discovered she still had some nice sketches, in black and white, which, she said, she could use for this first article, until I get a chance to try my hand at food styling for photographs.

Styling ... I thought you simply had the food photographed on a nice tablecloth or *lappie*, and that was that. But I didn't ask any more questions. I didn't want Mary to know the depths of my ignorance.

Daniel was pleased and relieved that I had found a job which would take me out of the house: he fully realised I was too house bound and frustrated.

I soldiered on with the new job. I could experiment and do most of the work at home, dreaming up recipes, improving on those of others. Some mornings I went in to the office; there were suddenly things to do and people to see. But always, at the back of my mind, were my babies' wellbeing. At odd times I would wonder what they were doing. And the high point of any day was still the moment I parked under the shady old plane trees in Linden, went to ring the bell at the nursery school door, and saw my bright-eyed, pink-cheeked boys running towards me.

South Africa had by then already changed to metric measurements from the old Imperial system, but it was a battle to convince readers that metrication was easy. All the older recipes I wanted to use I had to metricate with a calculator and then test again. Often I gave up the battle and kept them as I had them in my scrapbooks, in cups, tablespoons and teaspoons. The older readers liked this: they understood it; there was a great unwillingness to learn grams and millilitres.

One morning at the office I had a visitor. Those were the days of Big Brother the Government, with its many tentacles which reached out stickily and touched everything. Big Brother told you what to do and how to live. So, of course, a Metrication Board had been in existence for a while. Maybe some people will still recall an even earlier time when we switched to rands and cents from pounds and shillings, and a jingle played over and over on the radio: "I'm Decimal Dan, the Rands-Cents man …"

"I'm from the Metrication Board," my visitor said, and introduced himself. I asked him to sit, offered coffee, which he refused, and sat down myself across the desk from him. I wondered what this was all about.

He carried a sinister black briefcase. He was youngish and fairly pleasant-looking. But he wore an ugly brown suit, matching waistcoat and dull tie.

Without preamble he said accusingly, "We have noted that you do not consistently use metricated recipes. You often revert to cups and spoons or pounds and ounces. That is not allowed."

I shared the office with other journalists, but they were all out. I felt a *frisson* of fear, that old Calvinist awe of authority. Then I rallied.

"No, I don't use metricated recipes all the time. Many of our readers relate much better to cups and spoons. Anyway, many old recipes are better off unmetricated!"

"You're not allowed to do that." He was no longer pleasant-looking to me, as I could discern that he didn't possess a glimmer of light-heartedness or a sense of humour.

"Look," I said, "You must understand. When I develop recipes, I do metricate. But people are still very used to the Imperial measures. They understand pound far better than half a kilogram. All the best recipes in my scrapbooks are still in Imperial measures. You can't expect …"

"Yes, we do," Brown Suit said with tight lips. "You are not allowed to use anything but metric weights and measures."

He had now used the term "not allowed" three times.

"You can't tell me what to do."

"Lady, I am from the Metrication Board and I *can* tell you what to do. We are trying to inform and train the people of South Africa on the new system. It is not allowed in the media to use Imperial weights and measures any more. Or cups and spoons. If you carry on being obstinate about this, we can take steps against you."

I could hardly believe my ears. Steps against me? I think my mouth dropped open. What was this: the Metrication Police?

"Since when are cups and spoons either Imperial or metric measures?" I asked in disbelief.

"You have to be precise. You have to use precise measurements. For example, a tablespoon is 12.5 milliliter."

"No, it's not! It's madness to work with such clumsy calculations! I have given the readers metric charts, and in my book a tablespoon is 15 millilitres. A cup is not 225 millilitres, but 250! It makes no difference to the recipes and it's simply easier! I will not work with half grams!"

He didn't answer. His mouth was now a compressed slit. He rose.

"I see you're a hard-headed lady."

"I want to do the practical thing. It'll take time, this metrication ..." I faltered. I've irritated a tentacle of the State. I'll probably be imprisoned without trial.

He took his hard black briefcase, laid it on my desk and snapped it open. For a moment I thought he was taking out forms to fill in in triplicate: all my details down to my maternal grandmother's maiden name, so I could be prosecuted for Not Metricating Consistently.

Inside the briefcase were nests of measuring spoons and small transparent measuring jugs. If there were important papers, they must have been hidden underneath these cheap, innocuous plastic utensils.

He solemnly handed me a jug and a set of spoons.

"Goodbye," he said. "*Use* them!"

I laughed, thanked him, and took my leave of him. He was not amused. Then I sat back and stared in wonderment at the little two-cup – oops, 500 ml – jug, and the set of white spoons joined at the handles with a ring.

For a long time I blithely carried on switching between nicely metricated recipes and the comforting older ones using cups, spoons and occasionally pounds and ounces. They were, I admit, small acts of rebellion. I might have been naïve and uncertain, but I hated the thought that that insignificant man could come into my office and berate me about recipes, the format of which the Government did not approve. I was quite surprised, really, when in the end no steps were taken against me ...

It was a challenge, the entire food writing thing, but I loved it. It was great that food companies contacted me, offering beautiful food pictures in exchange for a small mention in a recipe, or that large importers of tableware gave me carte blanche to borrow their lovely dishes for food shots.

I taught myself food styling – helped and instructed in no small way by Republican Press's excellent photographers. Mary was pleased: the food pages were colourful, and well received by the readers.

The photographers and I had one running battle, however. I wanted them to photograph foods when ready, which meant at my house. They wanted me to lug it all to the studio at the offices. Sometimes I won, sometimes I lost. I was quite willing to do the food schlepp if it consisted of stuff easy to transport in a car, but I drew the line at stop-start city driving with delicate or hot food which could easily be damaged or spoiled.

Contrary to what happens to much food photography, we photographed the food as it really looked when prepared. It was never artificially touched up. All we ever cheated with was to use glycerine on raw fruits and vegetables to simulate fresh dewdrops.

By the time Stephen turned three, he could also go to nursery school in the mornings with Danny. So I now had personal freedom until 1 or 2 p.m. to pursue my small career.

The freelancing expanded to include stories for the (now defunct) Afrikaans magazine *Ster*. I also tried my hand at several décor articles for magazines in the Republican Press and Nasionale Pers stable, and for a while wrote a column for *The Motorist*. If I had time, I wrote short stories. Seventy-five percent was rejected.

Because of the kids, I'd become very aware of nutrition. Adelle Davis, the nutrition guru of the time, was my food prophetess. Many of her dictums hold true to this day, although her work is now out of date. I still have her falling-apart books like *Let's Cook it Right* and *Let's Get Well*.

"*Never* soak any vegetables," I cautioned my readers after Adelle's instructions, "and *never* soak lettuce leaves in cold water. Many of the nutrients will simply dissolve into the water." And, with great authority à la Adelle Davis: "Remember that the concentration of vitamins and minerals in deep-green leaves is greater than in any other type of fresh food …." And so on. You have to sound authoritative or your readers won't believe in you …!

I checked my old scrapbooks, the magazine cuttings yellowed with age. My first effort, the selection of salad recipes, now seems over-elaborate and frankly silly in an age in which, thank heavens, we prefer fresh, natural foods again.

∾ SALAD TIPS ∾

* Salad leaves should be as dry as possible. If you have to wash lettuce leaves, shake them in a colander and then roll up gently in kitchen paper. Even then there will still be water on the leaves. So I appreciate those pre-washed mixed salad pillow-

packs. They might not be as nutritious as buying whole heads of mixed lettuces, but they are so convenient! Nothing, of course, touches freshly picked young salad leaves from your own back yard bed.

* Salad dressing should be added just before serving, and then just enough to coat the leaves after tossing them, so that they glisten. No pool should form at the bottom of the bowl.

* Those little packets with dried "salad dressing refill" make quite delicious dressings. I use the following ingredients and measurements: Into a measuring cup, pour 50 ml water. Fill up to 125 ml with cider vinegar, not any other kind. It is healthier and tastier, without the sharp acidic taste of inferior vinegar. Add the salad powder of your choice, stir in well, and leave to stand for a while. Then fill up to 250 ml with a good, fruity virgin olive oil. Stir well, and pour into a salad dressing container. Shake well before each use. (If you don't like salad dressing packets, use the same amounts of water, oil and vinegar, and season with herbs and a dash of Worcestershire sauce and some freshly ground pepper.)

* When an iceberg lettuce is firm and healthy-looking, remove the outer leaves and cut out the bottom, which always looks discoloured. Rinse only over the top: don't let water get inside. Break open: if the head is tight and clean inside, with no discoloration, use as is and don't spoil the crispiness by washing. This might sound sacrilegious to the hygienically minded, but I've been doing that for years and so far no lettuce has harmed us.

∼ SALAD THINGS ∼

* It was a pleasant surprise some weeks ago to come across endives (or chicory) again. This is a vegetable which is not often seen in my neck of the woods. Endives are great wrapped in good ham and baked in a cheese sauce, but it works so well as a salad. When cut into thin rings, from the pointy pale green tops down to the pure white parts, it forms crunchy half circles which are delicious in salads. Perhaps chicory's finest moments are when the leaves are taken apart and filled with things … The leaves form perfect little white boats, which can serve as containers for the following, and are then fanned out prettily on a large platter and served with crusty, fresh bread:

- Finely chopped cucumber, olives, sweet onion and tomatoes.
- Quartered quail eggs, chopped peppadews and spring onions, with a dollop of mayonnaise in each.
- Taramasalata with an olive in each endive leaf.
- Tzatziki with a sprinkle of ground cumin.
- Thinly sliced and rolled ham slices.

* The "house salad" in this house is very plain, but that's what my husband prefers: lots of salad leaves, chopped tomatoes and onion. To this is added whatever is available: peppadews, sliced sweet peppers, baby marrow rounds, cucumber – whatever is fresh and salady. It's cool and crisp in summer and mostly eaten as a starter. If the meat dish is spicy, I like adding the soft sweetness of banana to salad. If it's a robust meat like Kassler chops, in go the gherkins. By great good luck we have a few garlic chive plants, which give off a delicious, faint garlic flavour when snipped into the salad.

* Should fresh green asparagus be classed as a "salad thing"? It's hard to say. As it is always an expensive vegetable I spend far too much money on asparagus when in season. Sometimes it's put into a pot with a little water, the protruding tops covered with foil. It's steamed for 3 minutes and eaten hot with pure butter, with great relish, or cooled and eaten as a salad, with a little olive oil and salt. (The white asparagus has never succeeded in seducing us.)

Easy Lasagne

During those years of kids and part-time work, recipes like these often fed us, while I dreamt up fancier dishes for the magazine readers. This is a quick version and does not even pretend to be the real thing. But for a busy mother it certainly beats the recipe I saw recently, which had a long list of ingredients and – horror! – a numbered "plan of action" on how to proceed from stage to stage.

About 375 ml cheese sauce*
500–600 g lean beef mince
250 ml soft breadcrumbs (use a processor to make them)
Worcestershire sauce
Salt or soy sauce
5 ml thyme or oregano
A pinch of ground cloves
5 ml coarse black pepper
A little milk or water
1–2 tins (about 400 g each) chopped tomatoes
Sugar
Pre-cooked lasagne sheets
Extra Parmesan or mature Cheddar cheese

* The cheese sauce: You can use shop-bought, but making it is quick this way. Use a small heavy-bottomed pot and a whisk. Put 325 ml milk in the pot, and add about 45 ml cake flour – 3 tablespoons, levelled. Whisk this into the milk over medium heat, until the mixture starts bubbling and thickens. Take off the heat, but whisk to cool a little. Add anything from 125–250 ml grated Cheddar (to taste), and season with a pinch of salt. I like to add a few drops of any chilli sauce at hand, which enhances the flavour. Cover and keep aside. A piece of wax paper pressed on the sauce prevents it forming a skin.

Preheat oven to 180 °C. Put the mince in a bowl, add the bread-crumbs, then a few shakes of Worcestershire sauce, and about 15 ml soy sauce. If you're not sure about soy, use salt instead: 5 ml might be enough. Add the herbs, pinch of cloves and pepper. Use a fork to break the mince apart and mix the additions in well. Add a little milk or water, enough to make the mince mixture soft and almost "spreadable".

Grease a fairly deep lasagne dish or square Pyrex oven dish (I find these a little shallow, though). Dump the tinned, chopped tomatoes on the bottom. Whether you use 1 tin or 2 depends on how much tomato sauce you need to provide an adequate bottom layer, which in turn depends on the size of your oven dish and personal taste. Season with a teaspoon of sugar, some pepper, perhaps a tiny pinch of salt, stir, and level the sauce.

Cover with a layer of lasagne sheets. I find I have to break the sheets to provide full coverage. They will splinter, but never mind, just patch it until the tomatoes are covered. Don't use more than a single layer of lasagne.

Now ladle the meat mixture on top, and level carefully – this is why the meat should be softened by milk or water. (Milk, by the way, is an excellent meat tenderiser.)

Cover with another layer of lasagne sheets. Then pour or scrape the cheese sauce over the top.

At this stage, leave the dish to stand for about 30 minutes. or more. Bake in preheated oven for about 1 hour or a little longer. Sprinkle with a handful of grated Parmesan just before it comes out of the oven.

Mom's Take-Away Chicken

For four to six people. The coating mixture
also works well when frying fish.

250 ml buttermilk

20 ml (or to taste) chilli-garlic sauce

Pinch of seasoning salt

1 chicken, in pieces, about 1 kg

125 ml flour

125 ml mealie meal

About 7 ml seasoning salt

20 ml or more chopped fresh or dry rosemary (or thyme)

Oil and butter

Preheat oven to 180 °C. Mix together the buttermilk, chilli-garlic sauce and seasoning salt. Add the chicken pieces, and toss to coat well. In another shallow bowl, mix the next four (dry) ingredients. The coating is enough for eight or nine chicken pieces.

Remove the chicken pieces one at a time, shake off the buttermilk, and roll in the flour mixture. Coat well. Repeat with all the chicken pieces. At this stage they can be stored in the fridge (in one layer in a shallow dish) until needed. If you use an ovenproof dish, they can go straight into the oven from the fridge.

Put the chicken carefully in one layer in an oven dish. Drizzle over a melted mixture of olive oil and butter. Or sprinkle it over, or try spraying with olive oil spray containing garlic. Roast for about 45 minutes or until golden brown.

French Onion Soup

Inspired by Robert Carrier, who evoked wonderful visions of the old Les Halles market in Paris when he described this soup. It made him think, he said, of the smokey workmen's cafés in Les Halles, where workers could warm themselves with deep, fragrant bowls of onion soup right through the night. Enough for six people.

6–8 large onions, preferably sweet onions, sliced into thin rings
10 ml sugar
60 g butter
1.5–2 litres beef stock

100 ml brandy or cognac
Salt and black pepper to taste
Bread, preferably good French bread
Gruyère cheese

Fry the onion rings, with the sugar, slowly in butter over medium heat. Do not hurry the process, and stir often. Don't burn, just let the onions sauté until a nice light brown colour. Then add the stock, bring to a boil, turn down the heat, cover pot, and simmer for 1 hour.

Just before serving, add the brandy, and taste whether it needs salt: stock is sometimes salty enough. Grind in pepper. Toast bread or slices from a French loaf, and put in the bottom of warmed soup bowls. You can either put a thick layer of grated Gruyère on the toasted bread, or ladle in the soup and then sprinkle a layer of cheese on the soup. Sometimes the cheese is quickly melted under a grill before serving the soup.

Cucumber Soup

*Surprisingly flavourful and sophisticated enough for any dinner
party. Serves six as a starter and four as a light meal.*

2 medium onions, chopped	125 ml thick fresh cream
3 large cucumbers, chopped	1 extra cucumber, for garnish:
45 ml butter	cut into neat small cubes
750 ml chicken stock	Salt and pepper
30 ml flour	Chopped parsley or chives
2 egg yolks	Sour cream

Fry the onions and chopped cucumbers over medium heat in
30 ml of the butter. After about 7 minutes, add the stock. Let
the soup simmer without a lid for half an hour. Pour soup
through a strainer and mash the pulp which stays behind. Put the
mash back into the soup. Or simply put soup in batches in a food
processor and process until smooth.

Melt remaining 15 ml butter, remove from heat, and stir
the flour into the butter. Add the processed soup slowly while
whisking, and return to heat. Boil for a few minutes until flour is
cooked and the soup has thickened slightly. Beat together the egg
yolks and cream in a small bowl, and then add a little hot soup
to the mixture. Stir this mixture into the soup – but do not let it
boil again, or it will cook the egg yolks. Just keep the soup hot,
and stir well, adding salt and pepper to taste. To serve, use warm
bowls, ladle in soup, and garnish with chopped raw cucumber,
chives and parsley and a dollop of sour cream.

CHAPTER 17

~ A BITTER CUP ~

TEA THAT HELPS OUR HEAD AND HEART.
TEA MEDICATES MOST EVERY PART.
TEA REJUVENATES THE VERY OLD.
TEA WARMS THE PISS OF THOSE WHO'RE COLD.

J. Jonker, circa 1670

I did not want to include Aunt Betta in these stories. And she was not my aunt.

She has been dead for three decades.

I have no idea why she, of all people, insinuated herself here, as she was very close to having no redeeming features at all. She was not even a cook; she didn't have a family to cook for.

On the other hand, perhaps that is why she is so insistent on getting attention: during her lifetime she knew how to cleverly foist herself on people, who became her reluctant friends, and often, later, her bitter enemies.

There she is, in an expensive pale green suit, silk scarf expertly knotted around her neck, matching handbag on her arm. Well, she might want to be included here, but then she will have to hear the truth about herself at last.

She got herself invited to the parties and dinners and family Sundays of her contemporaries. Then, afterwards, she often criticised the occasions savagely, and told scurrilous tales about the guests. Yet she inserted herself continuously into people's lives like a bookmark between the pages of their existence, almost inconspicuously, offering no riches of the spirit or gaiety of nature. She was accepted and catered to, at least at first, because such is the nature of people; most people are kind.

In the beginning they always felt sorry for Aunt Betta, for she came with negative baggage which she unpacked for them in short, clipped sentences, her chain smoking providing the punctuation for her tales. Her invisible husband, with whom she still shared a house, was an alcoholic who kept mistresses. That, in brief, was what she held up as her lot in life.

In the end she always became a problem to her "friends". In at least one incident she was chased from a house because word had reached the family that she had been slandering them behind their backs while regularly enjoying their hospitality.

Aunt Betta had no children, no particular interests, and no hobbies except shopping for clothes. She pried into private lives as a dentist might pry between teeth for signs of decay. She scurried from friend to acquaintance to friend, carrying her mean-spirited gossip with her like a hag's bag, which she would turn out with glee in other living rooms.

She was the only person I ever knew who had wall-to-wall carpets in her kitchen. Maybe she was the only woman in the world with a carpeted kitchen. When people exclaimed over this aberration, she said smugly that she never spilled anything and she was never messy. Her house was spotless but unwelcoming, and she did not encourage visitors. She made her gardener polish her garden taps with Brasso. Her obsessive neatness hinted at much deeper problems, but we were never quite sure what they were.

I inherited Aunt Betta from my mother-in-law. Mother-in-law Esther had, among her friends, a coterie she called her "lame duck contingent". She bore them with fortitude and generosity of spirit and invited them, always, to our family dinners and get-togethers. So for years Aunt Betta was always around: you could not escape her. Although she professed to be an excellent cook she never invited any of her "friends" to her home in return; we assumed it was because of the problematic husband.

When I got married it was, I suppose, inevitable that she would also become an uninvited guest in our very first home. By the time Danny was a toddler and Stephen still a baby, Aunt Betta was running out of friends of her own age. I was too young, naïve and polite to do anything about her badly-timed visits.

I was still working at freelance translating at home, in between bottles and dirty nappies and nearly useless home help.

When I recall those baby years, especially the many months of Stephen's colic, and never enough sleep, I sense my own despera-tion. I was exhausted. But many women have had a much harder time that I did: I confess to having been too over-anxious and stressed out.

Daniel spent his days and even weekends at the office, and taught two evening classes a week at the Technical College. He also joined the Citizen Force Navy again, which meant he was away on Monday and Thursday nights as well. I was a drowning woman forever battling to keep breathing, sometimes clutching uselessly at Sargasso weeds and sinking, until I worked up the energy again to kick and rise for another breath of air.

And somehow Aunt Betta forced herself into my hectic insular existence as she had done with all her other acquaintances.

She started turning up at my door, once or twice a week, and always at the witching hour of five o' clock.

Young mothers know that there is no worse hour than five o' clock. It is the hour of the fractious baby, the whiny toddler, the clamouring pre-schooler. It is the time of day when mothers prepare formula for the night, prepare kids' evening meals, and wrack their brains about what to cook for dinner later. It's the time when the colicky baby starts to grizzle. It is approaching supper and bath time for small ones, who are tired after their long day.

My babies wanted their mommy then, all of her: not this half-drowned woman whose husband must also eat when he eventually gets home, and who later might want sex, by which time all she will desire is to let darkness envelop her and to sink, sink, into sleep, perchance to dream … until a baby cries again.

Aunt Betta's Mercedes would draw up almost soundlessly and stop in front of the garage doors under the saffron pear trees. I would glimpse the car through the lounge windows, baby on arm, and my spirits would plummet.

Aunt Betta was no ordinary, helpful older friend. She held no truck with babies and their demands. She saw my five o' clock fluster as incompetence; after all, she had never had any children of her own. She never picked them up or soothed their tears; she bore their existence with unconcealed irritation. I never saw Aunt Betta touch a child in her life except to push it away from her immaculate self.

She did not lift a finger in other people's houses, like offer to make herself a cup of tea. She would enter my messy afternoon house in her designer outfit, plonk herself down on a couch, and demand: "Zuri … make tea." She would immediately take her cigarettes and lighter from her expensive leather handbag. She preferred Earl Grey, but I never had any. On one occasion she thrust a box of Earl Grey into my hands as she came in, and I was instructed to keep it for her visits.

On those afternoons I grew extra arms. I had to. The baby fussed, the toddler would do dangerous things on chairs. But a neat tray would have to be set for Aunt Betta: starchy tray cloth, best teacups. She always instructed me on the tea-making, shouting from the lounge to the kitchen.

"You must use only fresh water from the cold tap. And you must let the tap run first! Don't use the first water. And please, please, rinse out the electric kettle; you can't make good tea if there is 'old water' left in the kettle …"

She did not like tea bags. Decent tea was made with tea leaves, so there had to be a strainer on the tray, prissy in its little porcelain holder.

While I whizzed here and there (a minute with Aunt Betta, a minute in the kitchen, a minute to soothe a toddler's knee), she talked, gossiped, demanded my reaction, demanded my attention, much like the kids did. When she deigned to notice my efforts at trying to keep the kids to their usual evening schedule, she interfered.

"Oh *no*, for God's sake, you *never* give a baby leftovers from the fridge to eat! It's *death*! How could you?! You must make their food from scratch! And why is the baby crying so much? I can't stand it!"

I never explained that the leftovers were only a manifestation of her unwelcome visits: how can I cook fresh baby food, try to get a dinner for me and my husband on the stove, mix bottles of formula, and make tea and conversation, all at the same time? Something's got to give!

Why didn't I tell this battle-axe to leave me alone, to stay away, during those impossible hours? Why didn't I ask her to visit at a more civilised hour? I simply didn't know how, without giving offence, and Aunt Betta took offence very easily. Actually, I was terrified of her.

"The old lady is lonely," my husband said. "She's just looking for company."

"Then why the hell does she think she can find company with me at the godawful hours she visits here?"

Of course there is simply no good answer to hysterical questions like that.

As with all things, the situation improved with time. The kids grew older, Stephen's colic went away and he turned into a sweetie with blue angel eyes. Eventually they could eat a little later, and I could sit down with Aunt Betta for a while without having palpitations.

Aunt Betta did teach me one useful thing. She once told me how to make a real traditional tomato stew.

I'm from the Boland, and tomato *bredie* is more a dish from those parts than a northern dish. I craved it, but a long-distance phone call to mom to probe for the details would have cost too much, would tip our precarious budget. Aunt Betta grew up in the Western Cape, and she claimed that she knew the secrets of all Malay and traditional dishes.

So this woman with her carpeted kitchen, whom I came to … well, not detest, but dislike intensely, taught me how to make tomato *bredie* properly.

The pot was on the stove when she arrived one afternoon, because for tomato stew you use stewing lamb or mutton, which takes a long time to become tender.

"What's that I'm smelling?" she demanded.

"*Tamatiebredie,*" I replied, wiping a child's button nose.

"Let me see." She marched to the kitchen, and lifted the lid off the pot. "Oh no, no, this is all wrong! Too much liquid. Now you listen to me, and I'll tell you how to make it properly."

I had no other choice. I listened to her instructions. And if one has good meat and good tomatoes and it's made her way, it's the best *tamatiebredie* in the world.

That's all I can remember Aunt Betta ever teaching me about food, apart from the repetitive litany on tea-making. After her husband died, whom we suspected had never been nearly as bad as she had made him out to be, she inherited everything. For some unfathomable reason they never divorced: she had probably refused him a divorce, preferring the security of his home and his money while spurning him openly.

Was Aunt Betta, then, wholly bad? No, not really. She only suffered from the egocentric selfishness which sprang from a loveless and unhappy marriage which she clung to, to its bitter end. She really was deeply lonely and despite the invitations she received and her ubiquitous presence at the home of my in-laws, she had no real friends.

She often made us laugh with her coarse, cynical, below-the-belt humour. Somewhere in the recesses of her life lurked great misery, which she forever refused to acknowledge. There was dark talk of a baby lost when the miscarriage could have been prevented. She blamed it on her husband, but the details remain unclear. She and her husband, he always as elusive as a spirit, shared a house but lived different lives. There must have been some hell for both of them in whatever arcane vengeance it was she was wreaking on him. Once she said that they never had sex again after the miscarriage, which had happened shortly after their marriage. Yet in the material sense he looked after her well. She wore only boutique and designer clothes and drove an expensive car. He paid for it all. She was non-committal when he died; she carried on her life as before. She bought herself a new car.

"I'd love it," I said one day, only half joking, "I'd really love it if, one day, you leave me some of your crockery!" She had a kitchen and dining room full of expensive unused porcelain, flatware, and stacks of linen. I did not dare mention any of her other riches: the priceless original paintings, her lovely clothes, the Persian carpets, the money in the bank.

She sniffed softly, and smiled a little. "I think I'm leaving everything to a dogs' hospital."

"But you don't even like dogs!"

"Or to a university." She had never attended one.

It was her chain-smoking which killed her. She grew thinner. She ate less and less because food made her nauseous. Her olive skin developed a yellow cast. She died of liver cancer, which, the doctors said, had probably started in her lungs.

A male cousin of hers whom she barely knew inherited everything … including the crockery.

∼ AUNT BETTA'S TAMATIEBREDIE ∼

Use good stewing lamb. It must have fat, but shouldn't be too fatty. Use about 1.5–2 kg for four people because there's a lot of bone. You peel, slice thinly, and fry a large onion or two in oil or butter. Stir it, and don't burn it. Roll your pieces of mutton in flour. They must be well covered, because the flour helps thicken your sauce. Then start adding the pieces of meat to the pot. Add a little more oil if necessary. Don't put in too many at the same time, because it lowers the heat of the pot and the meat will start to steam instead of fry.

Fry your meat in batches. Take out a browned batch, then add the next few pieces, and so on. When all the meat has been browned, pour off the extra fat and oil, and then put everything – meat, onion – back in the pot.

Have about six big, ripe tomatoes ready. You will see soon enough whether the tomatoes are too many or not enough. You skin them first; you *must* skin them. Then you cut them into the hot pot of lamb – juices and all. The old-fashioned tomatoes like "Oxheart" are best for this. Don't use greenish, tasteless super-market tomatoes. They must be large and ripe and flavourful.

Stir well and turn down the heat. The tomatoes should provide enough liquid, but you should watch the pot – if it's too hot it will burn. It should all stew gently. Now you add a good teaspoon of sugar. The sugar is important – you *always* add sugar to tomatoes when you cook them, because otherwise your dish will have an unpleasant acidity. Add salt and white pepper. Put on a lid at an angle, because you do not want your meat to steam. Put in four or six peeled potatoes later. Stir now and then, but the meat mustn't break up completely, so do it gently. Your stew must go on simmering gently until the lamb and potatoes are tender.

Add a few chopped and crushed garlic cloves towards the end of cooking. If you have fresh basil, you can add that when ready to dish up, also a handful of chopped parsley. Your meat should be a deep reddish brown and the tomatoes should have reduced to a thick sauce. There mustn't be a lot of liquid. If there is, turn up the heat, stir well, and let the liquid evaporate. You never add water to *tamatiebredie* unless it threatens to burn, and then add only a little. You serve *tamatiebredie* over fluffy white rice.

CHAPTER 18

~ FOR BETTER ... AND WORSE ~

THOU ART TO ME MOST LIKE A ROYAL GUEST,
WHOSE TRAVELS BRING HIM TO SOME LOWLY ROOF,
WHERE SIMPLE RUSTICS SPREAD THEIR FESTAL FARE
AND, BLUSHING, OWN IT IS NOT GOOD ENOUGH.

Julia Ward Howe

For many years we had all been aware that, politically, South Africa was in a mess. We were living in a polecat country. But none of us knew what the solutions were. Our generation were busy bringing up babies, carving out careers, and living our predictable lives as best we could. It was the Seventies. Then the 1976 riot happened. We were shaken, but we were only bystanders in the political clash of cultures. "I'm so sorry," I kept apologising to Lizzie, my current domestic. "We are all so sorry."

We knew *sorry* would not help.

We were born during and after World War II. A child cannot judge a political or social system it had been born into because it has nothing to compare it with. We had to mature before we could see more clearly.

Most of us young Afrikaners had also been born into a Calvinistic, paternalistic set-up. If the Prime Minister said something, it must be right. If Daddy decided something, Daddy was right because he was the head of the household. Our White lives were protected – overprotected – in a chauvinistic manner, and thinking for yourself was not encouraged.

We were taught not to question our parents, the political set-up of the day, or the tenets of the Church. The elders knew best.

As a child I did develop a deep empathy for the Coloured farm labourers in the Hex Valley. I sensed that the gap between the rich farmers and these dirt poor people was too deep and dark. If they were paid better salaries ... If their children had easier access to schooling ... If they had better housing and electricity and running water ... Sure, many spent what little money they had on cheap wine and got drunk over weekends, but surely that might be a symptom of their culture of poverty?

But my conscience was on the socio-economic and not the political level, perhaps because the Coloured people I knew were not politicised then.

Only in the Seventies did the great political unease begin to stir in us, the generation who grew up after the war. The sanctions and boycotts against an unsustainable political system were becoming harder to bear. At our dinner parties long hours were spent arguing, trying out philosophical thoughts on one another, recreating a better South Africa. A *maybe* better South Africa. We discussed, condemned, praised, wondered. Deep down we also feared. It was as if things were building up towards a conflagration. But we had no choice but to carry on with our mundane lives, even if braver souls were embroiling themselves in various acts of rebellion against the government of the day.

Something else clouded my happy married life from time to time. I was abnormally anxious about Danny. It went way beyond the normal concern a mother has for her children's safety and wellbeing. It was a deep unease which had been there ever since I looked into his dark, wise eyes after his birth. There was no legitimate reason for it. Although not present every moment, it popped up, like a haunting wraith, this black dread, at the oddest moments. I told no one, because it was something too tenuous and insubstantial to verbalise.

The food writing was going well. I worked very hard, churning out two pages of recipes a fortnight. The income from this little enterprise was so low that, if the cost of ingredients, the electricity and petrol used were taken into account, it should have had a minus in front of the amount.

The fact that I had to pay for ingredients meant that I simply had to make use of advertorial sometimes in order to spend less on testing recipes. Advertorial are those hated articles where you get a lovely tranny for free, plus seven or eight recipes using a branded ingredient. This was free advertising for the brand, and saved me the intricacies of arranging for the food photographs. I always changed those recipes a little. They never sounded exactly right to me.

Being a food editor created a small personal problem. Friends and acquaintances believed I was now a *chef* kind of cook, who turned out amazing dishes effortlessly. But I wasn't, and it was no fun to hear a good friend say, "I can't have you to dinner, because I'm not a good enough cook."

As if I cared! It was great to sit at another table, eating food that I hadn't cooked, out of dishes I would not have to wash.

But I did fall into my own trap, trying to prove that I was one hell of a cook. It was a hard lesson and one I, thankfully, only had to learn once ...

Daniel and I had met a new couple. They were our age, and there were no children yet. They lived in a really gorgeous semi-Georgian house in Parktown. It was beautifully decorated and was, in fact, everything we wished for ourselves. They travelled overseas, apparently often, and the man, whom I shall call Marc, showed us his collection of French wines in a cute little basement cellar. No, he kept no South African wines: too plebeian, he said. Too ordinary. We didn't have any great wines in this country, he stated. He proceeded to give us a quick lecture on French wine regions, illustrating his lecture by whipping out a few bottles with choice labels, explaining the meanings.

Instead of hearing a tiny tinkling warning bell, we were deeply impressed. Such a suave guy, such a gracious wife, the blonde Christine, and the same age as us! What a worldly couple! Daniel might go overseas on work assignments twice a year and have seen something of the great big world, but I had never been further than Naboomspruit.

We decided we must have them to dinner. This was a friend-ship worth cultivating. We also invited an extremely erudite friend and his wife, the only people we considered might be able to converse on a par with our grand new friends: Willem and Marie.

The menu, the menu! It had to be perfect. It must be impressive. We could not impress them with our house or suburb, but per-haps we could impress with our abilities as host and hostess ...

For some reason best forgotten I decided on a starter with smoked eel as the main ingredient. What else was in it, I cannot bear to remember.

Duck would be the main course: I knew I could manage Duck à l'Orange and generally people liked it. Individual chocolate soufflés for dessert. A cheese platter.

I searched high and low for smoked eel. As South Africa was not a favoured nation, good imported produce was thin on the ground. Eventually I found, via the phone, a fish deli which had smoked eel. At last! She who seeks, shall find! Finding the deli with the eel meant, however, driving into parts of Johannesburg I had not known existed, getting lost, and frequently perusing a map of Greater Johannesburg after pulling off the streets into strange driveways.

I had never seen eel before in my life. Once I was back home with the strange-looking piece of leathery python, I discovered that it was still encased in a tough skin. This skin obviously had to be removed. It's a bitter memory which has faded at the edges: I recall sitting on the grass in the back yard with this smoked eel, close to tears of frustration. The neighbour's mongrel dog watched me through the wire fence with pricked-up ears. I could not figure out how to remove the skin. I did not even know whether this was what smoked eel was supposed to be like; whether this was edible. It could just as well have been something unidentifiable from an alien planet or an ancient frozen piece of mammoth trunk from the Siberian tundra. But there was no time left for other plans. The eel had been expensive.

Somehow in the end I managed to skin the eel. I threw the strips of skin to the neighbours' dog, who had watched my struggle so intently. He sniffed it, preferred not to taste it, and trotted away to fall down in a patch of shade and go to sleep. How I envied that dog its freedom not to battle with eel skin, and to simply decide it was time for a nap.

The guests arrived: Willem and Marie first, and a few minutes later our new trophy acquaintances, Marc and Christine. As they entered, I could not possibly miss Christine's eyes taking in our L-shaped living and dining area in nanoseconds: floors, furniture, walls, even the ceiling. We had bargain basement furniture and a bookcase built out of varnished planks and bricks. The only object of value was a large painting by a famous artist, given to us by my mother-in-law.

Neither could I miss the quick, meaningful glance between the wife and husband. A nauseous feeling formed in the pit of my stomach. We were bottom drawer, as far as these two were concerned. I also knew in that moment that it had been a mistake to invite them, or even consider them new friends. They were not of the calibre of our old, comfortable circle of pals, none of whom had lots of money or grand houses. Not to mention a cellar full of French wines. Too late for such thoughts, though.

The guests were introduced to one another and drinks were poured. The kids were admired, and put to bed by Daniel, and they behaved beautifully. Everyone chatted pleasantly and superficially while I puttered in the kitchen, getting my hopes up, vaguely, that the evening might work out after all.

Hesitantly I produced the cold smoked eel starter. It was a grey little dish which not even the chives and parsley could brighten up. Silence fell as they tasted it. And no, it wasn't because they were overwhelmed with awe at my cooking skills. After all the trouble I had gone to, it was not exotic-tasting at all, and I would have done miles better with a simple soup.

"What is it?" Christine asked at last. My sensitive ear did not like the cadence of her voice.

"It's ... ummm ... smoked eel."

Silence around the table. "How interesting ..." someone murmured in that polite tone people adopt when they do not feel like telling lies just to make the hostess feel better.

"Eel ... I've never eaten eel," Marie said.

Nobody finished the starter. I smiled bravely, gathered up the little bowls of grey goo and went back to the kitchen. Daniel poured more wine. I closed the kitchen door as there were still a few finishing touches to be added to the golden-brown ducks and their lovely orange-liqueur sauce. I dished up the vegetables and gave the salad dressing a shake. At least the main course would be a success.

I turned up the oven: in a while I'd put the individual chocolate soufflés in the oven. I carried in the platter of ducks in their sauce, complete with garnishes.

"Oh, what a feast!" Christine cried out, probably to make up for gagging on the eel.

But by now there were only three people left at the table ... and me.

"Hey, where are Willem and Marie?" I asked.

"They ... they left," Daniel said.

My mouth dropped open. "Daniel?" I asked, perplexed. "What do you mean, they've left?"

"They've gone home. Marie felt sick. Suddenly."

"Oh my God ... was it the eel?!"

"No, it wasn't. She's just not well. They apologised."

"At least Willem could have looked into the kitchen and explained to me too!"

"Drop it now," Daniel suggested. "She wouldn't have been able to eat anything more anyway."

I brought the rest of the meal to the subdued table. I sat down, anxiously pondering this abrupt disappearance of half my guests. "Why didn't they say anything to me?"

"Marie felt nauseous. She didn't want to be sick here."

It must have been the damned eel!

Daniel brought out some of his best red wines for the duck.

Insiduously, Marc now began needling Daniel about the wine. Why South African reds, he wanted to know? Daniel told him. We'd been down to the Cape to see my parents a few times. We'd done wine routes, tasted, and bought some wines. Marc went into another lecture about his French collection.

"South Africa makes excellent reds, and I'm interested in them," Daniel said somewhere along the line.

Marc was not impressed. He snorted lightly, then said, "One should be more adventurous ...!"

Daniel coloured slightly, at a loss for words. It struck me then, like a sledgehammer, that no matter what topic had been introduced so far, the new couple had swung it round to themselves. All their chat had been materialistic, superficial and self-centred. Still upset by the disappearance of Willem and Marie, I lost my temper.

"Oh, for heaven's sake! Surely it's better to get to know one's own wines before being pretentious about those of another country!"

A deep chill descended on the table. Every time Marc had taken a sip of wine tonight, he'd accompanied it by some remark about his own wine collection. His wine snobbery seemed to be his sole claim to fame. I hadn't heard either of them say a single intelligent thing about anything else so far. With Marc, it was wine and his new car. Christine talked about her pedigreed dogs and her "priceless" antiques.

When we'd met them, we'd heard their tales for the first time. Then it was interesting. Tonight we heard about the same subjects again and again. Daniel and Willem had introduced other subjects, such as politics and the future of South Africa, but time and again the conversation had made a U-turn back to Marc and Christine and their interests.

The duck was not fine, either. It was tasty enough, but it was tough. I'd fallen for a *special* on ducks at a supermarket and this was the come-uppance. They were third-rate ducks. They had the kind of stringy meat that sticks uncomfortably between your back teeth until you're dying for dental floss.

And as if to break the wine deadlock, Christine now asked, "What made you decide to buy a house *here*? You know, we have never been to this side of town. Had to look it up on a map. It's a rather … *neglected* little suburb, isn't it?"

"It was all we could afford. And I'm sorry the duck is tough."

"The sauce is great," Christine offered.

"Thanks."

Daniel did the rounds with a wine bottle, but Marc held his hand ostentatiously over his glass. Everyone masticated in silence. This main meal was not going to last long and there would be no seconds. I went and put four soufflés in the oven.

It was incredible how long drawn out an evening can be, I thought as I gathered the plates. Time for dessert.

There was something wrong with the soufflés as well. They were not as pretty and puffy as I thought they'd be. Oh, what the hell, I thought, and plonked them on the table and shared them out. We ate in silence.

Christine looked at her expensive watch as she put her spoon down. "Anyway, I think it's time we left. My mom is visiting and we don't want to leave her alone too long. It's quite a drive from here."

Yep. Quite a drive from the sticks to Parktown ... Bullshit – and I nearly said so. It was a fifteen minute drive at most. Our doctor lived in Parktown, so I knew exactly how long it took to get there. But it would be a relief to have an end to this evening. No cheeses and coffee, thank heavens.

Christine pulled her napkin from her lap and put it firmly on the side of her plate. "Marc, if you've finished ... can we go?"

Outside, we took our polite leave of one another.

"Can you believe," Daniel said once we'd closed the front door behind us, "that we could be so incompatible? We had nothing to say to each other after all!"

"And with Marie and Willem disappearing like that ... and the wine nonsense ... and then my crazy dinner," I wailed, "the biggest disaster of all! Can you believe the mess I made of the food?"

"What was that starter again ...?"

"Don't ever mention it again!"

~

Cheat's Starter Plate

Well, the only cheating here is that you don't get to do hard work –
or skin an eel. There is nothing very original about it, but it usually
looks very appetizing and guests love it. Everything can be bought
at deli's and supermarkets. I suggest the combination I like best, but
any cold meat can be used provided it isn't pink and plastic.

Mixed salad leaves
Smoked salmon
Carpaccio of beef (or venison)
Salad trimmings such as cherry tomatoes, cucumber, radishes
Chives or garlic chives
Chicken liver pâté
Vinaigrette dressing
Fresh bread

Arrange the salad leaves, salmon and carpaccio on each plate.
Decorate with a few cherry tomatoes, and so on. Dress up with
a few chives. Put the chicken liver pâté in small bowls and also
put on the plate. (It's easy to make ahead, or buy at a deli.)

Either drizzle the leaves, salmon and meat lightly with vinaigrette, or serve the dressing separately. Serve with slices of
health bread.

Curried Walnut Prawns

Buy the largest prawns you can find, preferably tiger prawns. Allow about four per person as a starter, depending on size of prawns.

Using kitchen or sewing scissors, snip through the prawn shell from behind the head down to the tail. Carefully cut off the shell round the tail and head and remove the shell, keeping the tails intact. Remove the thin dark membrane which runs down the back. If the heads break off, well, use them headless. That's why it's easier to work with huge prawns even if they are expensive. They simply look bigger and better with heads and tails on.

Beat well:

2 eggs, or more if necessary

Mix in a bowl:

250 ml flour	250 ml toasted and well-crushed walnuts or pecans
5 ml salt	5 ml mild curry powder

Mix separately:

Grated peel of 1 lemon	5 ml mustard powder
30 ml lemon juice	Pinch of salt
125–250 ml oil (or mixture of olive oil and butter) – amount will depend on number and size of prawns	5 cloves garlic, crushed and chopped

Dip each peeled prawn in the beaten egg, then roll in the flour-nut mixture; see that they are well covered. Arrange them side by side in a shallow cookie pan or similar oven tin. At this point they can be refrigerated for a few hours.

To prepare, heat the oven grill or oven to about 220 °C. Whisk the lemon-oil mixture well, and drizzle over the prawns. Grill or bake them just until they turn pink and curl up slightly. It will probably take about 4–5 minutes; do watch as it's easy to burn them. You could turn them over after three minutes, but it might cause the nutty covering to fall off. Do not overcook.

If the quantity of oil or butter does not seem enough, add more during baking/grilling.

Serve on salad leaves as a starter. It makes a wonderful main dish, if you can afford a generous quantity of prawns. Pile them all in a hot earthenware bowl and scatter with parsley. In this case, have rolls or bread on the table as well as extra butter.

French Seafood Tart

This is a wickedly rich, delicious French dish, which can be cut up while hot and served as a starter, or it can be part of a buffet. It should be served hot. It's very easy to make.

1 kg puff pastry	8 eggs
1 egg, beaten	Black pepper
2 kg high quality raw shellfish	Nutmeg
of your choice*	30–45 ml tomato purée
Butter or oil	Pinch of sugar
Seasoning salt such as Aromat	Garlic
Brandy or cognac	Finely chopped parsley
1 litre cream	8 tiger prawns
(4 x 250 ml cartons)	Gruyère cheese (optional)

Roll out the puff pastry until thinner, and use it to line a rectangular oven dish of about 30 cm x 20 cm. Build up the edges with strips of leftover pastry, fixing them in place with beaten egg. This will help hold in the filling. Or use a large flan tin. Brush the pastry all over with the egg, and put the lined tin in the fridge until needed.

Preheat oven to 200 °C. In a pan, sauté the shellfish quickly – just par-cooking them – in a little butter or oil. Sprinkle over some seasoning salt. Add a splash of brandy and ignite, if you dare. Take the pan off the heat and lift out the shellfish with a slotted spoon as you don't want extra juices in the tart. Scatter the shellfish over the pastry.

Beat the cream with the eggs, add about 2.5 ml ground nutmeg and the same of black pepper, beat in the tomato purée (I also add a pinch of sugar at this stage), crushed garlic to taste, and parsley. Pour this mixture over the seafood and decorate with the 8 tiger prawns to mark 8 portions. If you like, sprinkle the top with Gruyère cheese.

Bake for 25–30 minutes until puffy and golden brown on top.

* The shellfish: You can use small raw prawns, some mussels, and fresh firm line fish such as Cape salmon. Scallops, if you can find them, are great, and so is crab, but you can use the imitation crabsticks as well. Be wary of calamari, as the cooking time is too long for that and the calamari will be tough.

Angel's Hair Pasta

*A perfect starter to impress. It's so easy, it's just that the salmon
caviar is expensive, and these days even good old
lumpfish roe is an indulgence. Serves four.*

250 g spaghettini – not spaghetti
250 g good, fresh butter, at room temperature
200–250 g salmon roe
4 thin lemon or lime wedges
rocket leaves to garnish (optional)

Cook the pasta according to the instructions on the box, which,
if imported Italian pasta, is usually correct to the minute. Do
not overcook. Keep a bowl warm in the oven. Drain the pasta,
put in the bowl, and toss gently with the butter until the pasta is
glistening and coated.

Divide the pasta among four warmed plates. Top each serving
with a heaped tablespoon of the salmon roe and a lemon wedge.
You could also garnish with young rocket leaves on the side of
the plates.

Your guests should squeeze over the lemon juice before tucking
in. Don't be stingy with the caviar. You could use red lumpfish
roe, but if salmon roe is a poor cousin to real caviar, lumpfish is
the black sheep of the family.

This very easy way of timing and preparing a whole roast fillet of beef was given to me by an old friend. You cannot do this with a tiny piece of fillet. Use it when you splash out and buy one of 1.5 kg or larger.

Remove, carefully, the shiny, thin sinew which covers one side.

As a whole fillet usually has a thick part which tapers off to a thin "tail", I fold this back and tie it to the back end of the fillet so that the roast is equally thick all over. It also helps to tie the fillet with string at intervals. It will keep its shape better that way. Use the rub recipe below to prepare the fillet for the oven.

For rare roast, set your oven at 160 °C, and for pink or medium-rare use a 180 °C oven. Weigh the fillet. You need to roast it for 20 minutes per 500 g plus 20 minutes extra. Calculate as best you can, as no fillet is going to be exactly 1.5 kg …

Let it rest for 10 minutes before slicing.

Recipe for the rub: Mix together about 45 ml flour, 5 ml seasoning salt, some ground ginger, a pinch of cloves, 10 ml coarse black pepper. Rub the entire fillet with any good quality table mustard, then roll in, and cover, with the flour mixture. Put in the oven.

To serve: Mix 1 carton sour cream or a container of crème fraîche with 15 ml crushed green peppercorns, black pepper to taste and seasoning salt. Heat gently, using a whisk.

Australian Dessert Cake

*Easy and delicious. Must be made in advance, for the biscuits
to soften and the flavours to develop. Garnish a few hours before
serving. It makes about eight to ten slices.*

625 ml fresh cream

15 ml pure instant coffee granules

About 100 ml or 5 slightly heaped tablespoons drinking chocolate
powder – not cocoa, sweetened drinking chocolate

3 ml salt

10 ml vanilla essence

About 200 ml medium cream or sweet sherry

3–4 packets Boudoir biscuits

2 packets chocolate flakes, or flaked almonds, roasted to decorate

Use a flat rectangular dish. Pour cream into a bowl and add the
instant coffee. Whip the cream, adding the drinking chocolate
a spoonful at a time. Also add the salt and vanilla. Whip until the
cream is smooth and thick; do not overbeat.

Pour the sherry into a shallow bowl. Dip each Boudoir biscuit
briefly into sherry, and line them up side by side in the dish, in a
bread shape – about 10 biscuits. Spread a layer of cream over the
first row of biscuits. Repeat layers of sherry-dipped biscuits and
layers of cream, until you have four or five layers. (Usually, four
layers make the best shape.) Frost all over with the remaining
cream. Refrigerate for twenty-four hours if possible, and cover to
protect against other strong smells in the fridge.

CHAPTER 19

~ THE BUSHVELD FARM ~

PEACE WAITS AMONG THE HILLS;

I HAVE DRUNK PEACE,

HERE, WHERE THE BLUE AIR FILLS

THE GREAT CUP OF THE HILLS,

AND FILLS WITH PEACE.

Arthur Symons

In about the seventh month of my pregnancy with Danny, my father-in-law bought a farm in the Northern Transvaal, in the province now known as Limpopo.

Father-in-law was very much a city businessman, but his wife, originally a Free State farm girl, persuaded him that they needed a wild piece of Africa; that they both needed to own a piece of bushland. My father-in-law was doubtful about such a venture; certainly sceptical that he might cherish this same desire.

So Ma-in-law and Daniel's elder brother, John, cunningly carried on investigations, sometimes vanishing for a day. In due course they found a wonderful undeveloped bushveld farm for sale in the far reaches of the Waterberg, in an area called the Palala.

Father-in-law, albeit muttering, could not resist it in the end. It was not so much a farm as over a thousand hectares of indigenous bush, open veld, and dolerite koppies. There was a farmhouse – the kind which had begun as one or two large rooms under a plain corrugated iron roof. Other rooms had been haphazardly added as an expanding family or whim dictated. The house was square and plain. It had a cold water tap over the kitchen sink: the water came from a cement tank, which in turn was pumped full from a small natural dam lower down where the river ran. A rainwater tank on a corner of the house provided drinking water if you didn't feel inclined to drink dam water. There was no electricity.

My parents-in-law had no plan to live on this farm, however. Over Sunday dinners in Saxonwold, Johannesburg, as Joe, the white-jacketed gardener-dressed-as-waiter served us, the farm was eagerly discussed.

But first plans were vague: pie-in-the-sky dreams. A place to relax over weekends … maybe bring in some game, just for fun … No, no one was going to farm there, they were all too involved in business here, in the city … it was too far away to be farmed by remote control …

I was the only one who had my reservations about their dreams of sitting on the *stoep* of that farmhouse, drinks in hand, staring at the sunset over the bushveld koppies and watching a little herd of grazing impala.

We had been in our first home for only a short while. I listened to the descriptions of the bushveld farm at the end of a dirt track. Daniel, as excited about this new venture as his father, mother and brother, asked eager questions. Slight unease stirred in me. The idea of, perhaps, trekking to and from a remote, isolated bushveld farm on weekends, with a newborn baby, did not appeal to me at all.

These city dwellers had bought a huge tract of land which required nine hours to get there and back again. And there were labourers on the farm, dependent on salaries and provisions … Yet they kept on weaving fantasies of game that would come and eat in the yard, of long walks into the koppies to see where the cycads grew, of swimming in the river pools.

"You can't possibly leave a farm like that lying fallow," I ventured one Sunday. "It doesn't work like that! And not with labourers living there."

They laughed at me. What did I know about the Bushveld? "You're from the Boland; all you know is grape farming!" I knew nothing about wild undeveloped land in the Bushveld, but then neither did they – and I recognised a problem when it stared me in the eye. Yet Daniel's blue eyes shone when the farm was discussed, and how could I blame him? It was all so new and thrilling, this acquisition. My in-laws, and therefore also my husband, had a new toy and they could not wait to play with it.

With me being heavily pregnant we did not make the four-and-a-half hour journey until later.

In fact, John's wife Hayley was also pregnant with her third baby, due about six weeks after ours. And they already had two toddlers.

One Friday afternoon after office hours I found myself sulking on the back seat of John's car. Daniel was next to him, and we were off to this farm for Daniel's first glimpse of the Promised Land.

Danny was sleeping in a carrycot beside me on the seat. For me it was an interminable journey into the unknown night. I was breastfeeding Danny, which made things easier, but disposable nappies were not commonplace then, and at the best of times a baby requires you to travel with a mountain of luggage. I was not a happy camper.

Hayley was at home with her three small children: her new baby was only two weeks old.

We reached the farm at 10 p.m. The first thing that struck me when we stopped next to the house was the utter blackness of the night. After so many years in a big city you do not realise how used you get to lights and reflected light. In a city or town, however secluded your house, there is always indirect faint light, from street lights, from a distant highway or shopping centre. It is never, completely and entirely, night. And the moon plays a small part in a city: with all those artificial lights I had been barely conscious of moonlight for years.

There was no moon on our first night on the farm. When we emerged from the car the darkness was tactile, delicate as black silk. Suddenly jackals howled close by, in the *koppie* behind the house: a primitive and savage sound which startled me. John and Daniel switched on flashlights to unlock the house and find lamps. An eagle owl hooted eerily from an invisible tree. I waited on the porch, Danny sleeping peacefully in his carrycot. The dense black air was still and fresh and very cold. I peered into the night, and at last discerned tiny lights flickering faintly against the opposite hillside.

"The dying cooking fires of the *stat*," John explained, coming out with a lit oil lamp. "That's where the Pedi's live. There's a cluster of huts there. Come on in."

Inside, the yellow lights of the lamps flickered on the walls and threw strange shadows. The smokey smell of paraffin took me, momentarily, back to Ouma Greta's house: when last had I seen a paraffin lamp? There might be, I thought reluctantly, a certain charm to this place.

By that time Ma-in-law had already equipped the house with all the basics. The beds were made up. My first distinctly unromantic mission was to search for a pail and draw some cold water from an outside tap to drop Danny's used nappies into.

Through the years that followed I developed a love-hate relationship with the farm in the Palala. And of course, I had been right: the farm could not be left to lie fallow. Not long after our first visit, the first cattle were brought in. Corn was planted. It was farming on a small scale in those years, though. John was, from the start, the "main farmer".

John divided his time between his office and the farm. There were no camps yet, no drinking troughs or permanent water holes except for the river that ran through the farm. All these things needed immediate attention. Hayley dutifully schlepped with John to the farm on weekends with their three small kids. Ma-in-law dragged Dad away from the office; he could afford, at his age, to take days off. Gradually they spent more and more time up in the Waterberg. Dad, for the first time in his life, donned old shorts and puttered around planting fruit trees. Ma had a vegetable garden dug, acquired chickens, then mallard ducks for the long water trench in the old cattle *klipkraal* – the *kraal* with its drystone walls.

I loved the beauty of the unspoilt African veld. Behind the farmhouse the dolerite and granite *koppies* attracted lightning during summer storms. After the rains hundreds of tiny waterfalls splashed down and ran across the wide farmyard in brown rivulets. The summer sun was relentless. In winter the days were mild but the nights could be freezing. The long veld grasses faded from summer's olive green to winter's pale yellow. There didn't seem to be a spring or an autumn: simply a subtle transition with briefly gentle weather. The weather in Limpopo province must be amongst the best in the world. It can get too hot, too cold, too dry, but humidity is always low and there is seldom any wind, and most days the huge blue sky hangs above the still landscape like a celestial umbrella.

My dear Ma-in-law loved improving the humble house and bullied the men into putting in ceilings. Before, there had only been the naked corrugated iron roof above our heads. She painted the old pine cupboards in the kitchen bright red and hung gaily coloured curtains in front of the small windows, to go with the wood-burning stove with its red trim.

It was amazing, this trait emerging in Ma. In Johannesburg she was the sophisticated wife of a high-flying businessman. She lived a life of moneyed ease in her classic old house. She had a cook and a gardener. She had been an opera singer who had spent the years before the Second World War in Berlin. She could be haughty when circumstances demanded. She moved in high circles and sat on the board of the Operatic Society. She belonged to some fancy Afrikaner women's club.

But now she rediscovered her roots. She had grown up on a Free State farm. She was blissfully happy to be back on a farm, even if only part time. Here she went back to the simple life with the greatest of ease, and then, back in Johannesburg, swung round and became the grand lady again. It amused me endlessly: these two diametrically opposing roles she assumed so effort- lessly; these two people she was.

I adored the farm kitchen and that red-trimmed stove. It awoke the dormant memories of my grannies' kitchens again, and of black stoves in labourers' cottages in the Valley. And just like the stoves of my childhood, it cooked the most wonderful food. It wasn't long before Ma had a permanent gardener to plant and water. The vegetables were of the earthy kind: potatoes, sweet potatoes, pumpkins, squash, onions. Because the family could seldom be there during the week to oversee things, it was always touch and go for more delicate plants like tomatoes and lettuce. The baboons regularly raided the garden, fortunately preferring the mealie patch.

When they were "in residence", Ma had two Pedi women in the house to help. Martha cleaned the house and old Liesbet was in attendance in the kitchen. Before Liesbet went home in the afternoons, she made up the stove, and the fragrant woodsmoke would curl and twirl from the chimney, and scent the air outside. This kitchen became, as it should be, the centre of the house.

The best times were when all of us sat round the kitchen table at night, enjoying long dinners and enough wine to make sure we'll have a sound sleep. There would be Dad and Ma, John and Hayley, and Daniel and me. There were five kids eventually: our two and John and Hayley's three. We would feed them an hour or so before the adults ate, scrub off the day's dirt in a warm bath – two kids at a time – and put them to bed. The children adored the farm, and the great bonus for Hayley and me was that we had two willing child-watchers, two young Pedi teenagers, who played with them and saw to it that they didn't come to harm.

Around that table in the red kitchen Dad always sat at the head. He was a highly erudite man who had travelled all over the world and had met fascinating people. He would tell stories, endless stories, of people, of events, of incidents. He had a slow, reflective way of eating, and in between chewing on a chicken bone or dissecting his salad these stories would flow. I would wish, many years later, that I'd used a tape-recorder then. Now he is long gone and his wonderful tales with him.

Liesbet was a good cook, and at times when Ma was outside with her chickens, and Hayley and I were off in John's Kombi fetching milk from a neighbour for the children, she would start dinner. Nothing we cooked on the farm was ever elaborate. It was hearty, plain South African farm fare. There would be a mountain of gem squash, pumpkin with sugar and cinnamon, maybe a fragrant lamb stew with potatoes in an old iron pot. Even seasonings were plain – garlic, pepper, thyme from the garden. Hayley or I would put together a salad.

And somehow everything was lip-smackingly flavourful and the veggies fresh from the garden tasted faithfully of themselves.

Sometimes we brought prepared stuff like raw meatballs in a Tupperware, which could be pan-fried quickly on gas: we had kids to feed and often arrived too late to light the stove and wait for it to heat up.

For a time Hayley and I had to lug mountains of baby stuff to the farm, until the kids were big enough not to succumb to germs without bottle sterilisation, and could eat ordinary food instead of hygienically bottled baby foods. There was a two-plate gas cooker in the kitchen for quick meals, for the kids, or to cook breakfast on.

Breakfast was done in the time-honoured way of farming people. The three men would be out of the house until 8 or 8.30 a.m., and then come back for generous plates of eggs, bacon, bread, sliced tomatoes, sausages, fruit, coffee. Lunch was a huge salad

Hayley and I whipped up with whatever we had on hand or had brought from town. This we usually ate on the porch, with its view to the shimmery koppies in the distance.

The Pedi's on the farm had lived there most of their lives. They lived in groups of neat mud huts with clean-swept yards.

They cooked in their traditional way, in three-legged iron pots on open fires. Whenever any members of our family were on the farm, meat would be given to the workers to prepare for their lunch. One woman would cook, at an outbuilding near the farmhouse, when the men were at work. The Pedi woman would sit on her haunches in a shady clearing and feed a gentle fire which licked around the legs of the pots. There was something deeply comforting in this immemorial scene of a woman placidly preparing food.

In one pot she would boil water and salt, and add mealie meal to make their staple food: a stiff mealie *pap* or "porridge". And at lunchtime our kids sometimes joined in the communal eating, imitating the Pedis' way of taking a lump of pap, then dipping it in the meat stew before putting it in their mouths.

So, in many ways the farm was idyllic. I climbed the koppies behind the house, disregarding the dangers of mamba and cobra, clambering up further and further, seduced onwards by bushveld

Merops Apiaster

Encephalartos

Proteaceae

trees and shrubs I'd never seen before. I gathered seeds and leaves to try and identify them later from the illustrations in Ma's thick book on indigenous trees. I discovered a grove of enormous, very ancient cycads in the koppies. As they are often stolen – taken out and carted away – I can only hope that this group of ancients are too remote to be found by outsiders. Proteas – or *suikerbos*, as it is more often called – grew everywhere. Wild plum (*stam-vrug*) carried their small, mealy, oval fruits all along their main branches instead of in clusters at the end of saplings, as one would expect. In spring the long-tailed whydahs kept house near a marshy patch of the farm, fluttering awkwardly with those long black tail feathers, hampered in flight by their grand mating outfits. Colourful little bee-eaters showed themselves for a few seconds, pretty as butterflies, before swooping into the tangled bush again. Sunbirds flashed iridescent colours as they hung upside down in the aloe flowers among the thorny shrubs in the wild front "garden" of the old house.

The farm, at the end of a rough track, was a natural catchment area. A perennial stream ran through it, collecting its waters from the surrounding hills. It formed pools, where we swam in summer: even though the farm was in a bilharzia area, the farm waters were free of the parasite. A dam was built higher up and the one providing water for the house was enlarged. For drinking water there were now two rainwater tanks, Ma guarding the keys to the taps, making sure none of the precious clean water was wasted. But many times we forgot all about safe water and simply drank from the tap in the kitchen. We didn't fall ill, so the dam water could not have been too bad.

The children ran free, like little farm animals, with the two Pedi teenagers trotting behind to watch that they didn't fall into a dam or vanish into the dolerite outcrops. They invariably came home filthy and famished.

The only bathroom was out the kitchen door, to the left, tacked onto the house as an afterthought by a former owner. The bath stood on four curled iron feet. Hot water came from a "donkey". This was a clever contraption still in use on many farms today. It consisted of a forty-four gallon drum filled with water, suspended on its side between both natural and hand-packed rocks, a metre or so above the ground. The drum had a small tap in front, and was also equipped with a pipe which ran above-ground to the bathroom basin and bath. Under the drum, between the rocks, fire would be made at about five o' clock every afternoon, and there was always enough hot water so each of us could have a bath. The kids shared – it was much easier to scrub down two mucky little bodies at a time than to do it one by one, and saving hot water was a consideration. Even when they were much older, Hayley and I dared not leave them to it; we were still needed to help wash off all the dust and dirt of the day.

This bathroom was also the bane of Hayley's and my life, and a source of sniggering from the menfolk, because every morning as we came out in dressing gowns, with pale night faces, to get to the bathroom to wash and to brush our teeth, we would be confronted by the entire Pedi workforce, placidly sipping Ma's coffee at the back door before starting work. They'd curiously contemplate these two rumpled city women just out of bed. And naturally we had to smile and greet them; that was the proper thing to do.

But even worse was having to walk through the coffee-sipping ranks towards the outhouse ... This little den of iniquity stood in whitewashed glory some way up several natural rock steps which formed part of the *koppie* behind. So in the early morning you arose to the throne while many eyes watched your stiff, self-conscious back as you tried to keep your dignity.

The outhouse housed gecko's and lizards, spiders, bees and dung beetles. Hayley once had the unedifying experience of going up there with a flashlight one dark evening, while the rest of the family was chatting around the remains of supper at the kitchen table. Suddenly she let out a blood-curdling scream, pattered down the stone steps and hobbled howling into the kitchen clutching her skirt round her bottom but with her panties on her knees.

"I've been bitten by a snake! Help!"

John dragged her into the living room and inspected her behind, the scene of the crime. She'd been stung by a wasp. We laughed, to her chagrin.

Once during a school holiday Daniel and I took my parents and my uncle and aunt (who were visiting us in Johannesburg) to the farm. The very first evening we were all having drinks on the front porch in the mellow dusk, and Aunt Nita took herself off to the outhouse with a flashlight. Then, suddenly, the jackals began howling right behind the house in the *koppie*, close to the toilet. No one thought about Nita. They were enchanted by the wild, eerie cries.

After a while she burst onto the porch, out of breath, red in the face, and highly upset.

"I kept screaming, 'Come feeeetch me! Come feeeetch me!' and no one came! I was terrified! Have you ever heard any sound so scary and primitive in your lives?!"

Oh, well. We couldn't hear her; she was, after all, on the other side of the house some way up the *koppie*.

"Have a drink," my uncle offered. "It's only jackals."

But sometimes I hated the farm. Not only was a weekend away a weekend wasted, in which I could do no writing, but the distance from Johannesburg was a huge problem.

For Hayley and me, with young children, the four-and-a-half hour trip on a Friday night or Saturday morning, and then back again late on Sunday afternoon wasn't much fun. It could be exhausting. The new, straight N1 had not yet been built, and after we turned off the N1 at Naboomspruit, now known as Mookgophong, it was dirt roads all the way to the farm, roads which were extremely dusty for most of the year.

One night the kind of thing happened which you hope and pray never will.

It was Sunday evening at dusk when Daniel and I left the farm to return to Johannesburg. Dad and Ma were staying put until Tuesday. John and Hayley weren't there that weekend.

We were using the old Kombi, which was a general-use vehicle for the farm. Stephen was three months old, and slept in the old pram which had once been my young brother's. Danny was just over two years old. I had prepared an extra bottle of milk for Stephen, for the road, in case he woke up. We wedged the pram tightly behind the seats, and we made a kind of bed on the back seats for Danny to lie on.

After a thirty minute drive from the farm one came to a stretch where the winding road ran between mountainous ridges on either side. This part of the road was known as Bokpoort, a gorge which was especially dark at night because of the towering pinnacles on either side and the dense vegetation. There were no farms in this narrow area.

And somewhere in Bokpoort that night Daniel announced that something was wrong: the Kombi's lights were flickering.

He stopped, got out, and and investigated the engine, at the back, with a flashlight. The next minute I heard him curse and I jumped out to see what was going on. The engine or the battery had caught fire. He was throwing handfuls of sand from the road on the flames.

The fire was extinguished, but so was the vehicle ... We were stranded in pitch darkness, far from civilisation, in the middle of the bush, on a Sunday night. Cellphones were sci-fi then.

"We walk," I said. "We have to get out of this place with the children right now."

We hadn't the vaguest idea where we were, and whether the nearest help lay on the way back, or forward. We decided to go forward. I explained to Danny that the Kombi had broken down, and that we were going to try and find a farm to get help. We took the pram down and put Danny in with Stephen ... not that there was room for two on this horse. Poor Danny's legs had to dangle from the pram. Not very comfortable, but being Danny, there were no complaints.

I think Daniel was worried and anxious. His little family was now defenceless against whatever threats might lurk in the African night. We had no weapon, not even a knife. The flashlight was very feeble: Daniel switched it off to save battery power. The old-fashioned pram was low-slung and certainly not meant for pushing through dusty sand. The wheels went squeak, squeak in the dead silence as we started pushing it along the rutted, sandy road.

Around and ahead we couldn't see a thing in the pitch blackness. We could not see the edges of the road. If a farm track led off it, we would miss it. Daniel kept the flashlight off as long as he knew we were in the middle of the road. Pushing the pram was hard work. Now and then one of us would venture to the road edge hoping to faintly discern a name plate and a two-wheel track which would indicate a house somewhere, maybe with a phone … Nothing.

We walked and walked and walked. Silently we prayed that a vehicle might appear, but the entire Palala area seemed dead and desolate that night. Daniel checked the roadside at intervals: only dusty, thorny bushveld trees. We were still in Bokpoort, as evidenced by the greater blackness of the mountains against the darkness of the night sky. Even the stars above were faint.

I prayed that Stephen would not wake up crying. I'd put some clean nappies and the extra bottle of milk in the pram, but we didn't need a crying baby right now …

It seemed as if we walked all night, but of course we did not. After an interminable time we saw flickering lights deep in the bushes, and we heard sounds. But they were not particularly reassuring. It was the primitive, thousand-year-old sounds of Africa: chanting and the deep, rhythmic thrumming of a cow-hide drum. My skin prickled. Suddenly we were acutely aware of being white-skinned and vulnerable in the wilds of a continent we only thought we knew. The chanting around the fires, what did it mean? What message was being sent out by the moody, reverberating drumbeats? Instinctively we sensed that whatever ceremony was being held, it was private and alien. We thought of the turmoil seething beneath South Africa's seemingly peaceful surface. I wished the wheels of the pram wouldn't squeak so.

Then, at last, there was a slight lightening, a leavening of the atmosphere: we were out of the narrow pass. The mountains were no longer pressing in on us. Some way further on we saw lights in a farmhouse window through the trees, some way off the road.

Safe at last! Our throats were parched with dust and exhaustion. Yet it could not be very late. Daniel didn't wear a watch and I could not read mine. We pushed the pram with the two children up the almost invisible farm track towards the house, now apparent as a profile against the stars. As we came up to the porch of the old farmstead, dogs suddenly barked viciously and rushed at us.

The front door opened and a man's voice stayed the dogs just in time. "Who is there?" a deep, grim bass voice called out. In the light of the door behind him we could see that the man carried a gun of some kind. "Stay where you are!" he commanded and threw the light of a strong torch on us.

Daniel said our names and told him briefly about the trouble with our vehicle. The man hesitated, then said curtly, "Come in."

So this is local hospitality, I thought, amazed. Attacking dogs, a gun, a light in our faces ... We were neatly dressed for the trip back to the city; we hardly looked like gypsies – and we were pushing a pram! The farmer did help us lift the pram up the stairs to the stoep, wordlessly. I hesitated at the door: the cold wooden floors of a long passage gleamed in front of me. The wheels of the pram were dusty, and so were our shoes.

Doors led off the passage, like in many older houses. At the far end we found ourselves in a kitchen where a woman sat by a table with a linoleum top, listening intently to a radio. She must have heard the commotion and the voices, yet she hadn't stirred. She put off her radio reluctantly. I apologised profusely for intruding like this on their peaceful Sunday evening.

The two men conferred, and vanished. Yes, there was a phone: Daniel could phone his father on the farm. Fortunately there was an extra battery for the Kombi on the farm.

"I was listening to the church service," the woman said, and in my tired state I heard an accusing note in her voice which might not actually have been there. "Sit down," she said, at last, and I sank down gratefully into a kitchen chair. I explained again what had happened. Stephen woke up and grizzled, and I got up to find his bottle: fortunately he was used to drinking cold milk.

"I am so sorry to ask," I said, "but is it possible for me to put my toddler down on a bed somewhere until his grandparents arrive? He's so uncomfortable ..."

She seemed to relent at last. She took me to a room, where I put Danny down. He said he wasn't thirsty. As ever, he accepted the situation, turned on his side and fell asleep. I had an idea he'd not slept since we left the vehicle, as he'd asked several times whether "we were there yet".

I put a dry nappy on Stephen and discreetly wrapped the wet one in plastic. I was wondering whether I dared asked for a glass of water. The woman had made no move yet to offer us anything.

After some desultory conversation she asked at last, "Would you like a cup of tea?"

"Oh yes!" I said, almost tearful with gratitude, "I'm dying of thirst!" She made the tea, but she never offered me a second cup.

At long last my in-laws arrived with the extra battery, and the men disappeared into the night to fix the problem. We were intruding on what was supposed to be a quiet Sunday night, and when, an hour later, we could leave at last, the Kombi fixed, we were lavish in our gratitude towards our hosts.

"But can you believe their attitude?" I said angrily to Daniel later. "They treated us like scum when we arrived. Vicious dogs! A gun at the ready! A sharp light in our faces! And the guy could see we were pushing a pram! They were so ... almost surly. We had two babies with us! So much for South African *boere* hospitality!"

"You come from the Boland. The Western Cape is like a little bit of Europe. Hospitality on a dark night comes more easily there. The Palala, darling, is still wildest Africa. The farms are isolated. He was just being careful. And actually, they were nice enough in the end. What would we have done without them?"

"She could have lifted her bottom sooner to get me some tea! She never even offered a second cup!"

From the start John was more interested in the farming aspect than Daniel, and eventually he went almost every weekend, taking charge.

Later we would look back on those first years with nostalgia, and it is the jolly red kitchen with its large table and the singing wood stove which brings back the best memories.

Now Ma and Dad are both gone, and John and his sons, both married, are on the farm permanently. They have long since bought up more neighbouring farms, and it is now a prosperous commercial undertaking. But large parts remain as it was. A vast tract of land has been left almost as wild as it has been for hundred of years. Here log cabins have been built, a dam built and game brought in. Nature trails have been laid on by John's elder son, Nico.

The entire set-up in that once unknown Palala region has changed immeasurably since those early days when Dad bought the farm. The Palala has been discovered. There are now beautiful game farms and lodges luring the tourists, the roads have been tarred, and the area has opened up.

Baked Pumpkin Slices

*This is how Ma-in-law baked pumpkin. The rind or peel
turns into something resembling toffee: delicious.*

As many boer pumpkin slices as you like, unpeeled
Butter
Sugar, preferably brown or yellow
Salt
Ground cinnamon

Lay the slices, overlapping slightly, in any oven dish. The arrangement you use is not important, but make sure the slices will each get their share of sugar and butter.

Melt enough butter to be able to spread generously over the pumpkin. Strew over sugar, also with a generous hand. Sprinkle with a bit of salt, and then with ground cinnamon.

Bake for 45–60 minutes in a moderate oven. The slices should be soft, with a slightly chewy peel.

Farm Lunch Salad

This is not really a recipe. You need a large salad bowl, preferably one of those big round perspex or glass ones. This will serve about eight people. To change it from this cheap 'n cheerful suggestion to much more elegant, use flat platters and an expensive array of cold meats and fancy cheeses.

500 g garlic polony

About 250 g picnic ham

6 hard-boiled eggs, peeled

A cup of cheese cubes (any variety)

Lettuce – preferably 2 heads of iceberg or 2 packets of mixed greens

6 ripe tomatoes, unpeeled, sliced or chopped

1–2 green sweet bell peppers, seeded and sliced

Black calamata olives

Peppadews

Garlic

Vinaigrette dressing

Bread to serve with the salad

Chop the polony in chunks, not too small. Slice the ham into strips. Slice the eggs. Rub the bowl with a clove of garlic. Tear the lettuce into large pieces and put into the bowl. Add all the ingredients, and toss lightly with a shop-bought salad dressing.

CHAPTER 20

~ ARE WE THERE YET? ~

I MUST GO DOWN TO THE SEAS AGAIN,

FOR THE CALL OF THE RUNNING TIDE

IS A WILD CALL AND A CLEAR CALL THAT MAY NOT BE DENIED;

AND ALL I ASK IS A WINDY DAY WITH THE WHITE CLOUDS FLYING,

AND THE FLUNG SPRAY AND THE BLOWN SPUME,

AND THE SEAGULLS CRYING.

John Masefield

Once a year, of course, we went on holiday, as most families do. We would stay with my parents for a day or two, but mainly holiday meant the sea, the sea! It was the one aspect of life in Johannesburg that I missed dreadfully: being so far away from the ocean.

The boys were growing up fast. Before school holidays limited our options, we used to go to Daniel's late grandparents' old family house in Hermanus. We preferred the month of February, when we were assured of hot, still days. The skin cancer scare was not yet upon us, and although we were careful with the kids, we nevertheless spent hours in the sun and sea. The boys tanned to golden brown so that Stephen's bright blue eyes would be almost startling in his brown face. Danny had the skin type which rarely burned, and he tanned almost overnight.

We enjoyed our holidays to the hilt, and I always returned home in a small cloud of depression at the thought of leaving the sea.

The Cape coast can be very windy and cool in December, but as soon as the school holidays are over, the hot weather, with perfectly timed unjustness, arrives ...

Daniel took up angling, and bought himself a state-of-the-art rod and tackle, but up to this day he is not a good fisherman. During our times in Hermanus, and later in Keurboomstrand on the southern coast, his record remained dismal and the butt of many jokes.

It was on a day in Hermanus, when he turned up at the house, a little bedraggled, with a tiny fish at the end of his line – his only catch – that my wild desire, my lust, surfaced ...

We must find fresh lobster.

I'd actually been dying for fresh lobster for a long time. It was such a difficult sea creature to procure in a live state: either you dive for it yourself, or you can't get it. Certainly it hadn't been easily available for years. I suddenly knew how and where to procure sea-fresh lobster.

"Buy two bottles of sweet wine or cheap sherry," I instructed Daniel, who wasn't quite sure what I had in mind. He suspected that whatever it was, it wasn't going to be strictly to the letter of the law and was reluctant to do as I asked. "Put it in the boot of the car," I instructed.

Then we drove to Hermanus harbour.

It was about 10.30 a.m., and we saw the *bakkies* bobbing in – those small boats which used to be a feature of the Cape coast. They would have been catching linefish and lobster. They were allowed five lobsters each, but were not allowed to sell it to the public. The harbour seemed quiet; I saw no lurking men about who might be inspectors. As the small boats tied up, I bent and checked out their catches from the quayside as if I were merely an inquisitive tourist. Then I saw my quarry – an older guy who was handling five enormous, live lobsters with claws striking out futilely. He was putting them into a sea-wet hessian bag.

Squatting down, so as not to be too obvious, I negotiated with him. Two lobsters …? Please? Two bottles of sherry and so many rand …? He was reluctant. If any inspector was observing this transaction, he was a dead man, he said. We pretended to discuss his catch of *hotnotsvis* and steenbras, and worked out the plan. The car was parked on the quay, and all the windows were open because of the heat. He would walk past casually on the seaward side and chuck the two lobsters in the back. I would by then be busy "looking for something" in the open boot, and as he walked past, I would hand him his loot. He would not risk being seen actually handing me something and me handing something back.

He casually strung his fish on a line, rolled my two lobsters in old newspaper, the rest went into the gunnysack, and he strolled away after the men near him had left. As he passed our car, the newspaper parcel went lightning quick into the open back window, in front of the back seats. I heard it thumping to the floor. He paused briefly, tipped his hat in a pretend greeting, and just as quickly popped the wine and money I handed him into his sack. Sleight of hand. Deal done.

"Now we feast," I said happily. Daniel was less happy: he didn't like doing things illegally. "Gluttony knows no laws," I said and patted him on the leg.

The lobsters had freed themselves of the newspaper by now and were rustling about on the floor, moving their pincers and being generally scary. The kids clutched each other on the back seat in one small bundle, legs pulled up, yelling every time a lobster clicked a claw. "They can't get at you! Just hang on, we'll be home in a sec! They can't do anything! They're just lobsters!"

"They look like monsters! Ma, why did you do this to us?" shouted Danny, deeply offended.

As soon as the car stopped in the back yard the boys positively rolled out of it like curled-up armadillos. And I – also with a few screeches – gingerly carried the poor sea creatures to their doom.

It was only 11 a.m. No matter. I have desired, yearned, pined and dreamt about fresh Cape rock lobster for years. I do not deign to eat frozen lobster, as lobsters do not freeze well and lose their flavour.

There are many recipes, some very grand, for the preparation of lobster and crayfish. To my mind, this delicious seafood needs only the simplest of treatments.

It's hard to murder the poor creatures. But this is a time to be merciless for your own selfish sake. You can put them in cold water and heat it to boiling, and apparently they go into a coma (we hope) before the boiling water kills them. Or you could, like I did that day, send your husband down to the sea to fetch a pail of seawater, bring that to the boil in a large pot, and then dump in the lobsters. Slam on the lid – you can always put a heavy stone on top as they will definitely try to climb out. Sounds might emerge … apparently nothing more than the steam escaping from the shells – or is it? Turn away, cover your ears with your hand, run out the door, and say a prayer for the noble creatures you are sacrificing for the sake of your spoilt human palate. No wonder people turn vegetarian.

They die quickly, and, I only hope, without too much suffering. As soon as they turn that nice bright red, fish them out with tongs: that's twenty minutes cooking time for a large specimen, fifteen for a smaller one.

That day we had lunch at the ungodly hour of 11.30 a.m., complete with bottle of cold Riesling. We anointed our lobsters with pure butter which melted in yellow pools on the pure white flesh. We crunched open the claws and sucked out the sweet, sweet meat. We didn't talk. We were in heaven – Daniel was quiet about his scruples.

The kids had sandwiches, outside on the porch. Danny refused to watch us eat the lobsters. Neither of the two normally quite adventurous eaters would touch or even taste lobster. They had seen a pagan side of their mother which they did not know existed. She had broken the law, Daddy said, and then exposed them to alien monsters in the car, and laughed about it. Then she murdered the live monsters in a pot of boiling seawater. Then she had laughed again – or was it cackled? – as she cut open their backs with kitchen scissors.

One year in Hermanus I had a terrifying and inexplicable experience with regard to Danny, then about three years old. It did nothing to soothe my peculiar anxiety over this child. It was a particularly hot summer, too hot to take the children to the beach in the middle of the day. One morning very early, when Daniel and Stephen were still asleep, Danny and I went down to the nearest beach, a small deserted one just below the old Birkenhead Hotel.

It was that wonderful hour when the sun's rays were slanted and reddish and the rocks threw deep black shadows on the wet glistening sand. It was already hot, and we were both in swimming gear. Danny ran around like the first child on an undiscovered beach, entranced, preoccupied, inspecting each slippery black rock with its seaweeds, barnacles and mussels. When interested in something, he could concentrate very deeply. He wasn't worried about the small waves rolling in, because he had never been afraid of water. He didn't even glance at the sea.

The tide was coming in, and I kept a constant eye on Danny while standing higher up on dry sand, taking a few photographs.

The last image I had was of Danny bent over a sea-wet, weed-encrusted rock, engrossed in something he was inspecting in a fissure, perhaps a crab.

For maybe three seconds I concentrated on the camera. In those few seconds a huge wave crashed in seemingly from nowhere. When I looked up, the rock where Danny had been standing was invisible under churning sandy waters.

My child was gone. I screamed and ran towards the rock, towards the sea. He had been so absorbed that he would never have seen the wave coming. He was only a tiny child, unaware yet of such dangers.

The wild waters retreated and there was nothing. I looked around wildly: my child was gone.

"Danny! Danny!" I yelled, hysterical. I ran into the sea: there must be a small body being churned around and around in those waves … but I could see nothing. Could he have been swept further out? "Danny!!!" I looked behind other rocks. Nothing. By this time I was screaming and crying with tears running down my face. Danny had vanished. Only the gulls wheeled overhead. There wasn't another human being in sight.

I swung round again, a madwoman, aware only of my terror, of my guilt. For two, three seconds I'd not had my eyes on him.

Then a small figure, placid and unaware, strolled towards me from an area higher up – where a moment ago there had been empty dry sand. The wave didn't wash that far.

I grabbed him, this precious child with his perfect little body. He had been gone; in the moments I'd fiddled with the camera he could not possibly have moved so quickly to where he was now! Not a three-year-old! One moment he was bending down over the rock, then there was only the wild water. Now here he was, safe, on drier sand … How was it possible?

I hid my shock but I was shaking. Danny had no explanation and was unmoved when I said I thought that big wave had yanked him into the sea. We went home. I never mentioned the incident to Daniel. I felt too guilty. I felt there was nothing to tell. And I believed, anyway, that an angel must have spirited him to safety before the wave struck. It was the only explanation.

Once Danny was in school, we could only go away during school holidays.

I had a dear uncle who farmed apples in the Langkloof, and now we made use of his log cabin at Keurboomstrand during the Easter holidays. This village lies just east of Plettenberg Bay, a narrow strip of land between sea and indigenous forest. Keurboomstrand was not yet the exclusive little resort it is now.

The ancient Knysna forest ensures an almost subtropical climate for most of the year. Sometimes during the night a gentle rain would drip-drip, and then disappear before dawn. The log cabin was pretty basic, but we had wonderful holidays there. The boys learned to fish with rods made by Daniel from sturdy sticks: lines, hooks and sinkers attached. They tested their talent in rock pools, and their excitement when they pulled out a hapless little *klipvis* was wonderful to see: the shining eyes, the yells: "Look, look, I got one!"

One day, in an anglers' shop in Plettenberg Bay, Daniel gave in to the kids' greatest desire: he bought them real, small-sized, fishing tackle.

The amazing fact from those halcyon days was that the three of them actually caught fish every time they went on the rocks. Or, at least, the two little boys did even if Daniel didn't have their luck! We took it for granted then: if you go fishing, you come back with fish. Not all three hooked fish every single time, but one, maybe two of them would catch a fish. The kids could not cast far and had to be helped when they had a fish on the line, or they might be dragged off the rocks.

During our last two holidays in Keurbooms the two boys had styrofoam boards to play with in the surf. But Danny, as usual, aimed for more. Aged eight or nine, board under the arm, he would watch the huge waves breaking some way off shore, then race in to catch them. I would be jumping up and down and screaming for him to come back, and he would pretend not to hear. He would laugh at my anxiety: he had no fear of the sea whereas I dreaded those blue-green walls of water, top-heavy and wavering, seconds away from tumbling down in a white mass of foam.

I can still see him, this tiny tanned boy, splashing towards those frothing mountains, disappearing, this time forever, I thought, into the angry sea. But he didn't. He came in riding them triumphantly, lying on his styrofoam board, laughing with glee.

He was an otter, a dolphin. The waves would pull him under, maul him, hide him, but he emerged laughing, always laughing, as if he never even swallowed a mouthful of sea water, as if he had hidden gills which took over from his lungs when he was in the water.

Stephen was Danny's follower, up to a point. He was much more careful in his physical activities because he wasn't as athletic as Danny. He was also a neat, meticulous little boy. In all the years, for instance, I never had to tell Stephen – as I did with Danny – to do his homework. He'd come home from school, eat, and settle down to his homework religiously. Danny would make promises of "later, later!", get busy with something else, or slip out to a friend.

They were attractive, kind boys. Danny had a deep well of empathy and understanding of others which went far beyond his years. He loved animals, and they instinctively loved him back. Stephen was more practical and down-to-earth, and his quick temper tended to betray him.

Once, at Keurboomstrand, I witnessed an amazing scene. Lots of monkeys lived in the ancient forest which covered the high hill behind the village, and whose green tentacles sneaked down among the houses. These monkeys were naughty and would steal food from porches, but they were very wary and wild. One day my mother, my aunt and I, with Stephen and Danny, went on a forest walk. We surprised a troop of monkeys, chittering above our heads in the tangled branches. Most of the little mothers had tiny babies, which they held to their skinny chests with one arm. It was a heart-warming sight, but only lasted a moment as the monkeys fled from us, away up the hill, deeper into the tree canopy. We walked on.

After a few minutes I noticed that Danny was not with us, and I turned back to find him. I came upon an amazing scene. In a small clearing Danny sat on his haunches, with a number of the monkey troop about two metres from him in a half circle. He was talking to them in an undertone, and they seemed to be listening. The cute little babies clung to their mothers.

Unfortunately they saw me, and scattered in terror again. How had Danny managed to lure them back to him, and "talk" to them? He shrugged and said nothing, and I felt awful for having walked into that clearing and spoilt his intimate moments with the monkeys.

He was still the same wise old man he had seemed to be when he was born.

∼ CASUAL FISH MEALS ∼

Like my Ouma Sannie, my mother and my aunts before me, I would seldom bother to fillet a fresh fish just off the hook, unless they are big and too difficult to handle in a pan or the oven.

It is deeply satisfying for an angler, and especially for a very small angler, to arrive home sticky with sea and salt and sun, smelling of bait, and triumphantly bearing a fish or two. It is just as satisfying for the woman who perhaps stayed home and waited, to accept a supper free from the sea. It is, however, normally impossible to convince little anglers that their catch is actually edible, nice, and good for them. "Too many thorns," Stephen complained. But if their helpings can be carefully lifted off the bones at table, they might be persuaded to taste it.

It is less pleasurable for the mother to clean that fish.

But someone must do it … It has to be scaled, the insides and gills removed, perhaps the spiny fins cut off (but not the heads) and thoroughly rinsed. A fish of 20–25 cm should, in this holiday atmosphere, be kept whole.

At the Keurbooms cottage my aunt kept an enormous pan. This was great for making really flavoursome pan-fried fish, which we then ate from the pan. (Well, this wasn't Buckingham Palace!)

If you absolutely must, fry some sliced mushrooms alongside the fish, or some chopped onion and bacon. For extra juices, a tin of chopped tomato, to which you add a pinch of sugar, will also be fine. But it's quite sufficient to roll the fish in flavoured flour. A mixture of flour and mealie meal works even better. Season it with black pepper and seasoning salt. Season the cavity and head with a seasoning salt, and put in some chopped garlic and parsley, if available. Heat a mixture of butter and olive oil (or butter and any other oil) to a depth of about 1 cm. Heat well, and put in the fish, which should sizzle. (In a smaller pan, fry one fish at a time.)

Usually, for a roughly 22 cm fish, three minutes per side should be ample. Rather undercook fish than overcook it. It keeps on cooking while it waits to be eaten.

Such plain fried fish eaten with the pan juices and a squeeze of lemon is delicious with a fresh seed loaf or wholewheat bread, ripe tomatoes, and a few glasses of cold white wine. You get to clean out the pan juices with pieces of bread, swallowed down with cold wine. And you watch the sun setting on the sea.

～

CHAPTER 21

~ Oh Kitchen, My Kitchen ~

MY BLACK CAT SITS ON THE SILL AND PURRS,
PONDERING THE MYSTERIES OF LIFE, AND THE POSSIBLE CONTENTS
OF THE PLOPPING POT ON THE STOVE.
SHE MEDITATES ON THE MANY WAFTING SCENTS
IN THIS KITCHEN WHICH SHE SURMISES TO BE HERS ALONE,
AND STRETCHES GRACEFULLY IN A SUDDEN BEAM OF SUN.
A friend's incomplete poem

We moved to a new house after eight years in the first one.
We procured this house in rather a dramatic way. We had been
house-hunting – for a bigger, better house, closer to the schools
– for nine months. Or, to be correct, I was house-hunting. Daniel
hardly had time for riding shotgun with property agents day
after day.

After nine months of fruitless searching I was exhausted.
It was plain: there simply wasn't a single house for sale in the
Johannesburg or Randburg suburbs which suited us. Not only
were we picky, but we had a certain price range above which
Daniel would not go.

The agents were getting fed-up with me, but not halfway as fed-up as I was with them. Our requirements were not excessive. Price: middle-of-the-range. Position: not far from the schools. Danny was in primary school and Stephen in nursery school: these two were within blocks of each other. House wanted: preferably in a quiet street, preferably open-plan, preferably airy and fairly modern.

One would think that the agents, having been in this game for so many years, would "read" their clients like books and know instinctively which houses would suit which people. Not so. For nine months I was schlepped to dark antiquities with creaking floors and probably several resident ghosts, to those ubiquitous dwellings which needed *tender loving care*: which spelled restoration or improvements costing a fortune. I saw ugly square, tiny houses on busy roads which made our present humble house look like a small palace. At one place, about twenty kilometres from the nearest school, the owner tried to sell his house to me on the strength of one rare flowering bulb in his dusty garden. "You'll never find that lily again! Never!" he said threateningly as I left.

We met houses we liked, not loved, and might have considered if they weren't so far above our means. Time and again I found myself in houses where little broom cupboards were called bedrooms and the lounge looked into the neighbour's main bedroom.

One day, as I was being taken home by yet another agent who was as tired of me as I was of her, I decided that I was giving this house-hunting a rest for a while. I could not waste any more time like this; it was becoming more and more difficult to keep up with my job.

As I was cogitating on all this, she suddenly turned into a leafy side street.

"I'm sorry, but I quickly have to see a seller about her house as it's on our way. I hope you don't mind. Just, please, don't fancy this house, it's sold. The buyer is signing the contract tonight."

We stopped halfway around a crescent street in front of a flat-roofed house with pale beige walls. As we walked up the outside brick stairs past the tumbling shrubs and neat lawn, I thought, omigod, this looks like the house I've been searching for for nine long months … My heart sank.

While the agent talked to the lady of the house, I shamelessly wandered around. It was perfect! I'd heard the two of them mentioning the price, and I could not believe that this gem could actually be slap bang what we could afford …

The house had a U-shape and was built on several levels, so had steps up to the lounge, steps down to the TV room, and some interesting nooks. The floors were shiny brown quarry tiles. The lounge was huge. The lovely TV room had built-in planters in which green plants flourished. From all sides large French doors opened on to a stone stoep, which gave onto a secluded lawn and a real *klipkoppie* garden. The bedrooms and bathrooms were upstairs.

And what a kitchen! Two large wall ovens. A window behind the hob, which had a view into trees, over roofs, and as far as Muldersdrift. A separate scullery, with enough space for my chest freezer, and, beyond the scullery, a pantry! A pantry, in this day and age, cool and dark because an ivy blocked some of the light at the single window. Perfect, I thought, for Daniel's wines …

That was when I started praying. Please, God, let something happen. Please don't let us lose this house. Please …

"He must sign before midnight tonight," I heard the agent say to the pretty blonde owner. I couldn't hear more of their conversation, but I gathered that there had been some problems with the buyer.

I phoned Daniel on the white kitchen phone after asking the owner's permission. "You must come and see this house. You must. Listen …" and I gave him directions.

"But this house is sold," said the owner.

"I want this house," I said.

"My dear, it's too late," said the agent. "I'm going to phone the buyer as soon as I've dropped you off …"

"Just wait here fifteen more minutes!" I pleaded.

Daniel drove out to the house. And as soon as he walked in, he told me later, he had the same sensation that I had had, that this was our house.

Sometimes prayers, even such materialistic ones, are answered. The buyer had a deadline for signing the purchase agreement: midnight. As the afternoon hours dragged endlessly on, the agent could not contact the buyer. Night fell. At our house, we waited into the night. Then, some time past the witching hour, the agent turned up at our house. The buyer had missed this final deadline, and she could not trace him. He was not where he'd said he'd be, and he hadn't contacted her for days.

The house was ours. I felt a bit bad about it, but when the buyer was still AWOL days later, we were elated.

The new house was perfect for entertaining. The garden was a pure delight for the children. It was "wooded" as the property ads would say: on two sides there were old trees, newer trees and shrubs, forming ideal hiding places and playing areas. The plot was on top of what had been a hill, in the long-ago days when the area was still farmland. There was an overgrown rock garden close to the lounge, with a little path through the tangly shrubs. Again there were fruit trees: apricot, peach and a Santa Rosa plum. There was a tall acacia and an evergreen oak, and, on the kitchen side, a beautiful deodar cedar. The garden was full of birdsong. We bought a bird bath and leftover food and bread were put out for the feathered friends.

And at last I was lucky enough to find a young woman who would "sleep in" and be a full-time house help: Thandi Mabandla. Thandi would be with us for the next nineteen years, getting married in between and having two daughters. Thandi was very short and plump – facts she never stopped bemoaning – but she had the innate dress sense of a designer. She wrought miracles with what little she had, and dressed like the social A-list of Jozi. Sometimes she showed the melodramatic personality of a showbiz diva.

And she didn't do cooking … If she didn't want to share our food – she had many dislikes – she'd throw some beef chunks in a pot of water and boil it up. The smell was awful, so I begged her to add an onion, as food smells quickly permeated the open-plan house. And she would always cook herself a small pot of *pap*, the stiff mealie porridge without which most black people do not consider a meal complete. "*Pap* is fattening," I said. "I love my *pap*," she would say, shrugging her round shoulders.

We would often sit at the kitchen counter and gossip. She quickly got to know everyone who worked at all the houses in the crescent street – housemaids and gardeners. They, in turn, knew everything about their employers. It was as if invisible rays of communication, like the web of a spider, threaded from one back yard to the other, conveying the latest information. The So-and-so's only came home at 4 a.m. the other night and had a drunken fight in the street. They'd been to a party. "The Millers also had had a biiiig fight," Thandi said, arms thrown wide to indicate the size of the domestic squabble. "She threw him with plates and broke them all." A certain other neighbour was hitting the bottle badly and had been seen driving in a zig-zag way up a nearby street. Another family was totally dysfunctional, with the naughtiest kids in the neighbourhood.

We had a great informal security system. As soon as a stranger entered the crescent road at one end, the dogs on that side would start to bark. The barks would be picked up by the other mutts as the "intruder" continued round the crescent. They didn't bark at the residents, the gardeners, maids or kids. So, as crime escalated in Johannesburg, we knew to keep our ears open, and we would be forewarned by the dogs when someone we didn't know entered our circular street. It was a very effective alert.

We were really very happy in our new house. Two of my best friends now lived a few blocks away. Although I preferred fetching them, the boys could easily walk home from school. Suddenly Daniel's office in town was closer, not so much because the distance was less, but because the roads he now used to reach his office were quieter. We invited our friends: it was easy to entertain at this house. We made plans to build on a large study for Daniel: the original architect said it would actually enhance the property. We thought about a swimming pool for the boys. Danny was a good swimmer and we got a bit weary of all the summer trips to the local municipal pool.

One hot Saturday we were at the pool again, where I watched anxiously as Danny, now seven, pretending not to hear me shout, "No!", dived in at the deep end and swam the length of the enormous pool to the shallow end. Just a while later Stephen ran round the pool edge, slipped in a puddle, and fell very badly. His entire left side was badly abraded and bleeding. After some basic first aid given there we went home, where I dressed the poor crying child's bleeding and oozing wounds with the most effective dressings I knew, because they didn't stick to wounds: thin cut-up sanitary pads kept in place with micropore tape.

The cuts and abrasions must have burnt like hell. Stephen went, still sobbing, to curl up in a chair to collect himself.

A little later Daniel and I were busy with something else when we heard the unmistakeable laughter of both our sons from across the wall dividing us from one of our neighbours, and the splash of water. They were in a pool again!

"But Stephen's so sore!" I said disbelievingly.

When the two arrived back home, not a single dressing was left on Stephen's body.

"What happened to the dressings?" I was aghast. His left side was blotchy with red mercurochrome and all the cuts and bruises were exposed again.

"Oh, they fell off," he said.

So my dear neighbour Anneline, and probably her husband and children, had to pick bits of sanitary pads from their pool and lawn.

I was still disturbed by the fact that Danny seemed to have no concept of personal safety, or he was entirely fearless. He lived each day to its fullest, cramming in as many activities as possible. Quite a number of boys lived in the houses on our crescent, and Danny, Stephen and these little neighbours were often up to mischief of which the parents were unaware. Once they decided to lay walkie-talkie links from one house to the other, and lifted off manhole covers to crawl along stormwater pipes under the street – in summer, when thunderstorms hit suddenly.

The acacia on our back lawn was very tall. The house itself was situated on a small escarpment: Greater Johannesburg is not flat, but an undulating landscape of hills, valleys and outcrops.

One day I went to play tennis on the local courts lower down in the suburb. On my return Danny said with great satisfaction: "I saw you playing tennis."

"That is not possible!" I said. "The courts are too far down, and totally invisible from here!"

It turned out that, to be able to see that far, over the roof of the house, he had climbed the monstrous acacia, easily three storeys tall, to its very top. I threw a fit. It was not a good climbing tree. The branches were far apart and it would take a lot of stretching, hanging on, swinging up, and other Tarzan-like manoeuvres to climb it.

Danny had played rugby since Grade One and was as fast as a lynx but often lost concentration on the field and made laughable mistakes. He was an excellent athlete who could outrun boys much older than himself.

Stephen wasn't the athletic type. He was shyer, more introverted and studious.

Skateboards were the rage one year. Danny was the top skater in the crescent, against our wishes, because it was dangerous to skate in the street. He came into the kitchen one day and casually said, "Ma, can you do something? I scraped my leg on the tar."

I let out a small scream when I saw the abrasion. Heaven knows how, but he'd neatly peeled a rectangle of skin the size of a saucer off his outer thigh. He was unfazed.

Regardless of being a food editor, I was still having cake flops. No amount of tweaking to compensate for Joburg's altitude made any difference. My cakes fell, or rose with points, or the texture was terrible. One of my new friends across the street was not much of a cook, but her elderly mother was, so when this lady came to visit again, I went to her and begged for two basic cake recipes. She's lived on the Highveld all her life. She gave me two simple recipes, one for a chocolate cake and one for a sponge, which I will tag on the end of this chapter. They both worked like a charm.

Nouvelle cuisine had slowly invaded the foodie world. The foods in top restaurants were now too pretty to eat and too little to satisfy. And it was an expensive fad. "Half the food for double the money," was the saying at the time. The sophisticates liked to dine at the Three Ships at the Carlton Hotel or at Tollman Towers, which also had a popular Japanese restaurant called the Sukihama.

On our second Christmas in the new house I invited over my in-laws as well as a divorced friend with her little girl, for a Christmas Eve dinner. The house looked very festive and I had gone to lots of trouble with the food and the little gifts.

Later in the evening, with the giggles of the children in the background, my friend Natalie said to me, "I envy you all this. You have these two beautiful children, you're happily married, and your house is gorgeous." Then she sighed. "You know ..." she shrugged, "it's ... almost too perfect."

A shudder of apprehension snaked down my spine.

~

Caviar Mousse

Use a small round bowl or mould for this. It is delicate in taste,
easy to make, and this recipe will serve about six
as a pre–dinner snack or as a starter.

3 large hard-boiled eggs
125 ml tangy mayonnaise (Koo is tangy)
5 ml Worcestershire sauce
15 ml finely grated onion
15 ml gelatine softened in 65 ml water
10 ml lemon juice
50–100 g red lumpfish caviar – or the more expensive salmon roe
Optional: white pepper, Tabasco
Lemon wedges, chopped parsley and extra caviar to garnish

Grate the hard-boiled eggs as finely as possible. Add the mayonnaise, Worcestershire sauce and onion, and mix well. Stir the gelatine into the water, heat while stirring, until the gelatine melts completely. Add the lemon juice. Stir this into the egg mixture. Fold in the caviar gently. The quantity you use depends on your budget! Taste the mixture: it will probably need something extra like a shot of Tabasco or some seasoning salt or pepper.

Spray a small mould with nonstick spray. Ladle the mixture into the mould and chill for about 3 hours. Turn out on a plate and garnish with lemon wedges, parsley and caviar. If you can get it, salmon caviar is the ideal garnish. The mousse can be sliced thinly quite easily. Serve with melba toast and salty crackers.

Marinated Beef Strips

This recipe serves four. You could buy the beef at a deli, or do a fillet yourself.

250 ml sour cream or crème fraîche
15 ml wholegrain mustard
15 ml lemon juice
1 clove garlic, crushed and chopped
15 ml finely grated onion
Salt and black pepper
250 g cold rare roast beef, preferably fillet
Capers and red onion rings to garnish

Whisk the cream with the mustard, lemon juice, garlic, onion and seasonings. Slice the beef into thin julienne strips, and marinate in the dressing overnight or for a few hours. Divide among four plates. Garnish with capers and onion rings and serve with hot, crusty rolls or French bread.

Marinated Calamari

*Serves four as a starter. Calamari shrinks when cooked,
so 500 g sounds like a lot but isn't.*

500 g calamari, preferably South African, cut into rings	About 125 ml virgin olive oil
Oil and butter	Aromat
30 ml lemon juice	Freshly ground black pepper
30 ml runny honey (heat in microwave)	Capers
10 ml good table mustard	Black olives, pips removed
	Chopped green pepper

Sauté the calamari in hot oil or butter, or a mixture of both. Do it in batches, as you need full control over each piece: they need literally seconds in hot oil, just until the nanosecond they turn opaque. Remove with a slotted spoon and drain on kitchen paper. Tough calamari is the result of overcooking.

Whisk together the lemon juice, honey, mustard and olive oil. Season the calamari lightly with Aromat and pepper, put in a bowl, and mix in the dressing. Cover and leave in the fridge until needed.

Garnish each helping with capers, halved olives and chopped green pepper, and grind over black pepper. Serve with crusty bread and chilled white wine.

Spinach Roulade

*This is much easier than it sounds. It's a nice side dish,
and, served with dolled-up tinned chopped tomatoes for a sauce,
ideal for vegetarians*.*

250 g frozen spinach, thawed and drained	5 ml seasoning salt
A generous handful of parsley, finely chopped	Tabasco or chili-garlic sauce
	Freshly ground black pepper
65 ml cake flour	5 ml grated nutmeg
250 ml milk	4 very large eggs, separated
125 ml grated mature Cheddar cheese	Pinch of Cream of Tartar
	Grated Parmesan or pecorino cheese

Preheat oven to 180 °C. Grease and line a fairly small swiss roll tin with nonstick baking paper and grease again. (If your tin seems too large, make it smaller by folding heavy foil to make a "rim" and reduce the size.) The spinach can be defrosted overnight or in a microwave. Drain it very thoroughly: I find the best is to squeeze it by hand. Mix the chopped parsley into the spinach. (You can also use 500 g spinach and leave out the parsley.)

Use a wire whisk to beat the flour into the milk, in a pot on the stove. This is my way of making a white sauce: I seldom bother with the butter and so cut down somewhat on fats. There is nothing a wire whisk cannot do, and it does make a white sauce without lumps. Whisk while heating to boiling point, until the sauce bubbles and thickens.

Off the heat, stir in the spinach-parsley mixture, then the cheese. At this point, add the seasonings suggested. Beat the egg yolks lightly to mix, using the same whisk, and add, stirring in.

Use clean electric beaters to whisk the egg whites. Add cream of tartar. Beat until stiff – the whites should hold their shape if you turn the bowl upside down.

Fold into first mixture with a spatula, although I often whisk in instead of folding in – it's easier and doesn't seem to make much difference to the end result.

Pour into the prepared pan and spread evenly and into the corners. Bake for about 15 minutes or until puffy and beige on top. Turn out on a clean, dampened kitchen cloth sprinkled with grated parmesan or pecorino. If unavailable, use dried breadcrumbs.

Remove baking paper carefully, roll up with the towel, and leave to cool.

FILLING

1 large onion, chopped	About 8 green olives, chopped
1 red bell pepper, seeded	1–2 cloves garlic, smashed
and chopped	and chopped
oil for frying	250 g crème fraîche (or
Salt or seasoning salt	creamed cottage cheese)

While the roulade bakes, fry the onion and bell pepper in oil until soft. Season to taste. Take off heat and stir in the olives, garlic and crème fraîche or cottage cheese. Unroll the roulade, spread with filling, and roll up again. It's best served warm, but do not overheat.

To serve: Slice – you could use one or two tins of flavoured chopped tomatoes, heat, add that indispensable half a teaspoon of sugar, season with ground black pepper and basil, and serve as a sauce.

* If vegetarians are not around, I like to fry 125 g chopped bacon with the onion and pepper as well.

Biltong Mousse

There aren't many recipes utilising this South African perennial.
This should serve four to six as a starter.

15 ml gelatine softened in 65 ml water	3 ml ground coriander
	15 ml flour
125 ml beef stock, preferably made with beef stock powder	125 ml milk
	2 large eggs, separated
100 g finely grated biltong	45 ml cream

Dissolve the gelatine in the water, add to the stock, and simmer while stirring, so that the gelatine dissolves. Add the biltong and coriander. With a wire whisk, whisk the flour into the milk, and heat in a small pot while stirring. When it boils and thickens, cook for a minute, then remove from the heat. Cool for 30 seconds or so and whisk in the egg yolks. Add this to the biltong mixture and combine well. Chill the mixture until it thickens slightly. While it chills, whisk the egg whites until stiff and whisk the cream as well. Add both to the biltong mixture. (It should not need salt due to the biltong and salty stock, but do taste first.) Pour into a suitable oiled mould or small bread tin, and leave in the fridge to set.

Fill a plate with shredded lettuce and turn out the mousse. Garnish with a few nasturtiums for colour. Serve with melba toast or thin toast triangles.

Tannie Joubert's Chocolate Cake

This was the first recipe which really worked for me at Gauteng's altitude. And it works at sea level as well. This is the type of simplicity we're always looking for. I have not metricated her recipe because I prefer to write it as she gave it to me.

1⅓ cups sugar

1½ cups flour

⅓ cup butter (this is about 85 ml or 5 tablespoons + 2 teaspoons)

3 eggs

½ cup milk

3 teaspoons baking powder

Pinch of salt

3 tablespoons cocoa powder

1 teaspoon vanilla essence

Preheat oven to 180 °C. Put everything in a mixing bowl and whisk well for 3 minutes. Bake for 25 minutes.

Those are her instructions. The baking time sounds a bit short, so test with a skewer first.

Tannie Joubert's Sponge Cake

1½ cups sugar

4 eggs

¼ cup butter (about 4 generous tablespoons)

1 cup milk

2 cups flour

4 teaspoons baking powder

Pinch of salt

2 teaspoons vanilla essence

Preheat oven to 180 °C. Beat sugar and eggs for 10 minutes. Melt the butter in the milk; bring to boiling and remove from heat. Sift dry ingredients over egg-sugar mixture. Add the hot milk-butter mixture. Add vanilla. Fold all in well and bake for about 45 minutes.

Please note that the cake tins would without a doubt have to be greased well and the oven has to be at the correct temperature when the cake is put in. Older, experienced cooks did not think it necessary to explain every step – or even put the ingredients in the order used! Her instructions were extremely brief. Creaming butter or eggs and sugar is a job I hate. You could substitute castor sugar for granulated, which makes the job easier. Use an electric mixer and cream it until it is pale and thick.

CHAPTER 22

~ FATE STRIKES ~

... ALL OUR PLEASANT HAUNTS OF EARTHLY LOVE
ARE NURSERIES TO THOSE GARDENS OF THE AIR;
AND HIS FAR-DARTING EYE, WITH STARRY BEAM,
WATCHING THE GROWING OF HIS TREASURES THERE.
WE CALL THEM OURS, O'ERWEPT WITH SELFISH TEARS,
O'ERWATCHED WITH RESTLESS LONGINGS NIGHT AND DAY;
FORGETFUL OF THE HIGH, MYSTERIOUS RIGHT
HE HOLDS TO BEAR OUR CHERISHED PLANTS AWAY.

Harriet Beecher Stowe

Then the year began which was to be the watershed of our lives.

The strangest emotion held me in its grip on the first day: I feared this new year. This was an alien awareness for me, as I had never given much thought to the end or beginning of any year. I had never made a New Year's resolution in my life, and I was always pleased when the festivities and holidays were over and we could get on with life.

As that year progressed into February, March, April, my vague anxiety deepened and became hard to handle. I told no one, because I wondered if I were descending into depression. But it wasn't quite depression. It was an indefinable sense of threat, of doom.

With both children now at school until 2 p.m, I was a fulltime freelance journalist for several publications. I was also still food editor of *Darling*. I hardly had time for such strange afflictions. But I was now constantly worried about my children, for no reason. In the morning when I dropped them off at school and drove to the magazine offices in End Street, I was petrified with fear ... of what? I didn't know. One senseless thought recurred during those early mornings behind the wheel of my car: should the four of us be so far apart every day, in such dangerous and unpredictable times?

It made no sense. It was not a time of crime and hijacking yet. The kids were safe at school. And yet, and yet ... I only felt better when night fell and the four of us were all safely at home again, and would be for the next twelve hours or so.

There was obviously something very wrong with me. I was deeply miserable and the constant anxiety was like a fist clamping my stomach. Yet I did not seek professional help, because I had nothing to tell a psychiatrist. There were no personal problems to probe, or long-held childhood phobias to unearth. I was happily married, we lived in a beautiful house in a pretty, secluded suburb. As a family we were complete. Daniel and I adored our boys. We were not struggling financially any more. We had a wide circle of friends. On the surface, life was just fine and I was doing a job I loved. And when I thought of all this, trying to count my blessings, Natalie's words of Christmas Eve would come back to haunt me: "It's almost too perfect." Would life exact some retribution; even out things a little? But what?

During our holiday in Keurboomstrand during the April of that year we had the best seaside weather we had ever experienced. Every day dawned warm and pleasant, without harsh winds. Daily we explored the coast at low tide. The children fished and swam. There was never a cloud in the sky. Even the unnaturally perfect weather was like a premonition.

There was a moment during that holiday which I will never forget for as long as I live.

It was just another gorgeous blue and gold day, and I stood on one of the beaches watching the boys and Daniel playing in the waves. I looked across the windless deep blue sea, and suddenly an odd and very unpleasant feeling of absolute desolation and abandonment overcame me.

A foreboding surfaced like a black sliver of ice from a dark pool: that this might be the last time I'll ever stand here, like this, in this paradisiacal perfection. All this beauty, this happiness, might never happen again.

In those moments I felt wholly alienated from the glorious scenery and my frolicking family, as if I stood on a lonely island on a foreign planet, and all I saw before me was no more than a dream. And I was terribly, dreadfully afraid.

We returned to Johannesburg. I could not concentrate properly any more on the mundane, rather superficial world of interviews, articles, food and recipes. I lived on in my fog of constant inexplicable anxiety. I went for an annual gynae check-up, and to my own consternation I found myself confiding in this man about my state of mind. "It's like a black cloud hovering above my head," I explained in tears.

"It's strange …" he said as he watched me from across his desk. "You are so down to earth. I would not associate depression or such needless fears with you … You should talk to a clinical psychologist," he suggested. I never got that far.

On a bright and sunny Sunday morning in July, during the school holidays, Danny rode his bicycle out of the garage and straight into an oncoming motorcycle.

He never stood a chance. It was long before kids wore helmets when cycling. The head wounds he sustained were fatal.

Our unimaginably beloved child was dead less than two weeks before his tenth birthday.

There is no need to go into the aftermath. For weeks we were supported and fed and kept alive by our wonderful circle of friends, family and aquaintances. People went far beyond the call of friendship or duty to try and help, to be there for us.

Then there were, inevitably, the people who probably meant well but had no clue how to deal with our loss and only added to our grief and confusion. "Have another baby," some said, as if a child can be replaced like a broken toy. "God gave his only begotten son …" one old lady lectured. But we were not God! "I always pray for my children's safety," a friend said, as if implying we hadn't prayed enough …

The school grieved. Danny's rowdy friends were suddenly silent, sad little people, brought into contact with death too soon, too soon.

Stephen, who had adored his brother, could hardly comprehend the tragedy that had befallen us. He threw tantrums at God. He screamed at Jesus that he wanted his brother back, that no one had the right to take his brother away from him. And his father and mother had turned into hollow people, with so little to give, so little solace to offer him except the warmth of our arms.

I finished a few half-written articles and resigned as food editor. Mary had to rewrite my last column, in which I said good-bye to the readers. It was that badly written. I stopped working. I needed every gram of energy just to keep existing and to keep the remnants of my family together. If it hadn't been for Stephen I'd have committed suicide.

Maybe Daniel felt the same. A husband and wife, no matter how close, often cannot communicate after such an indescribable sorrow. It is too hard. If we discussed Danny's death, I thought, if we even mentioned the terrible lightless abyss we'd entered, we would start screaming into the Universe, become one enormous scream of pain which could not be stopped.

How obliviously we had lived before, with an almost arrogant if subconscious faith that we are specially blessed, and that we always will be. Now, God had deserted us. We had prayed daily for protection, for angels to watch over our precious sons, the two miracles we had somehow brought into being. And still God had struck at us like a cobra, with deadly accuracy.

For the first time we knew for certain that the lives we lead came with no guarantees. That to be born is to be plunged into uncertainty. I would be fearful for evermore, now that I believed life was no more than random chaos.

As I had had various psychic experiences in my life, I knew there was more to life than three dimensions and final oblit-eration. I began to read up everything on life after death. Some books I rejected instinctively. Others, I felt, told the truth. I went to see psychics. They were helpful, reassuring me that there really was a Hereafter; that it was "his time to go". That he was only meant "to be on this earth plane for a short while". I conveyed their messages of faint hope to Danny and Stephen. And there were signs and portents that Danny was alive in another dimension; that sometimes he was close to us. But of course we wanted him with us, back here, on this incredibly harsh planet ...

About nine months after Danny's death we decided that a break was necessary. We had to get away for a while.

~

CHAPTER 23

～ INTERLUDE ～

THE CITY'S ALL A-SHINING
BENEATH A FICKLE SUN,
A GAY YOUNG WIND'S A-BLOWING,
THE LITTLE SHOWER IS DONE.
BUT THE RAINDROPS STILL ARE CLINGING
AND FALLING ONE BY ONE –
OH IT'S PARIS, IT'S PARIS,
AND SPRINGTIME HAS BEGUN.

Sara Teasdale

Europe, like a beautiful woman, could be said to be overexposed. Her myriad attractions are displayed so often in the media and films that it is all too easy to imagine you have almost been there; seen that; it's all old hat. That's what I thought too. But nothing could have prepared me for the impact Europe had on me.

This was my first overseas trip, yet, weary of this world and of sadness, I expected to be disappointed.

But as we left Charles de Gaulle airport in a taxi, I suddenly became aware that I was breathing in unfamiliar air, with a smell unlike that of Africa. I sensed a totally new atmosphere. Out of the blue I had a completely irrational thought: *I've come home ...*

I stared out silently at utilitarian buildings on the outskirts of Paris, then with greater curiosity as the lovely old city revealed more of itself. I could not even speak French apart from a few words and phrases recalled from French I at university, two decades ago. Yet I felt convinced that this was some kind of homecoming to ancient roots.

Daniel would be attending a business conference in Paris for a week, and for that week we were staying in a fancy hotel paid for by his firm.

April in Paris! What a strange sensation it was to feel my spirits lifting. As we sped to the hotel, I caught my breath when we passed the beautiful Arc de Triomphe: bigger, whiter, and more imposing than I had imagined. Suddenly it was good, oh so good, to be in an entirely new environment for a while.

From the eleventh floor windows of our hotel room we had views towards the Bois de Bologne, towards the Sacre Coeur, towards landmarks I did not recognise. I went from one window to the other, over-excited, like a teenager.

Later, Daniel got me a *Carte d'Orange* for the Métro, a Métro map and a street map of Paris. I was set. I would explore on my own, while he, poor thing, had to dress in a suit for six days and sit in a conference hall.

"I think I lived here in a former life," I said.

Daniel grinned. "Maybe it's racial memory: French Huguenot forefathers!"

The remnants of our small family were still three fragile porcelain figures which had been shattered into fragments and clumsily glued up again. Our lives were brittle and slippery as if we had little grip left on reality and could at any moment plunge downwards into some black abyss.

A few days ago Daniel and I had stood at Johannesburg International airport watching a plane roaring down a runway, lifting, lifting, growing smaller. We were the bravest people in the world: Stephen, eight, was on that plane to Cape Town, to go and stay with my parents in the Hex Valley while we were overseas. With terror beyond words I watched that clumsy plane lumbering into the air and growing smaller and smaller – a frail and fallible machine carrying away our only remaining child, the beautiful boy with his clear blue eyes, pink cheeks and sturdy body. Please keep him safe, Jesus, I had prayed while watching that plane, and then recalled that I had no faith left anyway, and I knew now that life was as ephemeral as a soap bubble.

At least grandpa and granny would look after him well, and for a while he, too, would be away from everything that reminded him of Danny. They would spoil him with love and indulgence, exactly what he needed now.

As I walked the streets of Paris alone, I became ever more entranced by this city. I did not suddenly become a whole person – myself as I used to be – nor did my dark companion, grief, disappear. Neither would it happen for Daniel. Nothing was ever going to be the same again. But Paris was good to me.

In the coolness of one early morning, after leaving a Métro station and blindly walking, I discovered my first food market: temporary stalls as well as permanent little holes-in-the-wall shops. I wandered, enchanted, through a cornucopia of food riches such as I had never seen. As I walked and marvelled I wished fervently that I, too, could shop at the wonderful stalls, and cook a French meal.

For the first time in nine months I found joy again in these everyday things. I took photographs: neat stacks of perfect red tomatoes, of huge artichokes (did they really grow to such a size?), of barrels of all kinds of fresh produce. A tiny shop which could barely accommodate two people at the same time had shelves stacked with cheeses almost up to the ceiling, a paradise of cheese! Next door was a *boucherie*, a butchery, but like none I've ever encountered in my far-off country. The meats were delicate, cool arrangements of thin slices of breast of *dinde* – turkey – neat portions of rabbit, goose, duck breasts, pale escalopes of veal. The famous chickens from Bresse lay rather indelicately with their long, ticketed legs in the air. All the meat was so beautifully cut and cleanly arranged that the usual yuck-and-blood factor of a butchery was totally absent; this *boucherie* was a place of refinement, even elegance.

Next door was a small wine shop, then a *boulangerie* from which billowed clouds of fresh-bread fragrance. It was crowded, and in picture-postcard style people were emerging with long *baguettes* in bags and under their arms. A *charcuterie* breathed out the aroma of the smoked meats and sausages it sold: Parma hams hung like a fat, incongruous curtain above the door.

The fish and seafood amazed me even more. Paris is not on the sea but on the Seine, yet even fish like mackerel, which spoils so quickly, was laid out here, still a shimmering blue-green, as if plucked from the ocean a moment ago. On a plate of crushed ice an artful arrangement of seafoods gleamed, washed by a recent wave, surely: oysters, shrimps, langoustines, prickly sea urchins, scallops, shellfish, crabs … How did the French do it? I do not know to this day.

The women, many elderly and dressed in black, slowly moved from stall to shop to stall with their huge carry-bags. They argued with stallholders: what they bought, it was clear, should be nothing less than perfect. It was evident that they planned their meals as they shopped, according to what was best and freshest that day, or in keeping with what they felt like preparing. How I envied them.

The *pâtisseries* of Paris were endlessly seductive. I would buy a delicious lemon or cherry tart, or a slice of dense chestnut cake, and eat it on the street like Parisians do. Or I sank down, exhausted by kilometres of walking, at a sidewalk café and ordered black coffee and a slice of the *tarte du jour*, which could be apple or apricot or berry or plum.

My husband's Swiss colleagues invited us to dinner at a five-star restaurant. I remember nothing about the meal except that we had oysters as a starter. The oysters were very good indeed, but no better than our own Knysna oysters. For the rest, I concentrated so hard on being a good guest and battling to converse in my university German, that the food was secondary. Our hosts were horrified that I hadn't been to a single tourist attraction yet.

"You must not miss the Louvre!" they urged. "And Montmartre, and Napoleon's grave …" But this first time in Paris I skipped all those well-known places, needing to sense the spirit of place: to absorb the atmosphere and watch the people.

One lovely morning I stood on the ancient Pont Neuf with my hands on the blackened stone and dreamily watched the *bateaux mouches* at anchor downriver and the spires of Notre Dame on its island. Suddenly anguish and pain washed over me and guilt enveloped me like a grey blanket. Danny, perhaps a tall, dark-eyed young man then, would never stand here. He would never wander with a backpack down the maze of streets near the Sorbonne, drink a beer at a sidewalk café, or sleep in a backpackers' inn with his friends. How dared I enjoy all this, when my child was dead … The world dimmed.

No, no, Danny was in a better place now. To that conviction we must cling: it was inconceivable that his bright spirit, his old soul, could be anything but joyously alive in some unseen Paradise …

I walked on, crossing the old bridge. I had to go on.

The mellifluous tongue I heard around me made me wish fervently that I could strike up a conversation and ask questions: where do you live? Where do you shop? Or: may I see your kitchen? May I watch you cook?

Sometimes older people were rude to me when I spoke English, and turned their backs on me. "Speak Afrikaans," my husband advised, and from then on I relied on sign language and Afrikaans, and found the Parisians somewhat friendlier, because they thought I was from a corner of the Netherlands or Scandinavia.

After Daniel's conference was over we left for the southern parts of France on the TGV, the bullet train, then hired a car and meandered.

Daniel and I enjoyed this travelling together; it was a new experience for both of us. His previous trips had consisted of work, work, and no play. On the train carrying us down to Avignon we laughed out loud, once again, at something that Stephen had told us over the phone while we were in Paris.

Before he left on the plane for Cape Town, Daniel had buoyed up Stephen's spirits by telling him that drinks and snacks would be served free on the plane and that, although he would be under the care of an air hostess, he would be travelling "as an adult", all by himself.

Stephen was indignant: "I sat with other boys and girls in the front of the plane," he told us. "And as soon as the plane was waaaay up, the nice *tannie* came with a trolley and asked what we would like to drink. I asked for a Castle, and she laughed at me and gave me a Coke! Daddy, that was unfair! You said I'd be an adult up there!"

Our younger son who had to bear the unbearable with us was never far from our thoughts. We'd taken him out of school so he could go and stay with my parents. He was a highly intelligent little boy, and we had no qualms about doing what we felt was right for him at that time.

The other child … we did not discuss him yet. We never could open our hearts to each other about Danny's death anyway: I think it would have torn us apart; it might have shattered our fragile glued-together selves. It was better to *hou die blink kant bo* – and bolster each other up. Each knew, anyway, what the other was feeling.

The antiquity I saw everywhere in France, and which is so commonplace for Europeans, was hard for me to grasp. In our country antiquity is of recent date: here we seemed to be drawn back constantly into the long tunnel of time: medieval towers and arches, Roman ruins, stone walls a metre deep. Some ancient buildings along cobbled alleyways seemed to flow into one another. And in these stone fortresses people were living. Dim lights glowed in rooms glimpsed through narrow, secretive windows. Cats lay sleeping on worn stone steps. Flowerpots overflowed with red and pink geraniums and impatiens.

I kept touching these walls and sensing warmth, cold, joy, sorrow – a multitude of human emotions. Centuries of living had soaked into the ancient stone and left perceptible imprints.

It struck me then how small our lives were, how insignificant – really no more than candles in the wind – when considered in the context of all those countless centuries which had gone before and vanished into the mists. So the bitter thought rose like bile, that our mourning for one little life cut short was almost laughable compared to the immense human drama which stretched back into infinity.

"Yes," Daniel said quietly as I voiced this cynical thought at last, "but I still believe each life is precious and has purpose and design. And things happen for a reason … which we don't understand now." And he took my hand as we wandered on in silence.

Ever since our child died I'd been thinking back to that evening in Pretoriuskop in the Kruger Park, when I realised that I was pregnant again. Danny was barely a year old. I'd cried, and thrown myself on the bed in the hut, and ranted. I didn't want that baby. It was all so unfair! Daniel tried to console me, to no effect. I was no Earth Mother. I wanted only Danny!

But, I realised now, God, fate, karma – call it what you will – knew what it was doing. If Stephen hadn't been conceived unintentionally, we might easily have decided to stop at one child. And then? Where would we have been now, without our little blue-eyed blonde to keep us going, reminding us constantly how important it was to make his life as happy and secure as possible? Now he was the one still giving our life purpose.

This holiday was doing us good, even if our reality was overlain with a gossamer veil of sadness which never quite lifted. Still, we were able to laugh again, to experience moments of amusement and pleasure which hadn't seemed possible before.

A tattered red-eyed vagabond swayed drunkenly before us in a street and held out his hand for money. Daniel refused, and with some effort the man pulled himself up straight. In perfect, indignant German he told us that he was, in fact, a noble gentleman from Bonn who was travelling at the moment, a well-to-do gentleman, in need of a temporary helping hand, and we should respect that fact. He was standing right in front of a liquor shop. We moved away to chuckle where he could not hear us.

In Grasse in a decrepit hotel owned by three old biddies in black we were highly amused at the way they bickered shrilly and constantly amongst themselves, not caring whether their guests heard. They looked exactly like three small, bowed witches. Even a guest simply asking for his coffee at *petit dejeuner* could set off a howling quarrel in the kitchen. Poor little old ladies. They might have been three sisters caught in an impossible situation, we mused. Perhaps they had inherited the hotel from their father; it was their only source of income and although they hated one another, they had to carry on. Who knows?

Of course my interest in food, which had been dormant for a long time, had perked up again in Paris, and now with all the walking and exploring we did, we really enjoyed our food. France does not seem to suffer inferior produce – somehow a plain piece of roast chicken tastes better in France than anywhere else in the world. But of course you can also eat as badly in France as in a *platteland* café in South Africa. It's just that it doesn't happen often.

We paid for ourselves, so of necessity we stayed in fairly cheap hotels and ate at sidewalk cafés: plates of *moules marinière* with fresh bread, a glorious roast chicken with a stuffing of ricotta and spinach, a long *brochette* or skewer of grilled seafood over rice, bowls of brown, deeply flavourful Niçoise fish soup with aïoli …

One Sunday at midday we could not get a table in the only small restaurant in the tiny hill hamlet where we were staying. It was already full to overflowing. Spying a small deli which was about to close, I rushed in to see if there was anything left to eat. On a tray on the counter some round, white little cheeses rested in puddles of whey. Oh, the lady told me, they're delicious! So fresh! I bought two of the ramekin-sized cheeses which she wrapped in butter paper. I arrived triumphantly in our bedroom with our lunch. Daniel opened a bottle of Rhône wine. Cheese and wine – a French feast, *n'est ce pas*? Unfortunately not. The cheese turned out to be very, very rustic goat cheeses, acidic, smelling and tasting overpoweringly of billygoat. I hadn't noticed this in the shop. We could not bring ourselves to eat it after a first, tentative bite. And the wine was undrinkable, so dry and astringent that it puckered our mouths. Oh well … no Sunday dinner that day.

We were sitting at a table in a small cobbled plaza, having a glass of wine. I didn't want to go home. Daniel and I had become closer than we had been for nine months, and we'd been together for twenty-four hours each day: back home he would vanish to his office again in the mornings and return after dark.

I put my elbows on the table and rested my head in my hands. Enviously, I thought of the beautiful girl we'd spoken to a few days before, in her pre-medieval working room in Roquebrune. The room was cool and shadowy, and she sat there, serenely making lovely things from silk. I had bought a scarf from her. On the outside, the structure in which she lived and worked seemed to have no beginning and no end: a colossal stone edifice which undulated up cobbled steps. It was obviously somehow divided into apartments, because it had doors with numbers or names. It looked like something from a fairy story.

Into my mind a picture flashed: living simply in a place exactly like that, me doing pottery for a living while Daniel had an unde-manding office job. I would shop at a fresh-produce market every day, learn to speak French fluently and to make the wonderful Provençal dishes. We'd also acquire a fat cat and terracotta pots spilling over with geraniums. I told Daniel what I was thinking.

"Just think how terrible the plumbing must be in those ancient buildings!" he smiled.

"Trust you to shatter my illusions ..." But they had been shattered already by the disturbing realisation that both boys had momentarily been with me in this dream.

We caught a plane back to South Africa from Nice airport. "We'll come back," Daniel consoled me as the plane climbed into the navy blue night. "We will come back and see the rest of Europe too."

His words were small comfort to me early the next morning when the yellowing African veld appeared below us and the vacuum in our lives struck us anew. Yet, during this holiday in France some of the icicles in our hearts had, perhaps, melted.

Like all famous cuisines of the world, Provençal cooking arose out of poverty, out of "making do". Which they did, magnificently. It is a healthy cuisine of fish, garlic, olives, olive oil, onions, peppers, tomatoes. Herbs grow wild in the hills. In times long past truffles were commonplace; these days they are scarce and extremely expensive. Once I had an omelette with bits of truffle in it, but I honestly could not really taste it. Maybe there wasn't enough of it, or maybe it wasn't a very potent truffle which was used. I still don't know how a truffle smells or tastes.

To give Provençal recipes here would be presumptuous. So many wonderful cookbooks have already been written about this cuisine of the sun, and anyway, we do not always have the same products at hand.

∼

Quiche Lorraine

Not Provençal, but easier to make here and always delicious …
Like all classic French recipes there are many different convictions
on how a real Quiche Lorraine should or should not be made.
One famous cookbook writer, Elizabeth Scotto, states firmly that
cheese is never included in the traditional quiche Lorraine from the
Alsace-Lorraine region of France. Others, even a book with "secret"
recipes from Michelin-starred restaurants, do include Gruyère, the
cheese associated with this delicious first course.

Years after the first Paris visit we found ourselves in a restaurant
in Nancy, in the province of Lorraine, aptly called La Table
Lorraine. Naturally I had to have Quiche Lorraine, and it was the
best I've ever tasted. I asked the owner, a charming Frenchwoman,
for her recipe, and she gave it willingly … but in fast, spoken
French. I thanked her profusely for her generosity, but didn't quite
follow her quick speech, alas.

This recipe was once served at a restaurant in Paris' 7th
arrondissement and it appeals to me because of its decadent richness.

You'll need a flan dish of about 28 cm in diameter and at least
4 cm deep, or another appropriate oven dish.

SHORTCRUST PASTRY
200 g sifted flour (weighed before sifting)

5 ml salt

125 g unsalted butter

1 egg yolk

Ice water

Put the sifted flour, salt and butter into a processor (otherwise use your fingers) and process until the mixture is "sandy" in texture. Add the egg yolk and whizz. If too stiff, add a tiny bit of icy cold water. Be careful; it's easy to add too much. Process: it should form a compact ball which is not wet, but will not flake off either. Turn out, form into a ball, cover lightly and leave in the fridge for at least 1 hour.

FILLING

150 g Gruyère cheese, cut into tiny bits

150 g good bacon, chopped and fried until done but not hard

8 egg yolks

500 ml thick cream

About 7 ml salt

5 ml freshly ground black pepper

About 5 ml freshly grated nutmeg

Preheat oven to 190 °C. Roll out the pastry to a 4 mm thickness, and line the flan tin, scalloping the edges. Prick the pastry lightly. Sprinkle the cheese and bacon on the pastry, pressing them in very lightly, just so they don't roll around.

Beat the egg yolks, cream, salt, pepper and nutmeg together for 2–3 minutes with a wire whisk. When the oven reaches the correct heat, put the prepared pastry on a baking rack or tin and keep the tin half out of the oven. Now pour the cream mixture carefully into the tart without handling the tin, and slide the rack back into the oven. If you feel you have too much cream mixture, and it might cook over, don't use it all.

Bake for 45 minutes, lowering the heat to about 170 °C after 20 minutes. The baking time is very approximate, depending on the depth of your container and your oven. When done, the quiche should be golden turning to pale brown on top, and puffy.

Serve warm, in thin slices – it's rich, so should serve eight or more people as a starter.

The Provençal and Italian way of dipping fresh bread into fruity olive oil is one that appeals to me.

This idea is so simple that it is merely a suggestion which works, not a recipe. Tapenade, the classic Provençal olive spread, can be a little strong for some tastes, but people always like this bread dip.

Chop up pitted black Calamata olives, add a little finely chopped garlic and maybe, as they say, a *soupçon* of finely chopped parsley. Put in a small bowl and add enough good, fruity virgin olive oil to make a bowl of dip. Serve with any fresh bread, without butter, as a dip-cum-spread.

This is great when served alongside a thick, plain vegetable soup in winter.

CHAPTER 24

~ LIFE GOES ON ~

SO NATURE DEALS WITH US, AND TAKES AWAY
OUR PLAYTHINGS ONE BY ONE, AND BY THE HAND
LEADS US TO REST SO GENTLY, THAT WE GO
SCARCE KNOWING IF WE WISH TO GO OR STAY,
BEING TOO FULL OF SLEEP TO UNDERSTAND
HOW FAR THE UNKNOWN TRANSCENDS THE WHAT WE KNOW.

Henry Wadsworth Longfellow

A close, loving family who loses a child is never the same again. We would always carry with us, like a weight, our burden of longing and emptiness. People who lose a child do not "get over" it. They merely learn to live with it because they have no other choice. Eventually time softens the grief, but time does not "heal all wounds".

When making dinner I often took out four plates, four forks and knives … and then remembered. It was a stab in the heart every time. When the day was drawing in, when Stephen came in from playing with his friends, dirty as little boys are at the end of a day, the chasm created by Danny's absence struck home anew.

Just as kitchens were the solace of my earlier days, now the daily ritual of the evening dinner was the exact moment when our loss was felt the keenest. This was the time of day when we all came home, when we reassembled as a family. But one would never come back again, grubby, hungry, and with homework not yet done.

As far as we could, we pretended to each other that we were okay. Daniel and I cried apart, alone, as we could not offer each other much comfort. Stephen, at times, still shrieked out his anger at, he believed, an unfair God or Fate who had taken his brother from him.

But we still had our guardian angels, I suppose, who tried to help. I threw myself into a totally extreme passion for French food. This was, of course, ridiculous, but it was part of coping. I bought French cookbooks and French coffee-table books, over which I pored.

Daniel absorbed himself in his job with renewed vigour, because for those twelve hours or more a day when he worked, he didn't have much time for reflection. I enrolled for a year's course in French at Rand Afrikaans University. Never again would I set foot in France without at least knowing how to ask a few basic questions! The lecturer was excellent. I cared not one whit about being in a class with eighteen-year-olds: I enjoyed it. The next year I enrolled for an Honours degree in Afrikaans through UNISA. That same year I was asked to come and help out as substitute lecturer at the Johannesburg College of Education.

Other women's kitchens were now more comforting than my own. One of my best friends from university days, Lindie, lived in an unconventional rondavel house, with round rooms, which she'd furnished very artistically. I loved her kitchen. It was huge and circular, with a broad counter on one side and a "sitting corner" for lounging lazily. It opened onto a haphazard, charming garden area with a perspex roof where they held braais. Lindie had two kids and a hardworking husband, and she was also a lecturer at a college. Her kitchen was a warm and cosy space where all her friends congregated.

When microwave ovens were the new rage, Lindie went through a stage of microwave enthusiasm, when she microwaved everything. This was the one single thing we disagreed about. I disliked microwave ovens except for defrosting, heating food if I was in a hurry, and melting stuff like chocolate and butter. Lindie made cakes in her microwave. They were wonderful while still warm, but by the next day they were heavy and dry. She said I was trashing one of the wonders of the modern world.

Friends and kitchens and tea and women talk … I often fled to one of those friends, who opened their doors, who said, "Come with me and we'll make some tea." Or coffee. The sympathy and empathy were always implicit in the warm invitations. And that would bring Ouma Sannie to mind, and Ouma Greta, and my mom's cream puff kitchen. And I would think: all over this enormous city, women of all skin colours are sharing confidences, laughing, crying, over endless cups of tea and coffee, in all sorts of kitchens …

We should pity men: they have pals, acquaintances, drinking buddies in impersonal bars. They do not cry on a buddy's shoulder. They do not pour out their troubles. They keep up their manly fronts and have a beer or a whisky and slap one another on the shoulders, even when their hearts are breaking. Some might be great cooks, but they are not kitchen people. Men do not huddle around a kitchen table discussing other men, or lean with their elbows on kitchen counters sniffing sorrows into tissues.

About four years after Danny's death, a serendipitous thing happened. Out of the blue Daniel's aunt phoned him from St Francis Bay, where they'd retired to. She and her husband wanted to go away for three weeks in June, which would be during our winter school holidays. She had three cats. Didn't we want to come and house-sit for them, and have a holiday at the same time?

Did we! We immediately agreed, studied a road map, and we roped in Johnny, a friend of Stephen's from across the street, to go with us. St Francis Bay was, we discovered, some way off the N2 on the southeastern Cape coast. We'd never been to those parts.

It was winter, and I bought both kids waterproof windcheater jackets, in bright orange. It was not orange because it was my favourite colour, but because of my lingering insecurity: in that neon orange we would be able to spot the kids kilometres away on a beach or the rocks …

A bad gravel road ran the twenty-one kilometres from Humansdorp to St Francis Bay. And we were unprepared for the unspoilt beauty we found then: a bridge across a wide green river, and then a fairytale village of cosy white-walled, thatched-roof houses.

St Francis Bay at that time had one café-cum-shop. That, as I recall, was the sole commercial development. We loved that holiday. We played tennis on the courts next to the little shop. We swam and tried to find oysters; we didn't because we didn't know the right places to look for them. Like at Keurbooms, the Indian Ocean was warm enough for swimming in winter if the winds were not blowing. The kids loved the freedom of walking through the quiet little village to play on the beach. We adored the cats and once tried to surprise them with a supper of fresh *klipvis*, those small rock pool denizens we all fished for as children. But they obviously knew bad eating when they saw it, and only slapped the little fish around in short-lived amusement.

Often a momentous course of events in life is triggered by a small, insignificant incident.

One day it was rainy. I was reading a book. Daniel took Stephen and Johnny, and out of boredom and curiosity they drove the seven or so kilometres to the actual end of the gravel road which started in Humansdorp, and which for us had ended in St Francis Bay. But this road went further. It ended in a seaside hamlet named Cape St Francis.

When they returned, Daniel said with a laugh, "Good heavens, I've never seen an uglier place in my life!"

An ugly seaside village?

There was a very nice beach, though, Daniel said. And a lighthouse. "But the houses … some are shacks … a lifeless little place with one café, at the end of a forgotten road."

Intriguing. I had to see it.

A day or so later when the weather had cleared I took the car and drove to Cape St Francis by myself on the forested, shadowy road with its pools of rainwater.

At last the bush gave way and I could see the sea. To my right I glimpsed rocks: jagged palisades against which waves crashed quite spectacularly. Some nondescript houses hid among acacia bushes. Slowly I drove down the main street. Yes, the closed, shuttered beach houses were ugly – square, badly kept, with brown rust lines running down from metal windows. Then the street ended in a T-junction, right on the ocean.

A dreamy vista revealed itself here. Before me lay a small aquamarine bay. Across the bay, at the far end, a narrow stripe of white water indicated a rocky cape. To my left was an icing-sugar, sickle-shaped beach, empty of life. To the right, a few surfers rode smooth waves which rolled in evenly along a coast of flat rocks. And the crowning glory: there, on its rocky headland on my right, stood a tall and proud white lighthouse. Lighthouses fascinate me. They seem to me symbols of safety, warmth and protection.

I drove further along the seafront street, past the shuttered houses, and then further on, behind the low dunes of the long beach. Birds sang everywhere in the milkwoods, in the tangled trees and *fynbos*. Here and there were signs that a house was lived in year-round. Deep tranquillity hovered like a gossamer cloak over this entire place. The street ended abruptly against a wall of *fynbos* and yet more thick bushland, and as I stopped the car a graceful bushbuck stepped out of a thicket and glanced at the car as if it were an intruder, a curiosity. A *meerkat* sat up momentarily, peered at me, and shot off into the bushes. The sea whispered beyond the dunes.

"Please, it's my dream seaside village!" I said to Daniel. "It's something like Kleinmond when I was small. It's simple and quiet and undiscovered! Please, please, let's buy a stand there! It'll still be cheap!"

After a second, then a third look, Daniel realised how wrong he'd been to think it ugly, and the spell of the place fell on him too. We asked at the café, and found the village had one single property agent. Mr. Andresen was originally from Norway, and he had a fishing boat. Right from the start it was clear that he was far more interested in his fishing boat than in selling us a stand.

There were only four or five on the market. I wanted one on the sea. The only one available on the sea was perfect: it was where I'd first seen the waves crashing on the rocks. The locals called it "the Wild Side". The plot was dirt cheap. We put in an immediate offer, although Daniel said we didn't have money to build a house. I didn't care. We would have a small piece of soil we could build dreams on.

A few hours later the agent phoned us in St Francis Bay. The lady who owned the stand had pulled it off the market: she said it wasn't for sale after all. But we'll pay cash, Daniel offered. No dice.

I burst into tears.

We left for Johannesburg but detoured to Grahamstown to see the owner of the stand. She was a gracious old lady, a widow, but she explained, very reasonably, that the plot would go to her daughter, who had inherited almost nothing from her father's estate. She wanted her daughter to have that plot, as she realised it would increase in value with time. We left our address and phone number with her, but she wasn't really interested. There would be no sale.

Two years went by. I still lectured at the college. Stephen started high school. Daniel and I went overseas a few more times: we could now leave Stephen with friends or fly him down to Annie and her husband, who had a smallholding outside Port Elizabeth.

One afternoon the phone rang at home and I picked it up. It was the widow from Grahamstown. After we exchanged greetings, she came straight to the point. Were we still interested in that stand?

My heart stopped: "Of course we are," I said quietly.

"Well, that's why I phoned you. I'm selling it."

"How much do you want for it now?"

She named a price: it was now double what it was two years ago, but I wasn't fazed. I took details, and promised we'd phone her back as soon as possible. Then I phoned Daniel at his office.

"I don't care whether you beg, borrow or steal. But you must find the money, and we *must* have that stand."

Sometimes, never voicing it, we wondered: was Danny now one of our guardian angels? Did he want us to have this place by the sea? For there were many questions and no answers. Why did the old lady decide to sell, after explaining the situation to us years previously? Why did she go to the trouble of, I imagine, searching for our hastily scribbled names and phone number in Johannesburg? It would have been so much easier for her to simply hand it to a property agent. And even the price she asked …! When we went down soon after to have another look at our overgrown stand, someone from next door asked me what we had paid, and I told her. "But she'd *given* it to you!" she exclaimed.

So we had our perfect piece of soil on the sea. Three years later, when Stephen was in Standard Nine (now Grade Eleven) we had a small house built there. It had an open-plan living area with a kitchenette, and best of all, the main bedroom and its bathroom were upstairs and therefore private and out of earshot of rugby matches on TV and the chatter of Stephen's friends. The views were stupendous, and the seascape changed with the hours, the winds, the tides.

This small house was the best thing that had happened to us in years. Even my sister Annie was not far away: an hour's drive. And while we were up in Johannesburg, my ever-helpful brother-in-law Will came and planted a lawn for us on the sea side. The wonderful thing about this dream-come-true was that there was nothing except a footpath through the *fynbos* between the house and the sea. No road, no traffic …

I became a compulsive cleaner of this precious "sea-house" with its beige floor tiles and white surfaces on which every mark showed. Fortunately this obsession didn't last.

Stephen rediscovered his childhood love of angling. He would go off on his own with his rod and tackle to the wild, deserted coast west of Cape St Francis. I would worry, of course … one unexpected wave, one slip of a foot … My imagination could conjure up all kinds of mishaps for our only surviving child, now over six foot tall and due to go to university the next year.

But I believe those quiet hours on the lonely rocks meant a lot to Stephen. He learnt to like his own company, and to think and meditate on things, which he had no time for in Johannesburg, in the busy last year of school.

We swam, we gathered redbait, we walked, we entertained guests. Once Stephen was at university, there was never a shortage of friends who came with him; for whom we had to find a place to put down their sleeping bags.

The inevitable trek back to Johannesburg, and for Stephen back to Stellenbosch, was undertaken with a certain melancholy. We loved our Johannesburg house, our jobs, our friends … but there was something about this house, this area, which was very difficult to leave behind for another three or six months.

"I want to retire in a year's time," Daniel announced out of the blue several years later, on a dull July day in Johannesburg. "I'm *gatvol*. I know it's a few years too early, but I want to get out of this city. I am tired of the frustrations at work. Would you like to go live in the beach house?"

I was jubilant.

We warned Thandi: she had three kids by then, and was living in Alexandra with her husband and family. She would need to look for another job, but at least she'd have a full year to do that, and I was willing to place ads in the papers, but she wasn't interested. She was not enamoured with our plans at all. She made no move to find another job. One day in the kitchen, when I was a captive audience with my hands in a bowl of batter, she came up with a kind of Custer's Last Stand.

"There is a woman here in Johannesburg," she informed me in a deadpan voice, "who worked, just like me, for a family for many years. They also retired … and they left her the house, and everything in it."

"Thandi!" I exclaimed, "that can't possibly be true! A house is one's greatest investment! Only billionaires can afford to give houses away!"

She shrugged her shoulders and ignored me for the rest of the day. The urban legend was too attractive not to cling to.

By this time Stephen was a fully fledged chartered accountant, working in Cape Town for an international auditing firm. Our small nest had been empty for several years.

At the time it had been quite a battle for us to decide to which university he should go. We took him to different campuses to have a look, but no northern university appealed to him. Daniel then made the decision: "I want this child out of cities. He's going to Stellenbosch."

Stephen was aghast: now we were rejecting him! How could we even think of sending him so far away: the Western Cape was practically a foreign country! But the decision had been made. He was going to our *alma mater*.

In all the photographs taken in Stellenbosch that first time we took him there, he is either scowling or looking bitterly unhappy. After a few days of seeing old friends and revisiting old haunts, we left Stephen at his university hostel and left for home.

Not that I was particularly happy that my child was now so far away. It was hard to refrain from phoning daily. I still retained all my old insecurities. If he had a cold, if he failed to phone at an appointed time, I panicked.

But surprise, surprise: after a mere six months as a student in Stellenbosch he informed us that was never going to live in the Transvaal again. He'd fallen in love with the Boland, and he was enjoying every moment.

I myself had been in a new phase of my life by then. After a ten-year stint at the Johannesburg College of Education as substitute or part-time lecturer in Afrikaans, I'd been writing. Writing novels.

Ever since my teens in the Hex Valley I'd been walking around with an idea for a novel, the germ of a plot, in my head. It had no real shape or form, but it centred around a Coloured girl who had been my friend into my high school years. So I started writing that first novel when Stephen was a student and I had time to myself. It was, I found, hard, lonely work. And I had to exchange a trusty electric typewriter for a computer. I cried and cursed a lot at that computer. By the time we finally left Johannesburg, however, my fourth novel came out, and I was working on a fifth one.

We left Johannesburg with few regrets. One regret was having to leave Daniel's father behind. He was very old now and in precarious health. Dear Ma had died some years earlier. Dad lived in a secure townhouse, and an old acquaintance of Ma, a widow of long standing, was his housekeeper-cum-nurse, so he was in good hands, but still … Fortunately John and Hayley, who had retired to the Limpopo farm, still kept a townhouse in Johannesburg and saw him often.

We wouldn't miss the city, where crime was increasing at a frightening rate. But we would miss those friends who still hung on, we would miss our wonderful neighbours, and we would miss, more than we thought possible, our beloved house. Well, one can't have everything, but it would have been wonderful if we could airlift that house and plonk it down on the seaside plot …

∼ REDBAIT ∼

Any experienced sea fisherman and angler will know redbait. They live in the intertidal zone and cling to the rocks like dark grey, ugly, shapeless mounds. To get at the bait, this hard, gelatinous mass must be sliced off the rocks or sliced open with a sharp knife to get at the soft, orangey "bait" inside.

Anglers will shudder at the thought of eating redbait. It starts to smell within hours of being out of its "shell", and the penetrating stink of *vrot* redbait is not easily forgotten, although fish seem like to like it.

As a matter of fact, fresh redbait has a delicious smell, reminiscent of a ripe mango. There is absolutely no reason why redbait can't be eaten unless one is allergic to shellfish. It seems to be very rich in iodine.

I have eaten redbait on the rocks – literally – as the menfolk collected it. With a squirt of lemon and maybe a bit of bread it's a delicious snack.

One would naturally use redbait as straight from the rocks as possible, so try the following and serve it with drinks. You'll find it really is a tasty, exotic snack.

Rinse the redbait to make sure there is no sand on it. Pat dry with kitchen paper. Mix a little flour with a pinch of seasoning salt and a generous amount of freshly-ground black pepper. Cut the redbait into strips or snack-size pieces.

Heat a mixture of butter and olive oil, or whatever you have – but butter is best. Roll each piece of redbait in the seasoned flour, and fry quickly on all sides. Don't think – and this goes for all seafood – that you should cook it to biltong. A few seconds in hot fat will be fine. Drain briefly on kitchen paper, put on a plate, and serve as is. It needs no more than a little black pepper and a few drops of lemon juice, and even that's superfluous.

∾

Batter for fish and seafood

You don't need to deep-fry if you feel like using batter. You do need a wide cooking utensil – a wok does nicely. The oil needs to be really hot, and it's best to do the fish pieces one by one, or not more than two at a time. With calamari and prawns one could put in a few at a time. But this is a game where a fast hand is needed …

I've adapted this recipe from other batter recipes. They all look vaguely the same, but still I had to experiment until I decided this one had it all.

Your fish and/or seafood must be absolutely dry, otherwise the batter will not stick. Coat the fish/seafood well. If it's a whole fish, pick it up firmly by the tail with thumb and forefinger, and slide it into the hot oil. Just be very careful and it should not splatter. Keep a slotted spoon handy, and a wooden spoon to help you turn the fish over. A mere fillet is done in seconds: keep the heat high, and as the batter browns and crisps, turn it over, just once, give the other side a few seconds to brown, remove with slotted spoon, and drain on crumpled kitchen paper. Keep warm in the oven at low heat (no more than 70 °C) and do not cover! It's best to serve it immediately. The batter is thin and crisp, and all the moisture and flavour of the fish is retained.

250 ml cake flour
7 ml Aromat or other seasoning salt
5 ml coarse black pepper
7 ml turmeric
45 ml melted butter
250 ml beer
1 large or 2 smaller egg whites

Mix the flour and seasonings. Add melted butter to the flour, then add the beer. (When you measure off the beer, tilt the measuring cup and pour it in slowly to prevent too much foam forming. Fill up to 250 ml with the fluid, disregarding the foam, which will rise higher than that.) Whizz with an electric mixer (or wire whisk) until smooth. With clean beaters, whip the egg white until very stiff. Fold into the batter. If you battle, use the wire whisk and whisk it in. Then use as explained above.

Sosaties

*Real sosaties are not kebabs, and don't even think of using beef.
Skewers of indifferent meat plonked into a second-rate curry sauce
are not sosaties.*

*Real sosaties are made with lamb or mutton, pork, and a good
spicy curried sauce. Then, after they have been in their delicious sauce
for two or three days, they should be lovingly grilled over perfect
coals by someone who will not burn, overdo, or otherwise spoil them.*

*These days they are expensive to make, due to the price of lamb, but
they're really worth it. My recipe gives fairly exact quantities, but
in the end you should taste the sauce anyway, to make sure it has the
right tang for your taste.*

*Use a whole leg of lamb and cut the meat off the bone. Cut the
meat into generous chunks, very roughly about 3 cm x 3 cm. This is
not a precise science, so don't worry about the bits and flaps, and use
it all. The pork meat needed should be about half that of the lamb.
Do not cut the meats into too small pieces.*

THE MEAT

1.5–2 kg leg of lamb

Pork rashers or meaty pork belly or any fairly fatty pork,
bones and skin removed, and cut up like the lamb

Soft dried apricots

About 24 sosatie sticks (not the thin satay sticks)

THE MARINADE

1 very large or 2 smaller onions, cut into rings	10 ml salt
Olive or sunflower oil	200 ml white grape or apple cider vinegar (not spirit vinegar – too harsh)
30 ml coriander seeds, preferably roasted in a dry pan, then crushed in a mortar	125 ml dry red wine (Tassies will do fine)
5 ml ground cinnamon	15 ml fine apricot jam
5–10 ml ground ginger, or 1 heaped tablespoon grated fresh ginger	5 fresh bay leaves or 12 fresh lemon leaves, bruised to release flavour
5 ml allspice	Garlic to taste – if the nice, potent type, use 2–3 cloves, crushed and chopped
15 ml good-quality medium-strength curry powder	125 ml milk
75 ml (about 6 tablespoons) brown sugar	125 ml water – if necessary
15 ml cornflour (Maizena)	

Make the marinade first: Fry the onion rings in a generous amount of oil. Stir a few times. Meanwhile, mix all the dry ingredients in a small bowl: the crushed coriander, all the spices, the curry powder, the sugar, cornflour and salt. When the onions are pale brown, add these dry ingredients and stir-fry for a minute or two. This brings out their flavour. Then reduce heat and add the rest of the ingredients, except the milk and water. Stir, and simmer slowly until thickened – a few minutes. Now taste for seasoning: it should be tangy, neither too sour nor too sweet. Adjust the taste by adding either a tiny bit of vinegar or lemon juice, or sugar and perhaps a smidgen of apricot jam.

Cool the sauce. When cooled, stir in the milk. If the sauce is very thick, add a little water.

Thread the meat on the skewers, alternating mutton with pork, and insert about 2 dried apricots per skewer. There should be about 50 per cent more lamb chunks on each skewer than pork, but this can be a matter of personal choice. Pack the sosaties close together in a large rectangular dish – not metal, which reacts with the acid in the marinade. Pour over the marinade, turning the sosaties so all the meat has some contact with the marinade. Cover, and leave for two or three days in the fridge. Take out at least once a day, and turn the skewers.

Grill over medium coals and baste with the marinade. If you're a purist, use wood instead of charcoal. If necessary, rather let each person add more salt when the sosaties are served.

Hot Lemon Pudding

This recipe is quite well known, but one tends to forget how delicious it is. It is the perfect finale after a fish lunch or dinner. The pudding forms a light cake layer on top with a tangy lemony custard underneath. I have metricated this recipe as I have used it in food articles.

200 ml sugar
70 ml flour
3 ml salt
30 ml melted butter
75 ml lemon juice
Finely grated rind of 1 lemon
3 eggs, separated
375 ml warm milk
5 ml vanilla essence

Preheat oven to 160 °C. Mix the sugar, flour, salt and melted butter. Add lemon juice and rind. Beat the egg yolks and add together with the warm milk and vanilla. Whisk well. Separately, whip the egg whites until stiff. Fold into the mixture or stir in with a whisk.

Grease an oven dish, and warm some water in an electric kettle. Pour the batter into the greased dish. Using a larger container, place the pudding in it, and pour in warm water to reach about halfway up the sides of the pudding dish. Bake in the preheated oven, about 1 hour, until the top is pale golden brown and set.

Frozen Strawberry Dessert

This refreshing dessert or sorbet has only three ingredients!
Just make sure you use the very best strawberry jam,
not the cheap jelly-like types with almost no sign
of strawberries in them.

250 ml good strawberry jam
500 ml buttermilk
10 ml vanilla essence

Mix the jam with the buttermilk and vanilla. Freeze until firm.
Cut up the frozen mixture and, when a little softer but still half
frozen, whip with an electric mixer until fluffy. Freeze again in
a suitable container.

Great when served with fresh strawberries.

CHAPTER 25

~ ALMOST PARADISE ~

I THOUGHT OF AGE, AND LONELINESS, AND CHANGE.
I THOUGHT HOW STRANGE WE GROW WHEN WE'RE ALONE,
AND HOW UNLIKE THE SELVES THAT MEET AND TALK,
AND BLOW THE CANDLES OUT, AND SAY GOOD NIGHT.
ALONE ... THE WORD IS LIFE ENDURED AND KNOWN.
IT IS THE STILLNESS WHERE OUR SPIRITS WALK
AND ALL BUT INMOST FAITH IS OVERTHROWN.

Siegfried Sassoon

It is the pearly moments before sunrise. The sea is an endless platinum lake with silver froth near the rocky shore, the bowl of the sky is streaked with shades of pink: a scene on another, far more perfect planet than Earth.

This early, there is no wind, and the windsock with its gaily coloured ribbon tails hangs motionlessly from its pole, like an alien octopus hauled from that shining, breathing lake just beyond it.

Daniel is still sleeping deeply. I slip my feet into worn *stokies*, and go quietly down the staircase to make myself tea.

It is now twenty years ago that we first saw this piece of ground and coveted it.

Since then the entire St Francis area has expanded at a rapid rate, perhaps too rapid. Roads were tarred long ago. Instead of one small village with one small shop St Francis now has a real shopping centre, and the town stretches for kilometres along the coast: from the canals and the white-walled original village, through the Mediterranean architecture of Santareme, to Port St Francis, to end at the pretty Otter's Landing enclave where a narrow strip of nature reserve is all that separates it from the far end of the long beach of our own Cape St Francis.

Quiet Cape St Francis is still somewhat hidden away, somewhat protected from the greedy eyes of developers. The small permanent population is trying to keep it as it is: surrounded by nature reserve areas and free from ugly high rises and noisy commercialism.

We, the denizens of this side of Paradise, do not have burglar bars and we sleep with wide open windows. The only sounds we hear the livelong day are breakers crashing, the soft sounds of cars whooshing by beyond untamed hedges of bush, and birdsong. And, all summer long, the cicadas sing.

If you go on lone walks here, perhaps find a high rock to sit on, to meditate or just relax into the peace, you discover the spirituality of the area. Away from other humans, where only the sea and the birds can be heard, attuned to Nature, you sense the probability that a gateway to another dimension might open for a few seconds; that the diaphanous form of an angel might appear; that you might have a nanosecond's insight into the mysteries of the universe.

Taken to task, some years ago, why I never set foot in church, I reiterated that I am closer to God on these wild rocks than I have ever been in a church.

When winter rains have been plentiful, the uninhabited coastline to the west bursts into bloom: not as exuberantly as in Namaqualand, because our *fynbos* flowers are smaller, shyer, and tend to grow closer to the ground as defence against the scouring, salty winds. But it is rewarding to roam with a camera and photograph the tiny beauties, or to find formerly drab bushes now in full yellow bloom, a carpet of joy against the vast blue in the background.

This coastline is an angler's paradise. Naturally there are times when no fish bite, when the sea seems barren and ungenerous. But in time the shoals of shad, elf, will swim again around the lighthouse point, and the fishermen will clamber over the rocks with their pilchard bait and rods, while the seagulls scream joyfully over the waves and dive head first to grab a silvery form, until they are too satiated to fly, and drift upon the waves like flocks of snowflakes.

In the dusk of evening old men go to the beach and set up their rods on little tripods, and then contentedly wait for something to grab their sand prawn bait and judder the nylon line. Or young men wade into the warm dark waters to cast their lines behind the far swells, then retreat, rod in hand, to squat by a small fire in the sand.

It is rare for these anglers not to haul out at least a white steenbras or a *kolstert* – the latter so named because of the black spot near its tail. In winter our national fish, the galjoen, is often plentiful. And tasty.

Some people, for faddish reasons, do not like galjoen. Galjoen has greyish, flavourful flesh with tiny "threads" or veins running through it. It is marvellous eating – but not necessarily in summer, when they spawn and are thin, and which is the closed season for galjoen anyway. In winter galjoen is fat with splendid heart-healthy fat, and is delicious when butterflied and grilled over the coals. A simple marinade of lemon juice, garlic, black pepper and melted butter is all it needs.

Off the fishing boats come *kabeljou* (kob) and *geelbek*, the fish so erroneously called "Cape salmon". It has absolutely no connection to salmon, and is part of the kob family. Both *kabeljou* and *geelbek* make excellent eating, but the old adage remains: they should not be too big. A specimen of forty, fifty, sixty centimetres is fine. Older, larger fish have coarse, dry flesh. So often I see a visitor from up-country buy a metre-long yellowtail, *kob* or *geelbek*, exulting: "I'm going to braai this fish tonight!" Good luck, mate. Your fish is too big, and all three of these are white-fleshed fishes with too little fat for successful grilling.

Fish for grilling should be butterflied correctly, from the back spine. The tender inside flesh should be lightly seared over the coals first. Then the fish should be turned on its back, onto the skin side. Now a buttery marinade must be liberally sploshed over the flesh, and the fish slowly roasted without any more turning, so that the marinade stays where it's needed: on the white flesh. But that dear inlander is almost surely going to overcook that fish anyway …

This is South Africa's Calamari Coast. In a good season tons of calamari are exported from here, mainly to Italy and other Mediterranean countries. They prefer our more "fleshy", more *al dente* calamari to the softer, less tasty squid of Scandinavia and elsewhere. Visitors to our coastline marvel at the strings of lights on the night-black seas – the lights of the squid boats. The squid are attracted by the lights, like moths, and are then caught with handlines. The boats are state-of-the-art, and the squid is neatly packed and flash-frozen on board.

It's a hard life – the life of a chokka fisherman. Chokka is the local South African name for these cephalopods. Larger boats might stay on the sea for as long as three weeks, but "large" is a relative term … The chokka boats at anchor in Port St Francis harbour all look small and fragile and uncomfortable.

Here every woman who cooks, and all restaurants, know the secrets of preparing calamari. Calamari you order here should never be tough, and if it is, complain: the cook is probably from somewhere up-country …

Oh, all is not sweetness and sunshine!

We pay a price for living on a coast where the next landfall is Antarctica. Winds are salt-laden and can reach gale force in winter. In summer the climate is often hot and humid. These elements are hell on all electric and electronic equipment. Everything bar plastic and glass rusts or corrodes. Therefore the upkeep of house and contents is horrendous. The insides of our computers rust. The fridge in the kitchen has rust marks like industrial acne on its white surface. Recently we had to have almost all window hinges replaced, because some were so badly rusted that the westerly winds slapped them noisily to and fro and threatened to blow them all out when the next gale hits.

Electricity supply is iffy. We get brown-outs (two freezer compressors packed up) and power surges (three satellite decoders blew). If the wind blows hard, the power goes off. If it rains hard, the power goes off. And sometimes, on a bright, still day as I am working on my computer, the power goes off too …

I exchanged my electric hob for a gas hob recently, as gas is infinitely preferable in the circumstances. At least now we can make tea or coffee, and I can cook a meal, during the long hours of no electricity that we sometimes endure!

We miss our friends, and I miss the friends in whose kitchens I have sat. We are all mostly retired now, and spread out over a vast area of South Africa. You do not make intimate, kitchen-counter, listening, crying-laughing friends at our age. You make acquaintances. You may know the sweetest people, but you don't have a history in common.

We also have a small farm now, inherited from Daniel's father.

Dad, who passed away some years ago, bought this smallholding while on a visit to his sister in St Francis Bay – the same lady who asked us so many years ago whether we'd like to come and look after her house and cats.

Dad had bought this little farm for no known reason. The soil is poor and sandy; it is of limited agricultural or commercial value. It is not on the placid Kromme River or near the sea. But now it provides Daniel and me with a retirement interest: he keeps cattle, and I have free-ranging chickens, muscovy ducks, and an organic vegetable garden.

There is a house on the farm which we furnished with leftover stuff from the Johannesburg home and where we plonked down whatever we didn't have room for at the beach house. We do not want to live in it, as the house has great shortcomings – and we prefer living on the sea. It is great to have this extra house, however. It has been a free holiday haven for Stephen and his friends during many summers: it is so far away from any neighbour that the noise created by the young people could not disturb anyone. It also provides storage for our extra books and other paraphernalia, such as porcelain and glass I have not much use for now. Our farmlet is about ten minutes' drive from our beach house, and three kilometres from the sea as the crow flies.

There is a family on the farm: Thomas and Lizzie and their children. They are our eyes and ears when we are not there. Thomas, by now the owner of three calves – he gets every tenth calf born on the farmlet – watches over all the living things. Lizzie is an earth mother. Apart from her own two kids she is raising two foster children.

The farmlet has its own tranquil personality. There are old eucalyptus and pines in the yard. From the deep stoep we have a view towards the distant, pale blue mountains, the wide mouth of the Kromme River, and the sea – a blue line on the eastern horizon.

In the mornings and in the late afternoons flocks of guinea fowl run in single file through the grass to the muscovy duck pond to drink and to steal the ducks' mealies. Herons stand dreamily on one leg in the brown water, and small swarms of cattle egrets move like white dots among the multi-coloured Nguni cattle.

There is amazing bird life on the farmlet. Behind and above the house run sandy hills covered in shrubs, trees and scrub. In the pasturelands below the house two impenetrable thickets of bush have been left undisturbed, and two steenbok have taken up residence there. We see flashes of birds we cannot identify, and hear their sweet, strange calls, and wish we knew more about birds. We try and identify those we saw clearly, but the hundreds of sketches in our bird books soon confuse us, and we give up, frustrated.

In the ancient outbuilding next to the farmhouse, in a small room with signs of an older open hearth, stands a neglected Aga stove. An Aga! From time to time I stare at this stove and dream of having a working Aga – but where? The "sea house" is too small. The old stove needs major repairs. The Aga, therefore, slumbers on in rusty disrepair.

The original farm, *Goed Geloof*, of which our farmlet is now but a tiny part, was deeded to a Magdalena Landman in 1817. Daniel has a copy of the original deed, signed by Lord Charles Somerset. Magdalena was actually the widow of the first farmer in this area, Fredrik Potgieter. Why she obtained the deed to the farm only after her husband's death, is not known: it seems from the new surname that she married again. Or maybe she stayed on, farming stubbornly, and reverted to her maiden name.

Since then the huge farm has been cut up and sold off like pieces of a jigsaw puzzle.

We often wonder why the early White inhabitants at the Cape, with their tender European roots, were such intrepid explorers and adventurers. How, and why, did Fredrik Potgieter push on through primeval forests and across numerous river gorges to settle here with his family, in what was a godforsaken wilderness?

Magdalena and Fredrik had children, number unknown, who lived on *Goed Geloof* for five generations. The earliest known reference to the original farm dates back to May 2, 1785. An East Indiaman anchored in the Kromme River because so many of its crew and passengers were ill after the long journey from India. It is recorded that Fredrik Potgieter and his family provided help, lodging, food and hospitality to these travellers, who recovered well. Apparently their original farmhouse was some way upriver from the sea, near where the bridge over the Kromme is today.

When the lighthouse at Cape St Francis was built way back in 1885, a century after the Potgieter farm was mentioned in a ship's log, there had been no roads at all. Most of the St Francis area was an impenetrable, wilderness of sand dunes and bush. The building materials for the lighthouse had been brought in either by boat or on ox wagons. As late as 1983 the road from Humansdorp to the St Francis area was still a rutted gravel road.

So the mind rather quails at the thought of Magdalena Potgieter, stuck in such isolation, more than 200 years ago. One shudders at the thought of Magdalena giving birth, or having a seriously ill child: what did they do? Puffadders and even cobras are quite plentiful: were they ever bitten? What about farm accidents and bad wounds? Humansdorp might have been a mere trading post a weary wagon day trip away. Even Port Elizabeth must have been but a small outpost which could only be reached by a tortuous trail through forest and gorge.

The old outbuilding on the farmlet was quite clearly a family dwelling once. It consists of nothing more than five small rooms. There is no passage; one room was simply tacked on to the other. In the middle room stands the mute old Aga: this cramped space was a kitchen. Once upon a time a woman cooked meals here, fed her family and tended to her children. Once upon a time there was no Aga, just a much older open hearth. This woman, whoever she was, would have made a fire in there, daily, laboriously.

Our mysterious outbuilding is small and mean and must have belonged to a poorer family, or to Potgieter offspring. But the winds of time have blown away the history of these pioneers.

These early generations of women must have been tough mentally, as women can be. Men are only tough in the physical sense. All those aeons of mankind's domination over women have been a great injustice to the female sex. Women have never been the weaker link, yet they have often been – and in some places still are – slaves to men. Magdalena would have stoically borne her babies, suckled them, tended to the older children and used veld plants to treat disease. Perhaps she had a trusted servant family who accompanied them from the Cape into these wilds; it is doubtful that they would have had Xhosa helpers, as the Xhosas were still living considerably further to the east then, and anyway, relations between Boer and Xhosa were not amiable then.

Her husband might have tamed wild horses and hunted for the pot in the bush, but it would have been Magdalena who eventually cut up the bushbuck, preserved chunks of it with saltpeter and brine, and prepared it in a black iron pot over an open fire.

The soil here is unforgiving, the water hard and ferruginous. How did the family cope with the extra demands of that ship's ailing passengers on what must have been meagre resources?

Did Magdalena sometimes lower her face in her hands and cry quietly, for her hard life, her loneliness in this African outpost? I hope that she sometimes still walks the tranquil fields in her long white dress and observes how her wild world has changed and been tamed. But perhaps she does not approve; after all, her farm has been divided and cut up into as many lappies as one needs for a king-sized quilt.

~

Picnic Bread

This delicious bread has an entire breakfast in the batter! It can be made a day or two before using, cooled, wrapped and refrigerated. But eat it at room temperature. The recipe makes two small loaves, so one can be frozen. It's an excellent bread to send with your intrepid anglers, to give the kids as a snack, take on a picnic, or use as padkos, road food. It needs no butter. Before starting, prepare those ingredients which need a little preparation.

250 ml chopped spring onions, green part included
750 ml grated strong Cheddar cheese
2 packets (250 g each) rindless bacon, raw, chopped
8 jumbo eggs
10 ml Aromat or herb salt

Coarsely grated black pepper to taste
15 ml chilli-garlic sauce (or 5 ml Tabasco)
625 ml bread or cake flour
20 ml baking powder
30 ml melted butter
About 500 ml buttermilk

Preheat oven to 180 °C. You will need two small loaf tins, well greased. In a roomy bowl, mix all the ingredients except the buttermilk. Make sure that the pieces of bacon are well distributed through the mixture. Now mix in the buttermilk until you have a scone-like batter. Divide the mixture between the loaf tins and bake in the preheated oven for about 1 hour. Test with a skewer for doneness before removing.

Mussel and Vegetable Chowder

This recipe makes use of a brand name packet soup, but it really works well here … A deep yellow, flavourful chowder. Serve this with fresh bread. Oh, and about the vegetable quantities: this is not of great importance. Use as much or as little as you like.

Olive oil	1 packet Royco "Butternut &
Onion, peeled and chopped	Spices" soup powder
Carrots, scraped and chopped	300 ml water
Potatoes, peeled and chopped	300 ml milk
Celery, finely chopped	500 g frozen mussels in
Yellow and red peppers,	the shell
deseeded, cut in strips,	Juice of ½ lemon
and simmered until tender	Salt
About 6 rashers bacon,	Grated nutmeg
chopped	Tabasco or other chilli sauce

Sauté the onion, carrots, potato, celery and cooked peppers in the oil. If the oil "disappears", add a tiny bit of water, until the vegetables are soft, then let all the water boil away. Add the bacon and stir; reduce heat. Don't let the vegetables burn.

Mix the packet of soup powder with the water and milk. Add this soup to the vegetables in the pot. Stir and bring to a boil, then add the frozen mussels. When the chowder starts simmering again, let it cook gently for about 5 minutes. Take off the heat and season to taste: add salt, nutmeg and a few dashes of Tabasco. Squeeze the lemon juice into the chowder. Add salt or a seasoning salt, and stir in. Taste again. There should be a hint of chilli and a slight hint of astringency from the lemon. The flavour improves on standing, but keeep hot.

~ STUFFED PICNIC BREAD ~

Also ideal food to take when on a long walk, to a picnic, or to eat on the rocks by the sea. This is again a description, easy to follow, rather than a recipe set in stone.

You need one of those round breads supermarkets bake sometimes, or a fat, elongated bread.

When you have the bread, hopefully fresh, and nicely crusty on the outside, prepare a container of vegetables for roasting: peppers, thick onion slices, sliced baby marrows, eggplant, mushrooms, butternut … The choice is yours. Sprinkle over some salad dressing, or whip up some olive oil, prepared mustard, balsamic vinegar and a pinch of sugar. Don't leave out the garlic. Drizzle this over the vegetables. Roast as usual, until the veggies are tender and starting to singe on top edges. Do make enough vegetables as they shrink in the oven.

In the meantime, cut off one-third from the top of the bread, and carefully hollow it out, but you want a fairly thick "wall" of bread. Brush the bread on the inside, the "lid" as well, with melted butter or olive oil or a vinaigrette dressing.

Cool the roasted vegetables, and cut up a block of mozzarella. Stir into the vegetables. Season the vegetables if necessary. Add whatever else you like, such as freshly-ground black pepper and nutmeg. Drain off any extra juices from the vegetables.

Fill the bread shell tightly with this mixture, as tightly as you can. Put back the bread lid, wrap it all in foil, and refrigerate until needed. Keep it in the foil until you want to slice it. A glass of cold white wine will not go amiss.

There is a product on the market called "Liquid Smoke". I find this wonderful, as it adds a touch of smokiness to roast vegetables as used above. If you track down a small bottle, just be very careful as it is concentrated and can be overpowering. Experiment with its effect by adding a tiny amount to a tablespoon of water first, and sprinkling over the vegetables.

Marinade for Fish on the Braai

This marinade will not suit fine-fleshed fish such as kabeljou or geelbek, as it will overpower the delicate flesh. It is especially suitable for a large fresh vlekked (butterflied) snoek on the braai, galjoen or for a dry fish such as yellowtail or tuna.

125 ml olive oil

125 g butter

About 100 g fruity chutney

60 ml smooth apricot jam,
softened or melted

15 ml soy sauce

3 cloves garlic, crushed and chopped

60 ml lemon juice

Mix all the ingredients in a small pot, and heat gently while stirring, but do not boil. Mix well. Brush over the fish while grilling. A clean, broad paint brush will do the job well.

This is the kind of recipe any experienced braai cook prefer to tweak to his or her taste. For example, the soy sauce can be substituted with Worcestershire sauce, and then salt can be added when the fish is cooked. More apricot jam, for the sweetish tang, can be added. This recipe makes a scant 2 cups marinade.

Bread Pudding

By no means new or even original: my slight variation on an old favourite! But on a cold night when the west wind howls and whips up the waves, this is a comforting and easy dessert to make.

6 fairly thick slices white bread, not fresh	125 ml sultanas or seedless raisins
Butter	2 eggs
Apricot jam, preferably the whole-fruit type	500 ml milk
100 ml sugar	30 ml custard powder
	3 ml salt
	5 ml vanilla essence

Preheat oven to 180 °C. Butter the bread lightly, and spread each slice with apricot jam. Slice each into 4 or more squares. Layer these in a deep round or square bowl, about 16–18 cm in diameter. Sprinkle sugar and sultanas/raisins over each layer. You should have 3 (uneven) layers.

Break the eggs in a mixing bowl, and add the milk, custard powder, salt and vanilla. Whisk well, or use an electrix mixer. Pour evenly over the prepared bread. Don't bake immediately: this is the time to switch on your oven. Let the pudding stand for a while so the bread absorbs the custard.

Bake for about 45 minutes or until the pudding has puffed up considerably and the bits of bread sticking out are getting slightly burnt. Serve hot with vanilla ice cream, or plain. Enough for 4.

CHAPTER 26

~ CYCLES OF LIFE ~

HE WHO BINDS TO HIMSELF A JOY
DOES THE WINGÈD LIFE DESTROY;
BUT HE WHO KISSES THE JOY AS IT FLIES
LIVES IN ETERNITY'S SUNRISE.
William Blake

"Do you realise," Annie said, "that we are now where our oumas used to be, where Mom was decades ago? I'm a grandmother of three. Your Stephen is married …"

The fireplace crackles and spits out a tiny shower of sparks. In another corner of our living room Daniel and Will, Annie's husband, are talking male talk in serious undertones. Outside the winter wind howls and flurries of rain clatter against the windowpanes. Here, inside, it is warm and cosy and it smells of all the kitchens of long ago.

A pile of chopped *rooikrans* wood lies piled up in a basket: alien *Acacia cyclops* which are being eradicated from our nature reserves. The scent of woodsmoke is everywhere, like a comforting primordial memory from the time we lived in caves and the fires out front kept the beasts and the cold away. Everything in the house, including us, is going to reek of woodsmoke, but who cares?

"I'm not taking kindly to ageing," I say to Annie. "I so admire our oumas and the old ladies here, who grow old so gracefully, so contentedly. I am not content to grow older, to be overweight, to see my face wrinkle!"

"Oh, don't go there again … Isn't *this* the cake you're looking for?" Annie says abstractedly, scrabbling among cuttings and old scrapbooks and new cookbooks. She holds out two stapled pages, printed from the Internet.

"Yes! That's the one – but I changed the recipe, and it's that one that's missing!"

"Just bake it again and make the same changes," she says. "By the way, I found Mom's recipe book with the cream puff recipe when we visited them. I tried it, and it works, but they won't ever be Mom's cream puffs. They won't puff up as round and high as hers. They're good, though."

Annie is an excellent, instinctive cook, like Ouma Greta was. She is still the same no-nonsense person, this sister of mine, who has had a brush with breast cancer, and who was once that self-assured, impudent little girl who ate too much hotel bread. She's been thin all her life, like Ouma Sannie, like my parents. Her two married daughters have produced three grandkids between them. What a long and winding way we have come, all of us. Annie and Will are also retired and live in Blue Horizon Bay, an hour's drive away. But tonight, this wild, stormy night, they will stay here with us.

Someone puts more logs on the fire and the sparks fly upward.

It would have been nice to have our brother, George, and his wife here, too. Even Georgie's two children have flown the nest, and – it is difficult to comprehend – although he is twelve years my junior, he might be a grandfather in a few years' time!

I phoned our mother at noon. She and Dad watched a rugby test match against New Zealand earlier on TV and she has a crush on Percy Montgomery. "If I were a young woman," she said seriously, "I'd set my cap at him … What a lovely hunk he is. And oh, he was wonderful today! And those legs, when he kicks that ball! He really is a most attractive man!"

"Aren't you a little old for Percy? He's married, anyway."

"I'm not dead yet! I still have a good eye for a handsome man!"

"Mom," I said, "but you can't see that well …"

"I see what I want to see!"

Oh.

Presently we will have the seafood soup I've made, a Cape St Francis imitation of the bouillabaisse of Marseilles. Very tasty now after standing overnight, it's a broth full of seafood and fish, and in lieu of the lobster I'd have loved to have added, there's a whole red crab in there, which persists in bobbing on top of the huge pot of soup. The crab is for Will: he adores crab. The soup is heating gently, and there is fresh bread and a black olive spread to use as a dip.

This is my favourite weather. I love the gusts of wind, the tinkling rain against the windowpanes, the wild seas crashing against the rocks. Night draws in. Annie, Will, Daniel and I talk of many things, of seas and ships and sealing wax, of cabbages and kings. The fire snaps and crackles. The soup is now sending out kindly tendrils of fragrance. I put deep plates into the oven to heat, alongside the lemon pudding we'll have later. We pour wine. We drink a toast, to us, to Life.

Cape St Francis Seafood Soup

Well, real bouillabaisse can be had only in Southern France: our fish and seafood are different. This is a delicious imitation. It is best made the day ahead, as it becomes more flavourful on standing. The explanations here are lengthy, but the recipe is easy and it's more than worthwhile to make.

About 2 kg very fresh (or frozen when fresh) fish heads and backbones*

White grape vinegar

Water

2 onions, peeled and chopped

1 large potato, peeled and chopped into small chunks

About 3 thick smoked pork rashers, cut into cubes, or 125 g chopped bacon

1 tin chopped tomatoes

10 ml sugar

About 45 ml Thai fish sauce

About 45 ml oyster sauce

Coarsely ground black pepper

6 cloves garlic, crushed and chopped

Salt (or use soy sauce instead of salt)

Fresh or dried herbs such as thyme and oregano

1 punnet mixed seafood, defrosted

About 12–20 fair-sized raw prawns, peeled, heads removed

About 24 mussels, any kind, in or out of shells (fresh or defrosted)

About 100 g calamari rings

Nice to add, but optional: a whole lobster, whole langoustines, or a large crab

Olive oil

Use an enormous, fat soup pot. Rinse the heads well and remove any gills. Put the heads, bones (and if you have it, the prawn shells and heads as well) in the pot. It should be enough to almost fill the pot. Cover with water and add about 125 ml vinegar. Bring to a boil. If necessary, skim off scum. Simmer, covered, for 30 minutes.

Lift out the fish heads, bones, shells and whatever else is hard, from the stock with a slotted spoon, and keep in a bowl to cool. Do not discard! Strain the broth through a fine sieve into a suitable container. This will ensure that all small bones and bits stay behind in the sieve.

Wash the soup pot, and put back on the heat. Fry the onions, potato and pork cubes in olive oil until soft, stirring to prevent sticking. (Smoked pork rashers can be found in some supermarkets, and even a Kassler chop, cubed and deboned, will do.) Add the tomatoes from the tin, and the sugar. Stir through. Add the fish stock and stir. Note: for 6 people there should be about 3–4 litres of stock.

Add the Thai fish sauce, oyster sauce, pepper and garlic. Taste, as both these sauces are salty, then add salt (or soy) to taste. Add the herbs. Pull the pot aside and prepare the seafood.

This is the messy but necessary part: take off as much clean flesh from the heads and bones as you can. Avoid scales and be careful of small bones. Inside the fish heads are delicious bits of gelatinous flesh which should be added. Work until you have a small bowl full of fish bits, then discard the leftover bones.

Fry the rest of the seafood in batches, in olive oil in a pan, and season it all lightly with salt or Aromat. You have more control over the quality of the seafood if you fry them separately, rather than adding them to the stock and simply cooking them.

Be especially careful with the calamari: they are done in less than a minute, and goes tough when overcooked. Some cooks prefer their mussels on the half shell, others take them out of the shells for this soup. The choice is yours.

If using a whole in-the-shell seafood like lobster, langoustines or crabs, cook it in a pot of salted water for 10–15 minutes. depending on size.

Tip: I like frying beef marrow bones, at least eight, separately, adding a little water, until done. Then I remove the marrow, cut into chunks, and add it to the pot of stock.

Add the fish bits and the fried seafood to the fish stock, bring to simmering, stir lightly, and taste. This is a recipe with no rules, so add what you feel might still be missing: garlic, salt, Tabasco, more tomato, etc. If you had enough line fish heads, the soup should by now be very tasty. Lastly, if using, add the whole lobster or crab. Cool the soup, and chill overnight in the fridge. If it's winter, simply leave in a cold spot, covered.

To serve: Heat soup to a simmer for at least 10 minutes. Do not boil vigorously. Ladle into deep, warmed soup plates, and heap the seafood in the centre of each bowl. Serve with plenty of fresh French-style bread. Put the lobster/crab/langoustines in a separate, warmed dish, provide a nutcracker for the claws, a few warm, damp towels, lots of paper napkins, and voilà!

* It is absolutely essential that the fish heads and bones should be fresh. They are easily obtainable from a fishmonger. Some give it away, some sell it for a small sum. Any heads will do, but those of roman are best by far because they are gelatinous and make a superior stock. If you peel the prawns yourself, use the shells in the stock as well.

Special Day's Pork Roast

I am not very fond of pork. But this recipe is out-of-this-world delicious. Forget about dieting and fat, and try this just once – you'll be hooked.

A meaty pork belly with the skin (crackling) intact
Coarse black pepper
Balsamic or apple cider vinegar
Treacle sugar (the dark brown sugar)

If it hasn't been done by the butcher, score the skin diamond-fashion all over with a sharp knife, down to the fat beneath. A few hours or preferably the night before, put the pork in the oven dish you are going to use. It should fit fairly snugly. Pat pepper generously all over the piece of pork. Drench the meat in one of the vinegars mentioned, rubbing it into the scored skin. The skin side, of course, should be on top.

Now, with your hands, pat on a thick layer (0.5 cm) of treacle sugar over the scored skin. Don't be stingy: you will not have sweet pork. The top of the piece of pork should be well covered.

The next day, 8 hours before supper or lunch, set your oven at 120 °C. Now bake the pork, uncovered, at that heat for 8 hours.

Note that the size of the pork belly does not matter: the baking time stays the same.

After 8 hours you will have juicy, falling-apart meat. Only salt the meat after baking, or at the table. Best served with plain side dishes like boiled or mashed potatoes and green vegetables.

Although you can use other pork cuts for this dish, it must be quite fat. Pork loin or leg does not work, as it's too lean. A good butcher will be able to advise you on other suitable cuts if you can't find belly. I usually look for a meaty belly – not an overly fatty one.

To get a smoky flavour, buy the "liquid smoke" which you can find in some deli's in small bottles. It is concentrated, so use a teaspoon and add to the vinegar when you prepare the pork.

The meat usually needs no more embellishment than a little salt and perhaps a dab of mustard.

Annie's Cream Puffs

This is Mom's cream puff recipe which Annie copied from one of Mom's recipe books. She has made it often and says it works beautifully. Yet, she warns, Mom did have a way with it which only comes from years of practice. Annie says a fan oven works best, if you have it. This recipe is not fully metricated and I do not want to fiddle with it. One more point Annie makes is that the filling recipe is not quite enough for the number of puffs, and to make sure the puffs are filled to capacity, she increases the filling recipe quantities by 1½.

Put 1 cup boiling water and 125 g butter in a saucepan. Boil up well, and add 1 cup sifted flour all at once. Stir vigorously.

Remove from the heat as soon as a ball forms, and cool down well. Heat oven to high, 200–220 °C.

Mix in 3 to 4 eggs (depending on size), one at a time, and beat well after each one. (Annie uses a wooden spoon for this. She says to watch it: often 4 eggs make the batter too runny.) Add 2 teaspoons baking powder and beat well. The roux shouldn't be either too stiff or too soft, but keep its shape. Drop dessertspoonsful about 4 cm apart on a greased baking sheet. Shape each with a wet spoon into a round shape.

Put in the hot oven, and after 10 minutes reduce heat to 180 °C for 25 minutes until puffed up, light golden brown and thoroughly cooked. Cool. Slit horizontally to fill.

VANILLA CREAM FILLING

¾ cup sugar

3 tablespoons cornflour

Pinch salt

3 eggs, beaten

1½ cups scalded milk

1 teaspoon butter

½ tablespoon vanilla essence

Mix the sugar, cornflour, salt and beaten eggs, pour gradually into the scalded milk, keeping up gentle heat until thick and smooth. Do not boil! Stir in the butter and vanilla and whisk through.

Before serving, sift over a little icing sugar.

~ GLOSSARY ~

Antie – "Auntie": old-fashioned, polite way of addressing an older woman

Bakkie *(1)* – pick up

Bakkie *(2)* – a small wooden fishing boat

Beskuit – rusks

Biltong – spiced, dried thick beef sticks

Boerekos – traditional farm food

Boerewors – traditional South African farm sausage

Bokkems – salted, wind-dried small fish

Breekborde – china plates

Bredie – a meat stew with vegetables added

De Breede en de Smalle Weg *(Dutch)* – The broad way (to hell) and the narrow way (to heaven)

Die Suid Afrikaanse Kook-, Koek- en Resepte Boek *(old Afrikaans spelling)* – The South African Cooking, Baking and Recipe Book

Doekvoet – ragfoot

Dominee – minister, also called *predikant*

F.A.K. Sangbundel – a patriotic songbook, widely used in Afrikaans schools some decades ago. Published under the auspices of the then Federation of Afrikaans Cultural Association.

Frikkadelle – spicy meatballs

Fynbos – wide variety of wild plants, bushes and scrub limited to the southern and south-eastern Cape coasts. Most bear flowers in spring. Constitutes one of the six flower kingdoms of the world.

Gatvol – fed up

Goed Geloof *(old spelling)* – Good Faith farm

hanepoot konfyt – jam (usually with whole grape berries) made from the Hanepoot grape varietal

Hottentot *(fish)* – a type of South African bream which keeps to shallow coastal waters

Hou die blink kant bo – keep the bright side up

Kappies – bonnets

Keuken *(Dutch)* – kitchen

Klipkoppie – rocky outcrop

Klipvis – tiny fish found in tidal pools

Kraal – a shelter for livestock, often with drystone walls

Kom vang ons, Boesman! – Come catch us, Bushman

Lappie – a piece of cloth

Lappieskomberse – patchwork quilts

Melkkos – plain hand-made noodles cooked in sweet milk

Mieliepap – porridge made from maize meal

Natrossies – sweet grapes left on the vine after harvest

Padkos – food for the road

Pisvoet – piss foot

Platteland – countryside

Predikant – clergyman

Riempie seats – chairs strung with leather thong

Roosterkoek – bread cooked over a fire

Skinderbek – gossip

Snoek – South African pike
Soetkoekies – sweet biscuits
Ster – star
Stokies – elasticated cotton slippers
Stoep – porch
Strandlopers – tribe of nomadic beachcombers
Tamatiebredie – tomato stew
Tannie – colloquial "auntie"
Vetkoek – deep-fried dough
Vleisbraai - barbecue
Vlekked – flayed
Vrot – rotten
Waterblommetjie – edible flower that grows in dams and rivers
Witblits – strong, clear home-brewed liquor

～ RECIPE INDEX ～

~ Saffron Pear Tree ~

Perhaps the earliest cultivated tree in South Africa, the Saffraan Pear (*Pyrus communis*) is believed to have been brought from Europe during the time of Jan van Riebeeck in the 1600's. Over three hundred years later, the oldest tree in the Company Gardens in Cape Town is still bearing fruit, in spite of extensive "surgery" during its long and fruitful life.

Traditionally, the leaves were used to dye wool a distinctive saffron yellow and the fruits used in pickles and preserves. During the time of the settlers, many roads leading to Cape Dutch farmhouses were lined with Saffron Pear trees, although few have survived under the African sun.